The Fairmount Park
Motor Races, 1908–1911

The Fairmount Park Motor Races, 1908–1911

Michael J. Seneca

McFarland & Company, Inc., Publishers
Jefferson, North Carolina, and London

The present work is a reprint of the illustrated casebound edition of The Fairmount Park Motor Races, 1908–1911, *first published in 2003 by McFarland.*

LIBRARY OF CONGRESS CATALOGUING-IN-PUBLICATION DATA

Seneca, Michael J., 1973–
The Fairmount Park Motor Races, 1908–1911 / Michael J. Seneca.
p. cm.
Includes bibliographical references and index.

ISBN 978-0-7864-4592-9
softcover : 50# alkaline paper ∞

1. Fairmount Park Motor Race—History. 2. Automobile racing—
Pennsylvania—Philadelphia—History. I. Title.
GV1033.5.F35S46   2010   796.72'06'80974811—dc21   2003013574

British Library cataloguing data are available

©2003 Michael J. Seneca. All rights reserved

*No part of this book may be reproduced or transmitted in any form
or by any means, electronic or mechanical, including photocopying
or recording, or by any information storage and retrieval system,
without permission in writing from the publisher.*

Front cover illustration: "1909 Fairmount Park—Big George Wins Again," by Peter Helck
(collection of Richard M. Roy, courtesy of Jerry Helck). Back cover:
1908 Founders' Week Cup *(AACA Library and Research Center, Hershey, Pennsylvania)*

Manufactured in the United States of America

*McFarland & Company, Inc., Publishers
Box 611, Jefferson, North Carolina 28640
www.mcfarlandpub.com*

To my parents

Acknowledgments

I have had the privilege to meet many wonderful people during the course of this project, and I would like to extend my thanks to everyone who helped me along the way. Among the individuals who provided photographs, information, or leads to information are Jerry Helck, Elizabeth A. Robertson, John E. Kordes, Frederick A. Usher, Richard M. Roy, Joseph Freemen, Jim O'Keefe, and Louis Bergdoll.

I am grateful for the assistance provided by Mark Patrick and Laura Kotsis of the National Automotive History Collection at the Detroit Public Library, who supplied many of the photographs for this book. Stuart McDougall and Carl Rubenstein were equally helpful during my frequent visits to the Free Library of Philadelphia's Automobile Reference Collection. At Fairmount Park, I would like to thank Historic Preservation Officers Amy Freitag and Theresa Stuhlman, as well as Archivist Andrea Gottschalk.

Thanks to Sarah Weatherwax of the Library Company of Philadelphia; Joseph Benford of the Print & Picture Collection at the Free Library of Philadelphia; Theresa Snyder and Martin Hackett of the University of Pennsylvania Archives; Jean Caldwell of the AAA Archives; Kim M. Miller of the AACA Library & Research Center; Ward Childs of the Philadelphia City Archives; Janice Madhu of the George Eastman House; Indianapolis Motor Speedway Historian Donald Davidson; F. Michael Angelo of the Thomas Jefferson University Archives; Francis Waite of the Bucks County Historical Society; Ted Leonard of the Pennsylvania AAA Federation; Phil McCray of the Watkins Glen Motor Racing Research Library; the Society of Automotive Historians; the staffs of the Urban Archives at Temple University, the Balch Institute for Ethnic Studies, the Hagley Library, the Henry Ford Museum & Greenfield Village Research Center, and the Daimler-Chrysler Archives. I would also like to thank Diane Steele of Bailey, Banks & Biddle, and Susan Kindberg of Reed & Barton, who searched for information on the trophies that their respective companies produced for the Fairmount Park Races.

John Alviti, of the Franklin Institute, provided plenty of encouragement with his early interest in this book. Thanks to everyone at the Athenæum of Philadelphia, especially my friend Bruce Laverty. Whenever I needed an opinion on some aspect of the book, Bruce was always ready to listen and offer a suggestion.

My friends John and Joanne Seitter read a draft of the manuscript. I thank them for their comments and for being a constant source of encouragement. I am fortunate to know an historian with the experience of Rodney P. Carlisle. Rodney read the manuscript and offered a wealth of advice as I wrote my first book. I cannot thank him enough.

Last, but certainly not least, I would like to thank my parents, Michael and Joan Seneca; my brother Chris; and all of my family and friends. Without their love and support, this book would not have been possible.

Contents

Acknowledgments   v
Preface   1

1. An Unlikely Venue   3
2. Making Plans   19
3. The Founders' Week Cup   39
4. A Charitable Event   57
5. The Second Annual Fairmount Park Race   77
6. Surpassing Vanderbilt   99
7. The Third Annual Fairmount Park Race   115
8. Controversy   133
9. The Fourth Annual Fairmount Park Race   151
10. Opposition   169

Conclusion   187

Appendix   191
Notes   203
Bibliography   215
Index   221

Preface

On 9 October 1908, the day after the first Fairmount Park Motor Race, the *Philadelphia Inquirer* proclaimed, "When the history of motor racing in this country is written, much space must be devoted to yesterday's event." The reporter who penned those words witnessed the race and believed that it was one of the best that had ever been run. He thought that it was an important event in the city's history, that historians would record it, and that the story would be remembered. Unfortunately, that is not what occurred. In a city like Philadelphia, where so many historic events have taken place, a few are bound to be forgotten over time. This is especially so in regard to sporting events. Allegiances to different teams, athletes, or even the sport itself, can often be fleeting. The heroes of one generation are supplanted by the heroes of the next. So maybe we should not be surprised that an annual automobile race, which was only run annually from 1908 to 1911, could be completely overlooked by succeeding generations of historians and vanish from the collective memory of the City of Philadelphia.

Philadelphia history books make no mention of the Fairmount Park Motor Races, and even histories of Fairmount Park itself have completely ignored these events. If you were to read any of those books, you would think that the Centennial Exhibition of 1876 was the only event of any importance ever to take place in the park. If you asked any historian in Philadelphia, "On what day were there more visitors to Fairmount Park, than any other?" he or she would most certainly pick one of the days of the Exhibition, but that would be incorrect. The number of people that gathered in the park for each of the Fairmount Park Motor Races exceeded any single day of the Centennial Exhibition by hundreds of thousands. The races were obviously of great interest to the people of the city at the time, yet today, it's almost as if they never occurred.

Auto racing historians have generally glanced over Fairmount Park as well, in favor of more famous events such as the Vanderbilt Cup and the American Grand Prize Races. Fairmount Park may not have had Mr. Vanderbilt's famous cup, or the important title of the Grand Prize, but the racing that took place in Philadelphia is no less important than that which took place at locales such as Long Island or Savannah. In fact, Fairmount Park was the stage for some of the most exciting and successful automobile races that had ever been run.

For four years, the City of Philadelphia played host to the most dramatic of sporting events, and allowed the pristine and world-renowned Fairmount Park to be used as the venue. Philadelphians came out in droves to see early automobiles such as Locomobile, Lozier, Mercer, and Benz speeding through the park. Important names in the history of American motorsport such as Robertson, Harroun, and DePalma graced the entry lists. Fairmount Park was not an easy course to drive, and the story of these brave men, who risked life and limb to make the races such thrilling events, is one that deserves to finally be told. It is a story that is long overdue, and one which I hope will ultimately allow Philadelphia to assume its rightful place in history, alongside Long Island and Savannah, as one of the great road racing venues in the early days of the sport.

This book approaches the subject from the perspective of Philadelphia history. As I researched the races, I realized that the Philadelphia location, and Fairmount Park in particular, acted as both a hindrance and a blessing for the race organizers. I sought to discover what impact the Philadelphia setting had on the races, and what we could learn about the city by looking at its reaction to the event. Those who organized the races knew that there were social and political forces at work that could either help them or impede their plans. When one places the Fairmount Park Motor Races into the greater context of Philadelphia's social and political history, the reasons why the races came about in the most unlikely of places, and why the tradition was cut short despite its great success, become apparent.

1

An Unlikely Venue

The birth of the sport of automobile racing took place in Europe in 1894, when *Le Petit Journal*, a French newspaper, sponsored a trial run between the cities of Paris and Rouen. Not truly a race, per se, the Paris-Rouen contest was a point-to-point run during which the reliability and overall performance of the vehicles were judged. The following year another race was staged between the cities of Paris and Bordeaux. This time, the focus was on speed, with the first to cross the finish line being declared the winner. These contests were run on public roads, and the cars involved frequently clashed with horses, railroad crossings and pedestrians, sometimes leading to injury to the drivers, or those who strayed into their path. As a result of these encounters, the public decried this form of racing as being too dangerous. This was especially so as the cars became faster. Five mile per hour trial trips evolved into sixty mile per hour sprints through the countryside. When six deaths and at least a dozen injuries occurred during the 1903 Paris-Madrid race, the movement to the closed road course began.[1]

The closed road course was not really "closed" in the sense that we think of today. Like the trial runs that preceded them, road races were run on public roads, through rural areas, except in such races the cars traveled a number of times around a circuit, rather than traversing a great distance a single time. This allowed for some level of control in terms of roping off dangerous corners and keeping the public off of the course. *New York Herald* editor Gordon Bennett staged a series of international racing events in Europe, which began as point-to-point races, but switched to closed road courses in 1903. The success of the Gordon Bennett Races made road racing the most popular type of racing in Europe, and ultimately led to the staging of the first Grand Prix in 1906.

American automobile racing began one year after that first Paris-Rouen contest, when the *Chicago Times Herald* sponsored a race between Chicago and Milwaukee. It did not take long before trials and hill climbs were staged all over the country, but Americans also created their own form of racing—track racing. The lack of good roads in the United States left dirt horseracing tracks as the best available surface to compete on. The Brighton Beach Track on Coney Island is just one example of the many oval tracks that were commandeered by the automobile for sprint races and endurance runs. Road racing, like that which took place in Europe, was absent from the United States until 1904 when William K. Vanderbilt Jr. created a commission to stage a road race on Long Island.

The millionaire grandson of railroad tycoon Cornelius Vanderbilt, William was a frequent competitor in international racing events. Inspired by Gordon Bennett, he desired to bring an international race to the United States, using rules similar to the European events. His hope was that by staging a race of this type, he would promote a greater interest in automobiles. That, in turn, would lead to the improvement of the country's poor roads, and the development of better American cars. When it came to automobile technology, American manufacturers trailed behind their foreign rivals, and American cars generally did not perform well when they went head to head with European models in international racing events. The Vanderbilt Cup was a great success from 1904 to 1906, drawing Europe's best cars and drivers to Long Island to compete, but just like the trial runs, protests about the dangerous nature of the sport led to its cancellation prior to the 1907 race. The inability of the organizers to control the crowds, and the resulting deaths and injuries, were contributing factors.

At this point, Philadelphia was not that far behind the rest of the country when it came to motor racing. Local automobile clubs staged reliability runs between Pennsylvania cities, such as the Philadelphia-Scranton and Philadelphia-Pittsburgh trial runs sponsored by the Quaker City Motor Club. A one-mile dirt track, in the Point Breeze section of the city, was also the scene of automobile races from as early as 1901. It hosted sprint races, as well as endurance contests. The first twenty-four hour race at Point Breeze was run on 25 May 1907, but even a grueling twenty-four hour contest was a low profile event when compared to the Vanderbilt Cup. Just as Bennett had in Europe, Vanderbilt made road racing the premier form of the sport in America. This was the one type that Philadelphia lacked, that is until 1908, when the perfect opportunity presented itself.

Early that year, Mayor John E. Reyburn appointed a committee to determine the date of the founding of the City of Philadelphia. The committee was made up of government officials, as well as representatives of some of the city's learned institutions including the American Philosophical Society, the Free Library of Philadelphia, the University of Pennsylvania, the Library Company, and the Historical Society of Pennsylvania. After a thorough investigation of historical records, the committee determined that the official founding of the city took place in 1683, when William Penn, and his Surveyor General, Thomas Holme, first began to sell lots in the city. This meant that 1908 was the 225th anniversary of the City of Philadelphia. In their report to the mayor, the committee suggested a celebration of the occasion:

1. An Unlikely Venue

> Your committee makes bold to suggest that suitable recognition should be taken of the 225th Anniversary of the birth of our city, to the end that historians and the people at large may come to appreciate more than they have in the past the commanding influence of the province of Pennsylvania and the City of Philadelphia upon the history of the development of the United States of America.[2]

The mayor agreed with the committee's recommendation, believing that the proposed celebration would be an excellent promotional event for the city. At this point, Philadelphia had much to be proud of. Everyone knows of the city's role in the American Revolution and of the many historical events that have taken place there, such as the signing of the Declaration of Independence and the drafting of the Constitution. In those early years, Philadelphia was known as an intellectual city. Its most well-known institutions were libraries, hospitals, museums, and schools. In fact, a few of the institutions represented on the committee had existed since colonial times. Philadelphia's most revered citizens were noted intellectuals. They were doctors like Benjamin Rush, scientists like David Rittenhouse, or all-around learned men such as Benjamin Franklin.

By 1908, Philadelphia was a much different city. In the post–Civil War era, Philadelphia had become an industrial powerhouse. It embraced the Industrial Revolution as had no other city in America. At the center of this tremendous growth were the railroads, the Pennsylvania and the Philadelphia & Reading. They ferried iron, steel and coal into the city, providing the impetus for the creation of other businesses and bolstering traffic along Philadelphia's riverfront. As a result, factories appeared all over the city. They produced a wide variety of products, many of which were shipped across the country. Among these were many brands that would become very well known, such as Whitman Chocolate, Breyer's Ice Cream, and Stetson Hats. Baldwin Locomotive produced the nation's locomotives at their factory on North Broad Street. Sigmeund Lubin produced cameras, and filmed motion pictures, at his studio in North Philadelphia. The shipbuilding industry along the Delaware River was the largest in the country, and was second only to that along the Clyde River in Scotland. Firms such as William Cramp & Sons and Neafie & Levy produced modern steel ships, and the engines and boilers that powered them. Philadelphia would eventually come to promote itself as "The Workshop of the World," because no other city produced such a wide variety of products in such large quantities. When it came to manufacturing, technology, and commerce, Philadelphia was the place to be.

A large celebration of the city's 225th anniversary would be a chance to show the world just how advanced Philadelphia had become. In response to the committee's recommendation, the mayor formed another committee to plan a celebration. The mayor himself acted as chairman, and George W. B. Hicks, the Statistician to the Mayor, was appointed as its secretary. Nine sub-committees totaled 898 members. The result of their work was Founders' Week, a seven-day celebration of the city and its achievements, which would take place from the 4th to the 10th of October 1908. Each day of Founders' Week was assigned a theme, and appropriate parades and events were scheduled.

The opening festivities would take place on Sunday. Monday was to be Military

Day, honoring those Philadelphians who had served their country. Tuesday was Municipal Day, calling attention to those who worked in city government. Wednesday would be Industrial Day, a celebration of the city's aforementioned industrial growth. Thursday was called Medical Day, and also Children's & Naval Day. This day would celebrate Philadelphia's many pioneering medical institutions such as Pennsylvania Hospital, and Jefferson Medical College. It also gave school children a chance to participate in the festivities, and since a U. S. Navy fleet was scheduled to visit the city that day, a naval celebration was tacked on as well. Friday was Historical Day, reviewing all of the important historical events that had taken place in the city, from William Penn's arrival, to the Declaration of Independence, and up to Philadelphia's role in the Civil War. In terms of staging a race, Saturday was the most important day. Saturday was designated as Athletic & Knights Templar Day. The Quaker City Motor Club saw this as the perfect chance to finally stage a major road race in the city. Sporting events would have to be scheduled for a day celebrating athletics, and the club hoped that an automobile race would be one of them. Motor club officials canvassed Fairmount Park in search of a suitable course before they took their plan to the city government.

Obtaining permission to hold the race would not be as simple as asking the mayor for his approval. There was a law enacted by the State Legislature which set seven miles per hour as the speed limit in Fairmount Park. When a horse racing track, known as "The Speedway," was built in the park, a bill had to be passed by the legislature allowing the horses to go faster while on the track. Since there was not enough time to submit a bill to the legislature, there was some worry within the club that they would not be able to hold the race in the park. After some investigation, the club's lawyer, G. Douglass Bartlett, found a loophole in the law, which allowed local governing bodies to make exceptions for special events. "The law prohibits the use of firearms in the park, but the National Guard is never prevented from shooting there on holidays or special occasions," he pointed out.[3] So, as long as the Fairmount Park Commission gave the race its blessing, no laws would be broken.

On 14 August, Lewis E. Beitler, Deputy Secretary of the Commonwealth of Pennsylvania, acting as the representative of the Quaker City Motor Club, presented a letter to the Fairmount Park Commission. The commission's president, Colonel A. Loudon Snowden, was absent that day, so it was read by James Pollock. It began:

> Dear Sir,
> In a recent meeting of the Quaker City Motor Club, it was decided to take active interest in Founders' Week, and to that end we desire to present to you the following proposition for the consideration of your honorable body.[4]

The letter proceeded to lay out the Quaker City Motor Club's plans for a 200 mile road race which would take place in Fairmount Park, west of the Schuylkill River, during Founders' Week. This would require the commissioners to grant permission to use the park roads on the day of the race, and each morning for a week prior to the race, so that practice could be held. Club officials made it clear that they would handle all of the arrangements, and cover all expenses incurred in staging the event.

Beitler explained to the commissioners that the issue had not yet been dis-

1. An Unlikely Venue

The 10th Regiment of the Pennsylvania National Guard marches down Broad Street, as part of the Military Day Parade, in celebration of Founders' Week. The large ornate building with a clock tower at the left of the photograph is Philadelphia City Hall. A statue of William Penn stands atop the tower of what was then one of the world's tallest buildings. (1908). Photograph by William H. Rau, courtesy the Library Company of Philadelphia.

cussed with the mayor, who was vacationing with friends from the New York Yacht Club onboard his boat, the *Gretchen*. Beitler added that it had been discussed with George W. B. Hicks, the Secretary of the Founders' Week Committee, who stated that he was in favor of the idea. From the very beginning, the race was to be compared to the Vanderbilt Cup. Mr. Beitler stated, "that the club had adequate means to make the contest equal to if not to surpass the Vanderbilt Cup."[5] At this point, it was uncertain whether there would even be another Vanderbilt Cup Race. The Quaker City Motor Club only wanted their event to be compared to the Vanderbilt Cup in terms of its success and its popularity. They did not want it to have the same reputation when it came to the issue of safety. The letter from the Quaker City Motor Club to the Fairmount Park Commission is interesting in that it did not simply ask for permission to hold the race, and leave the details to be worked out later. The motor club anticipated possible objections, including comparisons to the Vanderbilt Cup's safety record, and attempted to address them in their letter.

They took nothing for granted. Even with Founders' Week as a good excuse to plan such an event, they knew that receiving permission to stage an automobile race was not a sure thing.

A close look at the letter reveals a few concessions by the club, the first of which was the proposition of the event as a stock chassis race. A stock chassis was basically a car that could be bought by the public in a showroom. The only alterations that could be made to the car were the enlargement of gas and oil tanks, the addition of softer springs, and the removal of accessories, such as running boards and headlamps. In comparison, The Vanderbilt Cup was a race for purpose-built racing cars. A frequent criticism of that type of racing was that it made no real contribution to the automotive industry, or to the public. Since the cars involved were not available to the public anyway, it wasn't seen as a good comparison between brands. By proposing a stock chassis race, the Quaker City Motor Club probably hoped to deflect that argument by claiming that the race benefited the public, because it was a demonstration of production cars, and not a purely recreational activity. The offer to cover all of the expenses involved in staging the race was also a good selling point. The Quaker City Motor Club would provide everything from the oil used to keep the dust packed on the roads, to the trophies awarded to the winners. They would also provide the officials and at least five hundred guards to keep the spectators out of danger. The city would get a high profile event for Founders' Week, at no expense, but perhaps even more important was the guarantee to repair any damage to Fairmount Park. Fairmount was no ordinary park, and its condition would have to be guaranteed before any event would be allowed to take place there.

The origins of Fairmount Park date back to 1855 when the city of Philadelphia first began to acquire land along the Schuylkill River north of the Fairmount Water Works. The original purpose of these acquisitions was to halt development in the area and ensure that the river, the source of the city's water supply, remained clean. The tracts of land in this area had long been home to the estates of many of Philadelphia's more prominent families dating back to the time of the city's founding by William Penn. The first piece of land acquired included Robert Morris' Lemon Hill Mansion. Later acquisitions included Benjamin Latrobe's Sedgley Mansion and John Penn's Solitude.

At the same time, the city was well aware that this would be a good area in which to lay out a park. The acquisition of land continued as plans were drawn up, and in 1867, the Fairmount Park Commission was created to administer the grounds. By the following year, the park had grown to 3,000 acres, making it the largest public park in the world. In 1876, Fairmount Park played host to the Centennial Exhibition, a world's fair of technological, scientific, commercial, and artistic development. Forty acres of West Fairmount Park were fenced off, and structures, most of which were temporary, were built to house the exhibits. An opening day crowd of 186,272 arrived to see such attractions as the hand and torch of the Statue of Liberty, and Alexander Graham Bell's first telephone. During a six-month period, over ten million people visited the exhibition.

After the Centennial Exhibition, Fairmount Park saw increased use as a public park.[6] Victorian-era Philadelphians enjoyed all sorts of outdoor activities. They took

1. An Unlikely Venue 9

This is a typical Victorian era view of Fairmount Park from the west bank of the Schuylkill River. A variety of activities enjoyed by visitors to the park can be seen in this etching. While some enjoy the shade of the trees, others boat on the river or ride their horse drawn carriages along one of the park's scenic drives. The group of buildings on the opposite bank is the Fairmount Waterworks, which supplied water to the City of Philadelphia. From J. Thomas Scharf and Thompson Wescott's *History of Philadelphia, 1609–1884* (Philadelphia: L.H. Everts & Co., 1884).

carriage rides, had picnics, and boated on the Schuylkill River. They attended concerts, and visited the nation's first zoo, The Philadelphia Zoological Gardens, which is located within the park's boundaries. An amusement park, known as Woodside Park, was also there for the people's enjoyment. Fairmount was the only park that had its own police force and its own trolley system. With the advent of the automobile, motorists could think of no better place to take a leisurely sightseeing drive. Unfortunately, this was something that they could not do early on, because automobiles were banned in the park. That changed in October of 1899, when the Fairmount Park Commission permitted automobiles on designated roads. In September of the following year, the commission permitted motorists to use all park roads except for the Wissahickon Drive and the West River Drive. Eventually, those roads would be open to automobiles as well, but permission did not come without objection. To some

Philadelphians, the thought of automobiles spewing smoke and tearing up park roads was unacceptable. The Quaker City Motor Club expected similar objections to their proposed race. Just as Fairmount was no ordinary park, the motor club knew that Philadelphia was no ordinary city, and that opposition was very likely, from some portions of the citizenry, no matter how good the club's proposal was.

The City of Philadelphia had a longstanding reputation for being resistant to change. A writer for *Harper's Magazine* commented, "The one thing unforgivable in Philadelphia is to be new, to be different from what has been."[7] This is not to say that the city has never experienced change of any sort. It certainly has, but it has not been without some level of resistance. This conservative attitude was not a characteristic of the general public, only of a small segment of Philadelphia's population, that of the Old Philadelphians, or the city's "old money." They were the city's upper class or aristocracy, and their influence was able to impede the best-laid plans. It was this group that posed the greatest threat to the Quaker City Motor Club. In his book, *Philadelphia: Patricians and Philistines*, John Lukacs refers to the class as patricians, a social class based on familial ties, rather than simply wealth.[8] This is an important distinction, because acceptance into this patrician society was most importantly based on ancestry. Therefore, Philadelphia's "new money," or those who made their fortunes during the Industrial Revolution, were not readily accepted into the social circles of the patricians.

Not all patricians were born into this social class. It was possible to be welcomed in based on stature, or achievement, as long as the person shared many of the same characteristics as the patricians. By looking at these identifying traits we can see why the Quaker City Motor Club feared that this conservative element would attempt to block the race from taking place in the park. For example, patricians lived in certain areas of the city. Those areas were considered "Philadelphia" to them, and everything else was inconsequential. These areas consisted of the streets Chestnut, Walnut, Spruce and Pine, between Washington and Rittenhouse Squares. By the early twentieth century, it was more fashionable to live closer to Rittenhouse rather than Washington Square, and many patricians had moved out of the city and built homes in the suburbs along the Main Line of the Pennsylvania Railroad. Those were the only acceptable places to live according to Nathaniel Burt, who in his book, *The Perennial Philadelphians*, dissected Philadelphia's old families. Burt asserts that, "if you lived north of Market Street you were on the wrong side of the tracks, 'Nobody lived there'."[9] The areas north of Market were populated, just not by anyone of any importance to the patricians. These neighborhoods developed as industry did, with wealthy industrialists building their factories and mansions, and the homes of their working class employees following soon after.

Patricians were also employed in certain professions, and industrial jobs were not on their list. Medicine and law were the professions of choice. They received their degrees from Ivy League schools such as Princeton, Columbia, Harvard, Yale, and the local favorite, the University of Pennsylvania. Patricians were very conservative in regard to money. They were more interested in maintaining their family fortunes than in trying to increase their wealth. Earning and keeping vast amounts of money were not overly important. In fact, they often sat on the boards of charitable organizations. A writer for *Munsey's Magazine* commented on the wealth of the patricians, saying, "At their root lie toil, thrift, and caution, and in these three things are their permanency. Seasoned millions are the best rebuke to speculation and hazard. It pays to be conservative."[10] This is where "old money" and "new money" differed. The patricians' neighbors north of Market Street were not conservative when it came to money and business. Industry required some level of risk, development and change in order to remain successful. The "new money" class was more willing to take risks, because of the new technologies and processes in which they invested, and were more eager than the patrician class to gain a great wealth quickly.

Patricians also tended to ignore the world outside of the city. They did not care to have Philadelphia on the world stage, and wanted none of the attention that other cities usually struggle to attain. They basically wanted to be left alone, which is probably why they disliked New York so much. Nathaniel Burt said of New York, "The whole aspiring, pushing, ostentatious, inhuman showcase quality of the city, the raucous glitter, the avidity for the novel, the insistence on the high pitch, everything about it in fact rubs Philadelphians the wrong way."[11] While they tended to dislike New York, and simply ignored other American cities, patricians admired Paris and London. It is no coincidence that Philadelphia resembles England with its mix of rowhomes and country estates. Patrician Philadelphians enjoyed the country life. They belonged to country clubs, and amused themselves with traditionally European sports such as fox hunting and cricket. Almost every home in the city had a garden of some sort and organizations like The Horticultural Society were very popular amongst this segment of society. This fondness for the country and greenery extended to Fairmount Park as well. In fact, patricians dominated the Fairmount Park Commission, even in the late 19th and early 20th centuries, when machine politics controlled the city government. According to John Lukacs, "it was tacitly understood that the commissioners could manage without interference by the politicians–in other words, [Fairmount Park was] a rare enclave of patrician administration."[12] They were happy to perpetuate William Penn's idea of the green country town, and they wanted none of the change or novelty of cities like New York.

Agnes Repplier, a Philadelphia essayist, quite famous in her day, called Philadelphia, "A droll city."[13] In fact, Ms. Repplier was welcomed into patrician society, and contributed to the city's drollness herself in some ways. A frequent target was Philadelphia City Hall, built on one of the city's five original parks laid out by William Penn. Construction of the building began in 1880, and when it was finally declared finished in 1901, it was the largest municipal building in the world, as well as the world's tallest masonry structure. It was built in the Second Empire style, and was covered with sculpture. It represented a city at the peak of its power; a technologically advanced city that could achieve anything it set out to do. Even before it was finished, there were calls from the patricians to tear it down because it was too extravagant. Ms. Repplier commented that "its only claim to distinction should be the marvellous [*sic*] manner in which it combines bulk with sterling insignificance."[14]

The patricians' distaste for City Hall stemmed from several issues. First, the Second Empire style was out of fashion by the time it was completed, making it a "novel" style. A small, unassuming red brick structure would have suited them just fine. Second, it was constructed on one of those original green spaces laid out by William Penn. Third, it was the product of the Industrial Revolution, and it was meant to attract attention. Industrialists built City Hall to showcase their growing industrial city, not the green country town laid out by Penn, and not the city as the patricians envisioned it.

A constant tug-of-war existed in the city between "old money" and "new money," and it wasn't just limited to the subject of the new City Hall. Whether it was architecture, music, theater, business, or sports, the conservative nature of the patricians was at odds with the rest of the city. With this social climate in place one can see why Philadelphia was such an unlikely place to hold a road race, and why the Quaker City Motor Club had so much to worry about when they proposed the idea to the patrician dominated Fairmount Park Commission.

In many ways, the proposed race bore the same characteristics as the new City Hall. First, not only was an automobile race perceived as a "novelty," but it too was meant to showcase the city and promote the products of "new money" industrialists. Automobile races sold cars, as well as tires, oil, gasoline, and a variety of other parts and accessories. There were a number of local industries that would benefit from a demonstration of the performance and reliability of automobiles. The second similarity was the location. In the past, trial trips were no bother once outside of the city limits, and the races at Point Breeze were confined to a track well outside of the city's center. This time, the Quaker City Motor Club was proposing a race, not only in the city, but in one of those green spaces that patricians held so dear. Third, a big event like an automobile race would be welcomed by most cities because of the visitors and income it would bring along with it, but this was not the case in Philadelphia. Just as they did not want City Hall to draw attention, the patricians would rather the attention from an automobile race be directed somewhere else. They were not impressed by the fact that people would come from near and far to witness the race. They would much rather everyone go to Long Island to see the Vanderbilt Cup, and with them in control of Fairmount Park, it seemed very unlikely that permission would be granted.

When the Fairmount Park Commission received the letter from the Quaker City Motor Club, they immediately referred it to the Committee on Superintendence & Police for review and recommendation. Since everyone expected a tough battle, this action was seen as a good sign. The *Philadelphia Public Ledger* reported, "Probably the very novelty of the suggestion to hold a race of this character on the roads of the largest public park in the world, from which automobiles originally were barred altogether, took away the Board's breath, as there was a surprising lack of comment on the project, but that little was deemed to be favorable."[15] The general feeling was one of relief. At least the commissioners did not vote down the idea immediately.

When the mayor returned from his vacation in New York, he was asked if he was in favor of the race. "I am assuredly in favor of the race," he replied, "and I believe all spirited citizens will agree with me that a motor car race such as the one proposed in Fairmount Park will do no harm at this time." He also felt that automobile racing was "extremely interesting from a sportsmanship viewpoint" and "beneficial to the trade."[16] On 20 August 1908, the mayor and other city officials joined members of the Quaker City Motor Club on a tour of the proposed circuit. The procession of fourteen cars left City Hall at four o'clock in the afternoon, and proceeded up North Broad Street to Spring Garden Street. This section of Broad was known as Automobile Row, because it was here that most of the automobile manufacturers had their garages and showrooms. The convoy of motor cars attracted much attention as it proceeded across the Girard Avenue Bridge, and into Fairmount Park. Mayor Reyburn rode in the first car, a Matheson owned by W. Wayne Davis, Chairman of the Founders' Week Automobile Committee. The group stopped on the South Concourse near Memorial Hall, which had been built as the main building of the Centennial Exhibition. This scenic location was chosen as the intended start/finish line.

After posing for photographs, the cars continued along the planned course followed by a convoy of reporters. All of the drivers were reminded that this was not a race, and that they should stay in line behind the mayor's car. They traveled down the South Concourse, circled around the Smith Memorial, onto the North Concourse, and then made a right onto Belmont Avenue. They passed behind Horticultural Hall through a twisting section that continued behind Memorial Hall, and then on toward Sweet Briar Hill. As the cars came onto the West River Drive, the temptation to speed was too great, and the order to stay in line was ignored. The cars kicked up a cloud of dust as they jockeyed for position behind the mayor. They turned onto Neill Drive through another twisting section that passed under the Philadelphia & Reading Railroad Bridge. From Neill Drive, they came onto City Avenue, heading back toward Belmont. They turned left on Belmont Avenue, veered right down Parkside Avenue and through George's Hill, before heading back onto the South Concourse. The course measured approximately 10 miles in length. After the trip everyone in the party was covered with dirt, except for those in the first car with the mayor, who joked to reporters, "at last I am getting back at you."[17] He again expressed his excitement about the race:

> Decidedly, I am in favor of holding a 200-mile race in Fairmount Park during Founders' Week. In the first place, automobiling is now the king of sports, and the one in which the people's interest is aroused at this time. There is nothing more thrilling or exciting than a well-conducted meet of the kind which has been proposed.[18]

Obviously, not everyone felt as the mayor did, because he added, "Some people object to the park being used for this purpose, but I believe it is the very best place in the city for such a contest."[19]

The next day the mayor sent a letter to the Fairmount Park Commission urging them to take action on the proposal, and asking that they grant permission for the race to be held. Due to the lengthy delay in making a decision, and the lack of comment from the commissioners, there was a growing suspicion that there were some on the commission who did not want the race to take place in the park. Meanwhile, despite the uncertainty, the Quaker City Motor Club continued to make preparations. *The Automobile*, an automotive trade periodical, pointed this out, saying, "they are going ahead with many of the preliminaries, just as if the desired per-

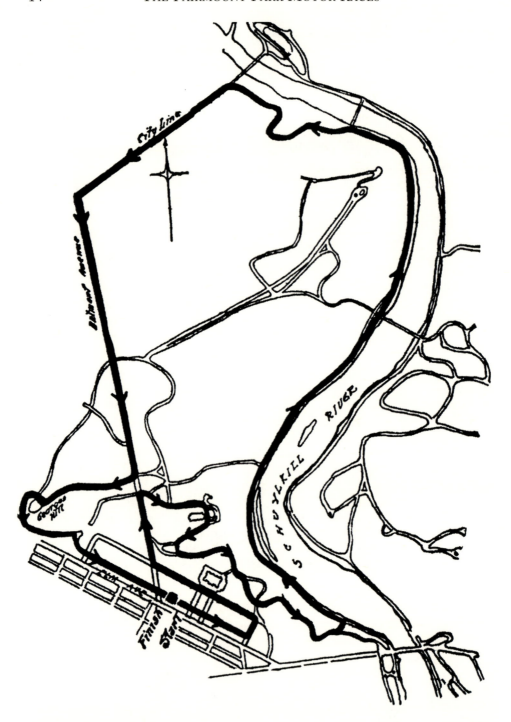

This is a map of the proposed course that Mayor Reyburn inspected on 20 August 1908. The starting point was on the South Concourse. Memorial Hall can be seen on the North Concourse, and a little further north is Horticultural Hall. From the *Philadelphia Public Ledger*, 6 September 1908.

mission was a matter of course."[20] It was almost as if they knew that permission would be granted.

This confidence on the motor club's part was no doubt due to their political allies in Philadelphia's municipal government. Since the Civil War, the Republican Party dominated Philadelphia politics. A political machine had developed under the leadership of Israel Durham, the State Insurance Commissioner. The Durham Machine was described as "Philadelphia's Republican Tammany."[21] It was said to be the worst in the country, especially when it came to municipal jobs and contracts. Durham "had developed the manipulation of public jobs and contracts for self-serving purposes to a level envied by other urban machines," writes historian Lloyd M. Abernethy.[22] One who had benefited greatly from this was State Senator James P. McNichol, whose construction company received a great deal of those contracts. In 1907, when Mayor Reyburn was elected, Israel Durham retired, and passed the title of "boss" to Senator McNichol. Like Reyburn, McNichol was highly in favor of an automobile race in Fairmount Park.

While the bosses of the machine were in favor of the race, this should not be seen as a political difference of opinion. In Philadelphia, almost everyone was a Republican. The differences were more social than political, and while one social class controlled the Fairmount Park Commission, another controlled the political machine. Mayor Reyburn was definitely not an "Old Philadelphian." He was born in Ohio, and moved to Philadelphia with his family when he was thirteen. The mayor's wife was from Kansas. Although he attended the University of Pennsylvania, and was a lawyer by profession, that was not enough to make him acceptable to the patricians. They might vote for him as their Republican candidate, but that did not mean that he was accepted socially. The fact that he was vacationing with friends from the New York Yacht Club when the race was proposed is evidence of this. No good Philadelphian would ever be a member of a New York club, according to the patricians. Besides, he also lived north of Market Street, on the corner of 19th and Spring Garden Streets, in that area that did not exist to the patricians. Reyburn's administration was defined by his plans to improve the city aesthetically and functionally. Known as his "Comprehensive Plans Movement," Reyburn's policies were designed to increase Philadelphia's notoriety and help its businesses. This plan would take the form of wharf improvements, the planning of what is now the Benjamin Franklin Parkway, and even events such as Founders' Week and the Fairmount Park Race. Reyburn wanted Philadelphia to lose its reputation as a slow, dull town, and help it obtain the credit it deserved for being a major commercial and industrial center. He was definitely not a patrician-style mayor.

The same was true of Senator McNichol, who lived on the 1600 block of Race Street, not far from the mayor. McNichol made his fortune as a contractor, a decidedly non-patrician occupation. As the city grew, McNichol's company was awarded the contracts to build power plants, subways, and other public works projects, both in Philadelphia and in New York. He was a hard-working, self-made man who would have identified more with Philadelphia's "new money," or even the working class, than he would with the patricians. After all, "Sunny Jim" got his start as a janitor in the Old City Hall.

Mayor John E. Reyburn sought to improve Philadelphia's reputation and make it a world-class city on par with New York and Paris. His efforts would take many forms, including his support for the Fairmount Park Race. From Frederick P. Henry's *Founders' Week Memorial Volume* (Philadelphia, City of Philadelphia, 1909).

Simply being politicians was enough to distance McNichol and Reyburn from the social circles of the patricians, who found the world of politics to be a low sort of profession. Evidence of this attitude is seen in the example of U. S. Senator Boies Penrose, a large figure in Philadelphia politics, and a leading member of the Philadelphia machine. Penrose was born into a wealthy Philadelphia family that had been prominent in the city since the colonial period. His father was a doctor and professor at the University of Pennsylvania. Boies was raised in a large house on the 1300 block of Spruce Street, almost directly between Washington and Rittenhouse Squares. By all definitions, the Penroses were patricians. Boies, however, chose a career in politics, and from that point on he was never accepted by the patricians, who, according to John Lukacs, "regarded him with considerable distaste."[23]

Philadelphia's government officials, as represented by the machine, obviously did not side with the patricians and they were known friends of business. W. Wayne Davis, the Chairman of the Founders' Week Automobile Committee, and himself the owner of the local Matheson automobile showroom, expressed his thoughts on the matter:

> I think that in as much as [the] Founders' Week celebration is largely a celebration of industrial achievements of our city during the past two and a quarter centuries, that nothing will be more representative of the business progress of Philadelphia than this exhibition of man's triumph in the world of mechanics.[24]

Mr. Davis was not being selfish in his support of the race. While it would certainly help his business, he also thought that it was something that the public would greatly enjoy. He said, "The entertainment value to the public, of course, is a great consideration, as it will give them an opportunity of witnessing such contests as have never before in their history been possible.[25]

So, while on the surface, its advanced industrial character may have made Philadelphia seem like the perfect place to hold an automobile race, it was in reality a very unlikely venue. There existed two influential social groups, each with diverging viewpoints over what type of city Philadelphia should be, and each held positions that could influence the decision about whether to allow the race to be held. The question before them wasn't really over whether or not there should be an automobile race, but over the same question that had always come between them. Should the city follow the example of the patricians, and take the conservative route, or should it follow its business leaders and take some risks in order to expand its commercial opportunities?

The Fairmount Park Motor Races may demonstrate this conflict better than any other event. What could be more bothersome to the patricians than an automobile race in Fairmount Park? On the other hand, what could be better for the city than to host an event that was expected to draw spectators from near and far? And, what could be better for Philadelphia business than to have a technological demonstration like this in the heart of the city?

If the patricians did not allow the race, the city would add to its reputation as a slow, boring, conservative town, but if permission were granted, it might put Philadelphia on the map for yet another great accomplishment. Philadelphia businesses would benefit from such a high profile demonstration of automotive technology, especially the showrooms along Automobile Row, and the local automobile manufacturers. If the city could pull off an event that would rival the Vanderbilt Cup, Philadelphia businessmen would also find delight in the fact that Philadelphia had upstaged their competition in New York City, even if the Vanderbilt Cup technically took place on Long Island.

With high-ranking members of the country's most powerful political machine in favor of the race, it must have been impossible for the Fairmount Park Commission to refuse to grant their permission. The decision rested on the fifteen members of the commission. The courts appointed ten of these, and the other five were ex-officio seats reserved for high-ranking members of the city government. These ex-officio seats belonged to officials who held elected or appointed positions, which meant that they were filled by members of the machine. Although they had stayed out of Fairmount Park business in the past, they were certainly able to exert more influence if they chose to do so. This is the last thing that the commissioners wanted, but the threat was there. *The Automobile* asserted that permission would most likely be granted because of the mayor and councils' support, "and last, but not least, 'Jim' McNichol, the 'boss' of the city, who owns several cars and will do all in his power to boost the game."[26] The mayor also threatened to get more involved. Although he rarely attended Fairmount Park Commission meetings, it was reported that, "he proposes to participate should any opposition develop."[27] So, with this insurance policy, the Quaker City Motor Club continued to make plans as they awaited the official decision.

2

Making Plans

On 1 September 1908, one commissioner finally spoke out on the issue of a race in the park. James Pollock, a member of the Committee on Superintendence & Police stated, "I'm sure I am perfectly willing the race should be held." He was quick to point out that he did not speak for the entire commission. "It's [*sic*] action I cannot anticipate," he said.[1] The Fairmount Park Commission was scheduled to meet on the 10th. An earlier meeting was impossible because many members were out of town for the summer, and a quorum could not be reached. The commissioners slowly began to trickle back into town, so on 9 September, the members of the Committee on Superintendence & Police held a meeting at City Hall to decide what their recommendation would be. "Personally, I considered it so important that I abbreviated my vacation fully two weeks in order to inspect the course and to be present at this meeting to-day," said Colonel Snowden.[2] The members of the committee quickly decided that their report would be favorable, and that being decided, they left for the park to tour the proposed track and estimate possible damages.

The next day, at the meeting of the full commission, they offered the following report:

> Your committee has given careful consideration to the application-going over the route proposed by the Motor Club, and whilst they realize that there is a sentiment of conservative people against granting the privilege, never-the-less, your committee believes that, with proper safe-guards thrown around it, and in view of the fact that it will afford a great deal of pleasure to many thousands of people without material injury to anyone, the application coming as it does with the endorsement of the Councils of the city, the mayor, and the Founders Week Committee, should be granted, with the distinct understanding that it does not establish a precedent for motor racing in Fairmount Park.[3]

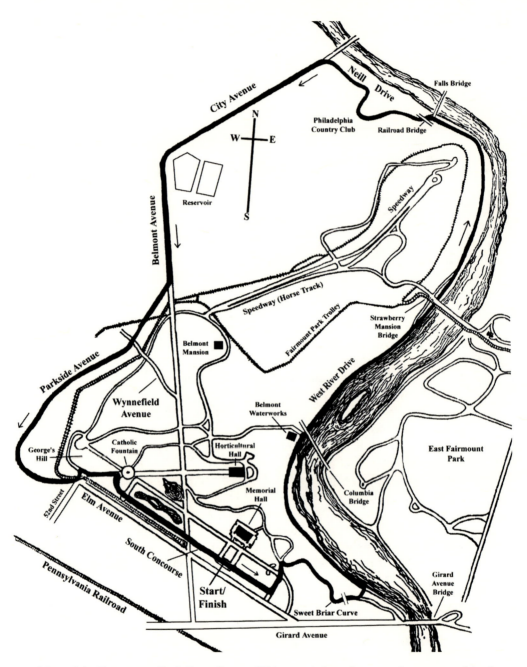

Map of the Fairmount Park Race Course. This map is based on one that appeared in the *Philadelphia Inquirer*, 9 October 1911.

Commissioner Pollock stated that during the past year more automobiles had entered the park than horse drawn carriages. "We must, therefore, give consideration to the motor car," he argued.[4] Except for the reading of a few letters in protest of the race, there was no further discussion or argument over the matter. The commission accepted the recommendation and voted to grant the permit. The Committee on Superintendence & Police was then put in charge of handling any further details.

There were a few conditions attached to the approval that had to be met by the Quaker City Motor Club. First, the commission recommended that the club be required to deposit $2,500 to repair damage incurred to the park. They also wanted $25,000 as insurance to cover injuries to individuals, or damages to personal property. Any monies that were not used would be returned to the club after the race. They also wanted the Chief Engineer of the park to approve the grade of oil used to sprinkle the drives in order to keep the dust packed down on the road. These were minor conditions, since the motor club had already agreed to cover all of the expenses anyway.

Another suggestion was that the route of the course be changed. Instead of turning back onto the North Concourse, and then making a right on Belmont Avenue, the cars would turn left off of the South Concourse, pass the Smith Memorial, and then turn right heading toward Sweet Briar. This cut out some of the more dangerous turns and kept the cars from traveling deep into the park, in the vicinity of Horticultural Hall. Some of the Park Commissioners must have felt that the original course layout was too much of an intrusion into the park. The changes "would be a great advantage to the Park as well as to the contestants," the commissioners explained.[5] This was yet another minor issue which the motor club was happy to agree to.

The approval of the race by the commissioners was not a vote in favor of the race. For an event that seemed to have little chance of being approved, the permit was granted very easily, with no debate over the letters written in opposition. They would have much rather the subject had never come up, but with the pressure from the mayor and the Republican machine, in addition to the urging from the Founders' Week Committee, they really had no other choice. If the commissioners had voted against it, not only would they have had to deal with the machine, but they would have appeared to be shying away from participation in the Founders' Week activities. The clause in the recommendation of the Committee on Superintendence & Police, that the race not set a precedent for racing in the park, was very telling. The commission only approved it because of Founders' Week and the commissioners wanted to make it clear that they were only allowing it this one time since it was a special occasion.

As soon as permission was officially granted, the local newspapers began touting the event. "The fact that an automobile race of 200 miles is to be held in a pleasure park right in the heart of the city has called attention once more to the fact that Philadelphia is the greatest sporting city in the world," proclaimed the *Philadelphia Record*.[6] The editor even thought that with the approval of the race, Philadelphia might lose its conservative reputation, saying, "of one thing there is a certainty, and that is that never again, in the automobile world anyhow, will Philadelphia be classed as a sleepy town or a city of the dead."[7] Philadelphia would now have a race to rival the Vanderbilt Cup, as Lewis E. Beitler of the Quaker City Motor Club pointed out:

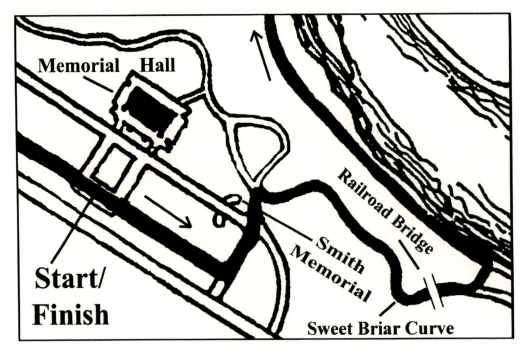

Detail of the southeast portion of the Fairmount Park Race Course.

> To give some idea of the importance attached to this race, I need only say that the promoters of the Vanderbilt Cup race considered it necessary to call off the elimination trials which were scheduled for the same day.[8]

Now that the Quaker City Motor Club had permission to hold the event, there was much work to be done. The race was scheduled for 10 October, leaving only one month to make the necessary arrangements. It was a good thing that they had been working on their plans prior to receiving permission because that gave them a bit of a head-start, but issues like preparing the course, creating awards, and finding entrants, were arrangements that could not be made until permission was officially granted.

On 12 September 1908, the Quaker City Motor Club distributed the official entry blanks for the race and announced that it would be run "under the rules and with the sanction of the Racing Board of the American Automobile Association (AAA)."[9] There had been much speculation as to whether the race would be sanctioned by the AAA or the competing Automobile Club of America (ACA). At the time, the two groups were fighting for control of motor racing in the United States. The ACA had been recognized in Europe as the official American sanctioning body since 1899. In 1902, the AAA was created because the ACA had become more of a social club for wealthy motorists, which did not deal with issues that were pertinent to the large majority of automobile owners. In his book, *The Car Culture*, James J. Flink describes the ACA's efforts as a failed attempt to gain, "highly centralized control over a national automobile movement by an elite group of automobilists."[10] The

AAA was intended to be a national organization that would focus more intently on issues that pertained to the average motorist. The AAA formed its own Racing Board, and moved to the forefront of automobile racing when they were awarded the sanctioning of the 1904 Vanderbilt Cup.

By 1908, the disagreements between the two organizations had flared up. One big issue was the ACA's awarding of its Grand Prize Race to Savannah, which would hold the race a month after the Vanderbilt Cup. The Grand Prize was attracting many of the international cars and drivers who would otherwise have competed on Long Island. The Quaker City Motor Club, while affiliated with the AAA, had a dilemma. The AAA had banned a number of manufacturers and drivers who participated in an unsanctioned race at Brighton Beach, which meant that a number of popular drivers might not be allowed to participate at Fairmount Park. There was also a chance that the ACA would ban drivers who participated at Fairmount Park from its future events, or those of other international clubs. The Quaker City Motor Club wished to remain loyal to the AAA, so before the officials made their decision they sent two representatives, G. Douglass Bartlett and Charles J. Swain, to visit both organizations in New York. Their goal was to find out what the feeling amongst the clubs would be, if one side was chosen over the other.

While it may have initially seemed like the Quaker City Motor Club was going out on a limb by choosing the AAA, the two rival clubs were not far from a peace accord, and it is likely that the Quaker City Motor Club's representatives learned this on their trip to New York. It was only four days later that the AAA and ACA made an agreement that recognized the AAA as the sanctioning body for national events, and the ACA as the sanctioning body for international events. The definition of these types depended on whether there were foreign drivers piloting foreign cars in the race. In other words, Americans could drive foreign cars and it could still be considered a national race.

Along with the entry blanks, the rules of the contest were also announced. As previously mentioned, the race was for stock cars only. They had to be the product of a recognized manufacturer and had to be listed in the company's catalog. All entries were subject to inspection to determine whether they were, in fact, stock chassis cars. The brand of tires was to be decided by the entrant, as long as they had standard treads. All repairs to the car had to be carried out by the driver and his "mechanician," with the exception of the changing of tires, and the addition of oil, water, and gasoline, which could be performed by the team during a stop. There was no limit on the weight or size of the car, and the driver and mechanician could be changed during the race if necessary. The deadline for entries was set for 7 October. The entry fee was $350 per car, but $100 would be refunded as long as the car actually started the race. No more than three cars of the same make could participate. All other issues would follow the standard rules of the AAA Racing Board.

As soon as the entry blanks were available, entries began coming in and speculation began as to which cars and drivers would be competing. Much of this speculation involved foreign cars, but for the first time in a major race, foreign cars were banned. It is unclear exactly when this rule was decided upon, as it was not in the original proposal. It seems as if the motor club wanted to have a race with American cars only, but left the door open to foreign cars as long as possible, just in case they did not receive enough American entries. The reason behind this decision may have been that the club did not want foreign competition since an American car had never won an international race. They may have felt that it would be just a bit embarrassing for a foreign car to win during an occasion such as Founders' Week. Another possibility is that they did not want to get tangled up in the rules that determined whether a race was national or international in character. With only American cars, there was no doubt that it was a national race, and therefore under the AAA's jurisdiction.

As late as 17 September 1908, owners of foreign cars were still promising to enter. They probably did not find out that they were banned until they went to the Quaker City Motor Club's headquarters at the Hotel Walton, on the corner of Broad and Locust Streets, to pay the entrance fee. Finally, on 26 September, the rule was announced. The club officials stated that they had thought about letting foreign cars enter, but that they could not, because one of the manufacturers had already made its entries on the condition that foreign cars remain banned.[11] Another late rule change involved the number of starters. The original number was to be twenty, but that was later changed to sixteen because of a AAA rule which said that there could be only two entries for every mile of the course. Since the length of the track was shortened from 10 to 8 miles, sixteen was the maximum number allowed.

The first entrant was Louis J. Bergdoll, well known across the country as a race car driver, but even more well-known in Philadelphia as a member of the Bergdoll brewing family. The Bergdolls had made millions producing one of America's most popular beers at their factory in the Fairmount section of the city, or Brewerytown, as the area became known. He and his brothers, Charles and Grover, also founded the Louis J. Bergdoll Motor Company in 1908, which had its showroom and offices on Automobile Row. Louis liked to spend his share of the family fortune on fast cars, not unlike his contemporaries such as William K. Vanderbilt. It was thought early on that Louis would enter his Benz, in which he had set a number of world's records, but since foreign cars were not allowed, he entered an American Locomotive car which he planned to drive himself. He was not a professional driver, but he had dabbled in racing, even winning a race at Ormond Beach, Florida in 1907, making himself well-known for someone who was not a full time racer. The American Locomotive car was the product of a locomotive manufacturer of the same name. They were based in Schenectady, New York, and had started producing automobiles in 1905. Louis' car was a 60 horsepower model.

The second entry to come in was from the Maxwell-Briscoe Motor Company in Tarrytown, New York, which entered one of its 28 horsepower cars without specifying a driver, as did the Hamilton Auto Company, which entered a 35.4 horsepower Stoddard-Dayton. Hamilton was a local distributor, which usually did not participate in racing, but decided to take part this time because the race was in their hometown, and they wished to help make the Founders' Week event a success. Their car, the Stoddard-Dayton, was the product of the Dayton Motor Company of Dayton, Ohio, a company that got its start producing tools and equipment for agriculture. P. F. DuPont, of Merion, Pennsylvania, entered a Peerless and named Bert

The Hotel Walton stood on the southeast corner of Broad and Locust Streets. One of the hotel's rooms served as the headquarters of the Quaker City Motor Club, and many club functions took place in the large ballroom. This photograph, from the year of the first Fairmount Park Race, is interesting, in that only one of the six vehicles parked outside of the hotel is an automobile. The rest are horse drawn carriages. (1908). Photograph by Byron, courtesy the Library Company of Philadelphia.

Maucher as its pilot, who was known locally as a very good driver. The Peerless was a very popular entry, described as being "a favorite with the most discriminating automobile buyers of Philadelphia."[12] They produced luxury cars that were well built and more expensive than most others. The combination of Maucher and the 38 horsepower Peerless was seen as an exciting combination and one to watch.

Another well-known local driver, Frank Yerger, was announced as the pilot of a 39.5 horsepower Studebaker, which was entered by the Studebaker Brothers Company of South Bend, Indiana. He had recently driven the car in the Glidden Tour, and a few other reliability runs, in which he produced good results. The Studebaker Brothers Company really wanted to gain a foothold in the Philadelphia market, and they believed that there was no better way to do so, than to enter one of their latest models in the race. The Palmer & Singer Manufacturing Company of Long Island City, New York, didn't even have to enter the race themselves. Charles A. Schroeder of Brielle, New Jersey, an automobile enthusiast, entered one of their cars, a 60 horsepower Palmer-Singer, which would be driven by William Wallace. Wallace was a twenty-one year old from Brooklyn, New York, who had been racing for about a year.

The Philadelphia Auto Company, local representatives of the Apperson Brothers, entered a 48.4 horsepower Apperson Jack Rabbit for driver George Davis. The Apperson Brothers Automobile Company had been building cars in Kokomo, Indiana since 1901, and the Jack Rabbit, so called because of its speed, was a popular car that they had been producing for about a year. By 22 September, half of the spots were filled, with the Welch being the eighth car entered. Erwin Bergdoll, Louis' younger brother, entered this car, which was rated at 51.3 horsepower. Erwin was an amateur, who had never driven in a professional race before. It was said that this would be the first time that brothers would ever compete against each other in an automobile race.[13] The Welch was the product of the Welch Motor Car Company of Pontiac, Michigan.

The Locomobile Company entered the next two cars. They were based in Bridgeport, Connecticut. Their local sales manager, Irving J. Morse, made the entries. One was for Joe Tracy, a famous Locomobile driver, and the other for Jim Florida, who worked for the local sales office. Morse had said just a few weeks earlier that Florida would not be participating in the race because he was "too valuable to the Philadelphia business to risk him."[14] The announcement of Florida as the driver must have meant that Morse had a change of heart. Tracy was a very successful driver and a veteran of the early Vanderbilt Cup races, who had retired, but Locomobile was hoping to coax him out of retirement for the race. This would ultimately not work out because Tracy planned to manage the Matheson team in the revived Vanderbilt Cup Race, and a preliminary event, The Long Island Motor Parkway Sweepstakes, was scheduled to take place the same day as the Fairmount Park Race. Locomobile would have to choose another driver before the race. Both Locomobiles were rated at 40 horsepower.

On the 26th two more cars were entered. The Acme Motor Car Company of Reading, Pennsylvania entered one of their 45-50 horsepower cars with Cyrus Patchke as the driver and James M. Munyon, another local automobile enthusiast, entered a 50 horsepower Chadwick car for Jack Harkins to drive. The Chadwick was a locally manufactured automobile, produced by the Chadwick Engineering Works in Pottstown, Pennsylvania, where the company had just recently moved. Previously, they were located in Philadelphia, producing cars in the city since 1904. Another local company, and one that was just founded in 1907, made the next entry. The Pennsylvania Motor Car Company, of Bryn Mawr, entered a 38 horsepower car and indicated that it would be driven by either the well known hill climber Len Zengle, or Robert Maynes, since one of them would have to represent the company at the Long Island Motor Parkway Sweepstakes Race.

H. A. Lozier of the Lozier Motor Company of Plattsburgh, New York, entered the next two cars through his local representatives. Herman Brill entered one Lozier for Ralph Mulford to drive, and W. B. Herbert entered another for Harry Michener. The two Lozier cars, while they looked very similar, were not equal. Michener's was a four cylinder, 45 horsepower car, while Mulford's was a six cylinder, 50 horsepower car. The AAA had banned these two drivers for competing in the unsanctioned Brighton Beach Race, but Lozier hoped to settle things now that the AAA and ACA had worked out their differences.

The sixteenth car to enter was a 40 horsepower Pullman entered by the Pullman Motor Car Company, of York, Pennsylvania through their local representative, L. Eugene French, and that car completed the list. Two other cars were entered as alternates after the list was closed. They were the Thomas, and Matheson cars. The Thomas Company of Buffalo, New York, was first reported to have entered one of their cars on 25 September. Their driver, George Salzman, had even traveled to Philadelphia with the car to take a look at the proposed circuit. On the 29th, the *Philadelphia Record* reported that the Thomas Company had still not paid the entry fee. This was the same day that the Pullman became the sixteenth car to enter, thus excluding the Thomas. Louis Bergdoll then entered the car for Salzman to drive, after the list had closed, perhaps because of the popularity of the Thomas car. A Thomas had recently won the New York–Paris Race, making it a very recognizable car to the public, who had tracked its progress daily in the newspapers. Having Salzman and the Thomas in the race would add to the event's stature. The Matheson Company of Wilkes-Barre, Pennsylvania also entered a car late, knowing that there was not much chance of actually finding a spot in the race.

Besides finding cars to compete in the race, the Quaker City Motor Club quickly got to work on preparing the course. Four club officials were in charge of overseeing the preparation of the course. They were Chairman Arthur B. Cumner, J. R. Overpeck, F. M. Johnson, and P. D. Folwell. They spent their days in the park trying to make sure that the course would be safe for both the drivers and the spectators, while still providing for the best possible race. They worked day and night to ensure that everything would be ready in time. The roads were rolled and oiled over and over to compact the dirt and create a hard and flat surface to race on. Some corners were also banked to allow the cars to carry a greater speed through the turns.

One problem area that the officials encountered was the West River Drive. Cinders from the Belmont Waterworks, on the corner of the West River Drive and Montgomery Avenue, were dumped on the drive, making it a cinder road rather than a dirt road. The laying of oil on the surface had no effect on the cinders, so only watering and constant rolling was able to compact it. The work on the West River Drive ended up making it the fastest part of the course. Although the Quaker City Motor Club was supposed to handle everything, the city government did help out in preparing the track surface. Even Mayor Reyburn took an occasional drive through the park to inspect the work, and offer his advice on different matters.

To keep the drivers on the course, the officials nailed large signboards to trees to alert them of upcoming turns and grade changes. These signs had large blue arrows with the letters Q. C. M. C. painted in yellow. Plans also had to be made for handling the crowds. A 1,000 seat grandstand was constructed along the Concourse for invited guests, officials, and anyone else who wanted to purchase a ticket. Spectators could also view the race from any other part of the course for free, by standing along the side of the track, or perching themselves on one of the many hills or embankments along the park roads. Only those who wanted to be on the Concourse were required to pay for a $5 ticket for a grandstand seat, $50 for a box, or $10 for a parking space. Cars could also be parked for free in specially designated areas. This had to be controlled and limited in order to prevent the vehicles from damaging grassy areas of the park.

In terms of safety, the entire course was roped off from start to finish to keep spectators from wandering onto the track. Telephone stations were constructed at all of the turns, and at other places around the circuit, and connected to the judge's stand so that information could quickly be relayed back to the officials. This allowed for an unprecedented level of control over all of the activities taking place around the course. Locations were sought out to place ambulances, and those stations were connected by telephone as well. In charge of the medical preparations was Dr. Hubley R. Owen, the chief surgeon of the city. Dr. Owen hired twenty-five additional surgeons to work with him. At their disposal were fifteen ambulances and eight patrol wagons, which were stationed around the course so that the injured could be quickly tended to and transported to the nearest hospital. In addition, an Army Hospital Corp. station was put together on Neill Drive to offer even more immediate medical attention. "Although we are not anticipating any serious accidents, we are nevertheless going to be prepared for an emergency and you may rest assured that anyone who needs it will receive the best possible attention," said Dr. Owen.[15] On 27 September, the doctors were taken on a tour of the course to see where they would be stationed and where the ambulances would be, so that they could plan their response to any accidents. Charles J. Swain, the patrol judge of the race, put out a call for volunteers from the state militia's Signal Corps. to act as flagmen during the race. These men would alert the drivers of obstacles on the track, and would warn the spectators of approaching cars.

Suitable prizes had to be prepared to offer to the winners, and the Quaker City Motor Club had very little time to design them and have them produced. The club did not place the order for the first place trophy until 28 September, leaving only eleven days for Bailey, Banks & Biddle to create it. The trophy was valued at $2,000. It was a silver cup, three feet tall and 20 inches across. A miniature figure of William Penn stood on its lid. "Founders' Week Cup" was inscribed across the front, and below that would be an engraving of the winning car, which would be etched on race day. On the back was inscribed, "The Quaker City Motor Club Stock Chassis Road Race, 200 Miles, Fairmount Park, October 10, 1908." The large cup sat on an ebony base emblazoned with a Quaker City Motor Club seal in gold and enamel. The *Philadelphia Record* reported that two shifts of artisans worked around the clock to complete it in time.[16] The MacDonald & Campbell Company, a Chestnut Street clothier, donated a large silver punch bowl as the second place prize, and Bailey, Banks & Biddle donated another silver cup, The Bailey Cup, for third place. Other prizes were offered by the city's many newspapers, such as The *Philadelphia Evening Times*, which donated a solid gold fob medal made by the J. E. Caldwell Company. This medal was to be awarded to the winning driver. In those days, all prize money and trophies awarded in automobile races were given to the owner of the car, rather than to the driver. The paper believed that the men who risked their lives driving the cars should be rewarded in some way, so they offered the medal as an extra incentive to win.

Despite any earlier worries, and the delay in getting the race approved, this was shaping up to be one of the most well organized races ever. Just the idea of preparing an 8 mile dirt road course in a month's time seems daunting unto itself. With the experience of the Quaker City Motor Club, and the assistance of the city government, everything went smoothly. The condition of the park also has to be taken into account. The roads were in pretty good shape to begin with, probably better than most of the city's normal streets.

The preparations were really a citywide effort, not just the work of the Quaker City Motor Club. Philadelphia's businesses stepped up to donate the trophies, and Bailey, Banks, & Biddle did a tremendous job in producing them on time. The medical community came together to help with the safety plans, and the railroads announced that they would be adding extra trains to the schedules to accommodate the influx of spectators into the city. Even the Fairmount Park Commission helped out in any way they could. There was no further talk of possible dissent amongst the commission members. Once the race was approved, they did everything they could to make it a success. As the officials continued to make preparations for the race, the drivers eagerly began their week of practice.

On Monday morning, 5 October 1908, practice began for Philadelphia's first big automobile race. Of the sixteen cars entered, ten came out for practice that morning. The first car to complete a lap of the circuit was the Pullman driven by Roy Staines. According to a reporter, the car passed the grandstand at exactly 5:38 A.M. "Her exhausts added a weird aspect to the surroundings as she pounded down the concourse and disappeared in the darkness towards Sweet Briar Hill."[17] It must have been a thrilling sight, to see a car speeding along the park roads in excess of 50 mph, when the usual speed limit was a mere 7 mph. George Davis, who completed a lap in 9:30, turned in the fastest time of the day in his red Apperson Jackrabbit. Edgar C. Ireland, who had been chosen to drive the Stoddard-Dayton, made the second fastest time of the day of 9:50, and Jim Florida made the third fastest time of 10:00 in his Locomobile. Other drivers to take to the course that day were William Wallace in the Palmer-Singer, Bert Maucher in the Peerless, Frank Yerger

After making the Sweet Briar Curve, the cars continued down Sweet Briar Hill and through the hairpin that led onto the West River Drive. In this photo, from the October 1911 issue of *Motor*, a regular touring car passes under the railroad bridge and into the hairpin. Notice the steep descent of Sweet Briar Hill. Courtesy AACA Library & Research Center, Hershey, PA.

in the Studebaker, Herb Bitner in the Maxwell, Louis J. Bergdoll, in his American Locomotive, and Len Zengle in the Pennsylvania. Some drivers would arrive later in the week due to their participation in a race at Brighton Beach on 3 October.

The only incident of the day was a close call between the American Locomotive, and the Pennsylvania. Bergdoll went wide on the Sweet Briar Curve and drove onto the sidewalk, nearly careening down a hill. He was able to straighten the car out and continue on, but the Pennsylvania was following close behind and nearly got caught up in the incident. Zengle turned off the motor and hit the brakes, barely avoiding the slower car. For the most part there were no risks taken that day. The drivers needed some time to familiarize themselves with the track before attempting to make a fast lap. The track itself made a good first impression. When the first practice rounds were completed, everyone agreed that the condition of the racing surface was very good. Only a few areas were considered soft and in need of repair.

The organizers were pleasantly surprised by the number of spectators who showed up on the first day of practice, despite the chill in the air and the early morning practice hours of sunrise until 7:00 A.M. More than fifty cars were parked across from the grandstands on the Concourse at the start of the session. As the morning progressed, this number only increased. Spectators also began to gather at Sweet Briar and other turns around the course. There were cheers and applause from the crowds each time a car sped by. For one individual, witnessing the events wasn't enough. A man from Bala, Montgomery County, took to the course in his own stripped down car, and proceeded to speed around the track. Noticing that the car did not carry an official flag, the park guards gave chase. They failed to catch him, but his identity was discovered, and a warrant was later issued for his arrest.

An unidentified car kicks up a cloud of dust and smoke as its driver makes his way through the twisting Neill Drive section of the course. The stone wall that lined the drive can be seen on the left of this photograph. On the right, spectators watch from an open area of the Philadelphia Country Club's property. Courtesy Print and Picture Collection, Free Library of Philadelphia.

The drivers awoke to a dark and foggy Tuesday morning, with visibility limited to only 50 yards. Nevertheless, the throngs watched as Bert Maucher's car pierced the curtain of fog and stormed down the straightaway at 60 mph. Onboard was a very lucky, or very unlucky, *Philadelphia Evening Bulletin* reporter. This was not the best day for a novice to experience the thrills of auto racing. "Hold on tight," warned Maucher, as the car passed the Smith Memorial and left the broad expanse of the Concourse for the twisting downhill run toward Sweet Briar.[18] Down the narrowing Sweet Briar Hill they sped, making the tight turn through the Sweet Briar Curve and under the Philadelphia & Reading Railroad Bridge. The car continued down the hill, and then made the double left hand turn onto the West River Drive. The Schuylkill River boathouses were barely visible in the distance as they flew down the normally scenic path. As they traversed the three miles of gently curving roadway, Maucher said, "Have to take your chances [on] a morning like this. You'd go wrong in this fog before you'd know what had happened."[19] The road made a bend to the right, then past the Belmont Water Works and under the Columbia Bridge. It then curved back to the left, passing under the Strawberry Mansion Bridge. At the end of the West River Drive, Maucher slowed the car down as the road made a sudden drop under another Philadelphia & Reading Railroad Bridge. Then it was right back on the power as they climbed Neill Drive. A stone wall loomed ominously on their right hand side as they made their way through the tight Neill Drive turns. On the left was the Philadelphia Country Club golf course, where spectators had a lot of room to view this tortuous section of the track. Onto the straight path of City Avenue, past the reservoir, and then left onto Belmont, the car accelerated, again reaching 60 mph. "Brace yourself, we're going some," Maucher warned the already terrified passenger.[20] The car dashed past the filtration plant, and the Methodist Episcopal Home, before following the trolley tracks down Parkside Avenue. It roared past the rowhouses and businesses that lined the brick paved street, before sweeping to the left back toward 52nd Street and Elm Avenue. A sharp left/right combination near George's Hill took them over the trolley tracks and onto a path that led toward the Catholic Fountain and back onto the South Concourse. After this harrowing experience, as the reporter attempted to clean the dirt and oil from his face, he remarked that he would not be riding again for quite some time.

Locomobile's second driver, George Robertson, made his first appearance on Tuesday. He was to drive the car that was originally entered for Joe Tracy. The crowds turned out to see Robertson, who had won the twenty-four hour race at Brighton Beach that weekend. Despite being only twenty-three years old, Robertson was one of the better known drivers entered. He had made a name for himself with his terrific drives in endurance races with the Simplex team. Robertson took one lap around the course as Jim Florida's passenger, in order to learn the course, and then got behind the wheel himself. He made one more lap and then parked the car in frustration because of the dense fog. An experienced driver like Robertson knew that it was not worth risking injury to himself or the car, under such poor conditions, when there were still three more days left for practice.

The fog was so thick that some people had trouble just getting to the park. Irving J. Morse, the owner of the two Locomobile cars, had a few close calls while on his way to the park to see his cars practice. Ultimately, he just stopped his car on the side of the road, and blew his horn until a passing motorist came along to help him find the starting point. Even with the thick fog, there were many more spectators on the second day of practice. It was believed that they numbered at least one thousand.

The course was much faster on Wednesday, allowing the drivers to really open up the cars for the first time. In addition to the drivers' greater familiarity with the course, an improved track surface also contributed to faster lap times. On Monday, the cars had dug a foot deep rut on the West River Drive turn because the dirt was too soft. They were also becoming airborne as they came down the Concourse and crossed Belmont Avenue because of a grade change. Over the first two days of practice, the officials identified such problem areas, and corrected them by rolling and

Officials, inspecting the road, pass under the railroad bridge that marked the entrance to the Neill Drive section of the course. The dangerous nature of this blind, downhill turn is illustrated in this photograph by the unforgiving stone wall that awaited those who misjudged the corner that would become known as "the dip of death." (c. 1908). Photograph by Nathan Lazarnick, courtesy George Eastman House.

oiling them to keep the dirt tightly packed. On Tuesday alone, thirty-six thousand gallons of oil was spread on the track.[21]

Ralph Mulford and Cyrus R. Patchke arrived at the track on Wednesday, both having participated in the Brighton Beach race. Mulford was an engineer from Asbury Park, New Jersey, who was discovered by the Lozier Company while he was employed as a mechanic repairing boat engines. Like Robertson, Mulford built his reputation in twenty-four hour races. He had won a twenty-four hour event at the Point Breeze track a year earlier, the first one in which he had ever competed.[22] After his first laps, Mulford said that he expected a slow race:

> Several turns must be made with extreme caution if one desires to remain in the race. Fastest time should be made on City Line and Belmont Ave., while high speed will undoubtedly be maintained down Parkside Ave.[23]

Patchke's car would not be ready to run until Thursday, because he crashed it through a fence during the Brighton Beach contest. He took a few laps around the track in a touring car to study the course, and then agreed with Mulford's assessment:

Ralph Mulford's No. 17 Lozier kicks up the dust as it speeds along the park course in this photograph from the November 1908 issue of *Motor*. Courtesy Automobile Reference Collection, Free Library of Philadelphia.

> There are too many turns which demand careful negotiation to expect the average speed to be good. While the worst ones will be allowed for by all the drivers, the apparently easy ones, if taken at speed, will cause no end of tire trouble, and possibly serious accident. I should say that an average of 45 to 48 miles an hour would win the event.[24]

The two Locomobile cars took the most laps of the circuit on this perfectly clear day. By the end of the session, Jim Florida's lap of 9:30 was the fastest of the day, matching Davis' time from Monday. His teammate, George Robertson, turned a lap of 10:45, but this was his first full day of practice, and it was very clear to those in attendance that he was holding back. Fast times were also made by Louis Bergdoll in his American Locomotive at 10:25, Maucher and Yerger each made a lap in 10:08, and Davis again made another lap of 9:30 in the Apperson. The spectators on Wednesday now numbered in the thousands. Nobody expected this many people to show up just to see practice. As a result, those guards and officials who were on duty had a tough time trying to keep people off the track, but they did a good job, and avoided any serious problems.

On Thursday, Florida upped the ante to 9:25, but the record would not last long. The crowd became increasingly excited by the consistency of the fast laps the drivers were making. Florida's next lap was 9:27, and then Robertson ran six laps of 9:31 before setting the fastest time of 9:23. His average speed for the lap was 51.15 mph. The Chadwick made its first appearance on Thursday, with Jack Harkins driving, as did the Welch of Erwin Bergdoll, and Cyrus Patchke's Acme. It was believed that the Chadwick would be very fast because of rumors that Harkins had turned some incredibly fast times in a "surreptitious nocturnal practice."[25] The rumors were most likely untrue, because Harkins' fastest lap was 13:15, not what one would expect from a driver who had already been engaged in illegal practice. Of the three newcomers, Patchke had the best lap at 10:15. Ralph Mulford turned a quick lap of 9:58, becoming the fourth driver to make a round in less than ten minutes. Davis did not take to the track on Thursday, and therefore could not make an attempt to regain the best time from the two Locomobiles.

Two accidents marred the day's practice, but neither was very serious. The first involved the Pullman car with Max La Roche at the wheel, substituting for Roy Staines. He had just passed the Smith Memorial near the end of the Concourse, and was heading toward Sweet Briar Hill, when a steering knuckle broke and blew out his right front tire. He found himself sliding toward the trees, but was able to slam on the brakes and stop the car. Soon after that incident, the Maxwell car of Herbert Bitner blew a tire exiting Sweet Briar, and turning onto the West River Drive. The car skidded and hit a culvert, breaking the right rear wheel. Luckily Bitner and his mechanician were uninjured. Both the Maxwell and the Pullman would be repaired and back on the track for Friday's practice.

Harry Michener took his first laps around the track in the Lozier on Friday. His fastest lap was 9:53, on only his fourth time around. Although he arrived on the final day of practice, Michener was an expert Lozier driver, and the crowds considered him a favorite to win the race. The two Lozier cars of Mulford and Michener were probably the most identifiable cars in the race. They were both painted white, and their drivers wore white driving suits with white hoods. They were often described as being "ghostly" in appearance.

Both of the Locomobiles stopped every other lap to practice tire changes, thinking more about race day, rather than making a fast practice time. Still, George Robertson beat his own record by completing a lap of 9:15, but even that time was eclipsed by Salzman, whose fastest time was 9:02 in his Thomas. Before practice on the course even began, Salzman had predicted that the average speed of the race would be 60 mph. His lap of 9:02 averaged only 54.79 mph. This was much slower than he had predicted, but it was the fastest time of the week. It would remain the fastest through the completion of the session, but the Thomas car was still a preliminary entry and there was no guarantee that it would be in the race. Then, toward the end of the practice session, Arthur B. Cumner, the chairman of the Quaker City Motor Club Contest Committee, announced that the original sixteen cars had all passed inspection and would be able to compete on Saturday. This was unexpected, since most believed that at least one car would be found to break the "stock" requirements, and create a spot for the Thomas.

The reason that all of the cars were found to meet the requirements was because there were no inspections. A *Philadelphia Evening Bulletin* reporter learned that although several cars were suspected of violating the rules, the technical committee was willing to accept a signed affidavit from each car owner stating that their entry met the stock requirements, as the only form of evidence needed to participate.[26]

Lozier driver Harry Michener sits behind the wheel of the No. 15 car dressed in the ghostly white garb that was the team's trademark. (1908). Photograph by Nathan Lazarnick, courtesy of the Detroit Public Library, National Automotive History Collection.

In other words, if the owners said they were in compliance, the technical committee believed them. When the announcement was made that all of the cars had passed, the spectators were very disappointed that the fastest car would not be competing in the race.

Davis did not try to regain the fastest lap with his Apperson. Instead, he spent the day testing a spare car just in case a problem was found with the primary car. George Parker took the Matheson car around for a lap, making a competitive time of 10:16, but like Salzman, Parker did not actually have a spot in the race.

After a week of practice, it was thought that the race would be an evenly contested one, despite the differences in the cars. Ten cars had completed a lap in less than 10:00 during the week of practice. There were different strategies at work; some drivers went fast early in the week, and then saved the car for the race; others went slowly over the course early in the week, but then turned in competitive times on Friday. In the end they seemed to be pretty evenly matched, and there were a number of favorites, such as Robertson, Michener, Mulford, and Davis. These drivers were favorites mainly because of their experience and the fact that they had been successful in other contests. Based on practice times alone, all of the drivers had a realistic chance of winning the race, with only a few of them off the pace. Another reason why it was thought to be an evenly matched contest was the rate of attrition.

Table 1. 1908—Fastest Time of Each Driver in Practice

Car	Driver	Time
Thomas	Salzman	9:02
Locomobile	Robertson	9:15
Locomobile	Florida	9:25
Lozier	Mulford	9:28
Apperson	Davis	9:30
Palmer-Singer	Wallace	9:38
American Locomotive	L. Bergdoll	9:45
Stoddard-Dayton	Ireland	9:50
Lozier	Michener	9:53
Pennsylvania	Zengle	9:53
Peerless	Maucher	10:05
Studebaker	Yerger	10:08
La Roche	Pullman	10:12
Acme	Patchke	10:15
Matheson	Parker	10:16
Welch	E. Bergdoll	10:40
Maxwell	Bitner	11:14
Chadwick	Harkins	13:15

Because of the nature of the course, it was believed that many of the cars would succumb to either mechanical problems or crashes, because of the tight turns. When a reporter asked Davis what his chances were, he quipped, "See me after the race, and I will tell you all about it."[27]

3

The Founders' Week Cup

Saturday was the big day, and the people of Philadelphia could not wait to witness their first road race. The start was scheduled for 7:00 A.M., yet just after midnight, the first spectators began to arrive in the park. Trolley after trolley arrived, each packed with eager fans wanting to find the best vantage point to view the race. Thousands of automobile enthusiasts parked their cars along the track. There had never been so many automobiles gathered together in the city before. The occupants climbed onto the roofs, hoods and running boards so that they would be able to see the track. These automobile owners were serious fans. Many wore driving caps, and carried signs in support of their favorite car or driver. Some were even carrying megaphones to cheer on their favorite. There were also some in the crowd who were so sure that their favorite would win, that they made wagers with others who were just as sure that they were wrong.

It was a cold and windy night, and many of the overnight arrivals brought blankets and robes to keep warm. Some entrepreneurs sold sandwiches and coffee for $.10 each and they did a very good business. As morning approached, the scene resembled "an immense army just waking to the day's activities."[1] Although it is impossible to know exactly how many people were gathered in the park that day, it was estimated that there were 400,000–500,000 spectators lining the track. This was based on the fact that the crowd lined the entire circuit, and in most cases they stood two deep. The papers reported that it was the largest crowd that had ever attended an automobile race.[2] Those who could not get close to the track, or who did not have a car to stand on, found spots on "nature's grandstands," the term that was widely used to describe the many hills, trees, and bridges throughout the park that provided good vantage points. Children also climbed onto fountains and statues to get a better view. The *Philadelphia Record*, adding a touch of humor to their report, pointed out that children "did not object to holding onto the ear or nose of a famous warrior of the past in order to see the mad pacing racers."[3] There were also several hundred rooftop spectators on Parkside and Elm Avenues, where the cars raced down city streets. Besides the main grandstands, and the Concourse, the greatest crowds were gathered at the end of the Falls Bridge, along Neill Drive, and at Sweet Briar Curve. Those were the places where an accident was most likely to occur. There is no denying that some people just wanted to witness the spectacle of an accident. Of course, by viewing the race from these locations, the spectators were also putting themselves at risk. Those who had gathered on the outside of the turn at the bottom of the Parkside Avenue hill were forced to move by the officials, who worried that if a car missed the turn, it would run right into the onlookers.

As the night went on, the area remained full of activity, as a constant stream of vehicles poured into the park. The officials were also busy all night, making last minute preparations to ensure the safety of the drivers and spectators. By 4:00 A.M. the teams had arrived at their stations along Belmont Avenue near the filter plant. They set up tents to house their equipment and built bonfires to keep warm, and then began preparing the cars. A few drivers took some slow laps around the course to gauge the track conditions and ready themselves for the long race ahead. In an interview with the *Philadelphia Public Ledger*, George Davis explained how drivers prepared for a road race in 1908. He said that drivers usually got very little sleep the night before as they were "extremely nervous" thinking about the race.[4] Even an experienced driver like Davis was not immune to the nervousness brought on by such a dangerous contest. Drivers visualized the course, turn by turn, so that they had an image of it in their head. On the morning of the race, they awoke to a light breakfast, just enough to sustain them for the duration of the race. Their arms and torsos were then wrapped with linen bandages to protect them from the vibrations of the car over the dirt roads, and their wrists were wrapped with tire tape to keep them from twisting.

Having so many automobile enthusiasts in one place was a great opportunity for automobile manufacturers, who set up displays of their latest production models to demonstrate to the public. Tire manufacturers were also well represented. Local representatives of the tire companies set up their own camps on Belmont Avenue to supply the cars using their brand. The local Continental representatives also put up $100 in gold as an award for the driver of the winning car, if that car carried their tires.

The night did not give way to sunshine, only a cloudy sky that threatened rain. As morning arrived, a surprise announcement was made. Salzman's Thomas, which held the track record after a week of practice, would be in the race after all. This drew a great response from the assembled crowd. Fortunately for Salzman, Erwin Bergdoll was only making average practice times in his Welch, and chose to withdraw. Since Salzman's Thomas entry was entered by Louis Bergdoll, it is most likely the case that Erwin withdrew because his brother's Thomas had a much better chance of winning. The other possibility is that the officials asked him to drop out because they felt he was not prepared to drive in a race like this one. Referee J. R. Overpeck had to approve the capabilities of all of the drivers to determine whether they were skilled enough to be participating in the race. It is entirely possible that Overpeck may have asked the amateur Bergdoll to withdraw to make room for the more experienced driver, George Salzman. A slow car on the course could be very dangerous to the other drivers, as well as the spectators. Because it was the fastest car in practice, the Thomas became the immediate favorite to win.

At 6:30 A.M., the cars were ordered to the starting line. This was difficult to accomplish since spectators were still arriving and blocking the track. Police with megaphones tried to get the crowds to move back with cries of "clear the way." It took at least fifteen minutes to clear the track as the crowds just did not want to move, but as it got closer to the starting time, they realized that the race would not be able to start if they did not move back, and so the crowds receded back onto the sidelines. The cars approached the start and lined up in rows of two, according to numbers they had drawn earlier. The unlucky #13 was skipped. For the next half hour, the cars tested their engines, revving them up and producing thick clouds of acrid smoke, which did not seem to bother the crowds at all. Just before seven o'clock, Mayor and Mrs. Reyburn, accompanied by George W. B. Hicks, arrived at their seats in the grandstand. Also present in the stands were the Fairmount Park Commissioners, Senator McNichol, and many other government and military officials. A brass band was also perched in the grandstand, entertaining the crowds as the start of the race neared. Then, an official with a megaphone ordered the drivers, "Start your motors!"[5] A series of explosions was heard and smoke filled the air, as the sixteen drivers started their machines. At 7:00 A.M., W. Wayne Davis, the starter of the race, blew his whistle and sent the Maxwell on its way. The rest of the cars were let go at thirty second intervals. This was considered a short interval compared to other races, but it was the largest possible due to the length of the track. In those days, cars started at different intervals for safety reasons. The officials really did not want them to be bunched together on the track, or to be jockeying for position. The second car off was the Apperson. Davis wasted no time as he shot away from the starting line. Then came Bert Maucher in the Peerless and La Roche in the Pullman. Car #5 was the Thomas, with Salzman at the wheel. He was followed thirty seconds later by Frank Yerger in the Studebaker. The Chadwick of Jack Harkins took off next, with three minutes now past since the start. The Stoddard-Dayton was car #8. This was the only car with its exhaust pipes on the right side of the car, and the crowds appreciated the light show that Edgar Ireland put on for them as he fired the car up and went on his way. The two Locomobiles approached the line next. Florida drove car #9, and George Robertson followed in car #10. Florida looked "as intrepid as ever, and filled with confidence," with Robertson "displaying all the sangfroid of the more experienced veteran."[6] Louis Bergdoll left the line five minutes after seven o'clock in the #11 car. Moments later, Wallace pursued in the Palmer-Singer, with Patchke's #14 Acme following close behind. Harry Michener piloted the #15 Lozier, and then came Len Zengle in the Pennsylvania. Zengle and his mechanician proudly wore sashes, emblazoned with the name of their car, over their white turtleneck sweaters. Ralph Mulford started last in his Lozier. Since this was such a short interval, scarcely had the last car turned the first corner, than the Apperson Jackrabbit turned the last corner and came into view to complete

Table 2. 1908—Starting Lineup

No.	Car	Driver	HP	Cylinder	Tires	Mechanician
1	Maxwell	Bitner	28	4	Ajax	Not Available
2	Apperson	Davis	48.4	4	Diamond	Not Available
3	Peerless	Maucher	38	4	Diamond	Not Available
4	Pullman	La Roche	40	4	Diamond	Not Available
5	Thomas	Salzman	70	6	Michelin	Mr. Winters
6	Studebaker	Yerger	39.5	4	Diamond	Bob Yerger
7	Chadwick	Harkins	50	6	Diamond	Not Available
8	Stoddard-Dayton	Ireland	35.4	4	Continental	Frank A.B. Harris
9	Locomobile	Florida	40	4	Firestone	Not Available
10	Locomobile	Robertson	40	4	Firestone	Glenn Etheridge
11	American Locomotive	L. Bergdoll	60	6	Fisk	Not Available
12	Palmer-Singer	Wallace	60	6	Continental	Charles Nauber
14	Acme	Patchke	40–50	6	Diamond	Jere Price
15	Lozier	Michener	45	6	Continental	Harry Lynch
16	Pennsylvania	Zengle	38	4	Diamond	Not Available
17	Lozier	Mulford	50	4	Continental	Fred Hall

its first lap. The Peerless and the Thomas pursued the Apperson, with the rest of the field following in short order. They all bunched so closely together on the track that fans and officials, normally accustomed to a separation of a minute or more, found it difficult to follow as each car passed the scoring stand. Three cars passed the Maxwell on the first lap. The least powerful car in the field, the Maxwell started first, but really had no chance of holding off its competitors, despite the thirty second interval. In terms of race position, the car held 13th place when it passed the scoring stand for the first time.

Salzman burned up the track with a record lap of 8:57 in his Thomas. Wallace made the second fastest lap of 9:27 in the Palmer-Singer, followed by Michener in the #15 Lozier with a time of 9:47. The #17 Lozier, driven by Mulford, skidded as it swung around the hairpin curve that led from Lansdowne Drive onto the West River Drive. A rear tire burst and the car plowed into a bank on the side of the road. Mulford and his mechanician, Fred Hall, made an incredibly quick tire change and continued on, but then stopped at their camp to pick up an extra spare. By the time they finished their first lap of 14:41, they lagged a lap behind the rest of the field.

As Mulford finished his first lap, his teammate Michener had a frightening incident near the end of his second lap. He took the turn near George's Hill too fast; so fast that the crowd gasped because they knew what was going to happen next. Michener lost control, and the car flipped over, throwing the mechanician, Harry Lynch, clear of the wreck, but pinning Michener under the car. It burst into flames, as Lynch and nearby police officers rushed to extricate the injured driver from the wreckage. They pulled him free of the car and laid him on the grass, as an ambulance arrived on the scene. Before they could put Michener in the ambulance, he said, "Don't take me to the hospital, give me a cigarette instead."[7] As the smoke cleared, there was Michener, "standing by the side of his demolished car, lighting a cigarette. A trickle of blood ran down his chin."[8] Michener and Lynch sat on top

3. The Founders' Week Cup 43

Len Zengle and his mechanician at the wheel of the Pennsylvania car. (1908). Photograph by Nathan Lazarnick, courtesy of the Detroit Public Library, National Automotive History Collection.

of their charred machine and watched the rest of the race. The lack of serious injury in this incident was attributed to the height of the seat in the Lozier, which acted like a modern day roll bar, and kept the weight of the car off of its driver when it flipped over. With the mishaps of the Loziers, the order on the second lap had the Thomas leading the Palmer-Singer by over a minute, followed by the #10 Locomobile of George Robertson. The leaders remained unchanged on the third lap, except that the Apperson worked its way up to tie Florida's #9 Locomobile for fourth place.

A number of cars encountered bad luck on the fourth lap. The Maxwell experienced it first, when the car's crankshaft broke while making the "S" turn on Neill drive. No one was hurt, and the police helped Bitner push his car to the side of the road. He and his mechanician worked on the car for over an hour before they decided it was impossible to repair, and officially declared themselves out of the race. Then the rear axle broke on the Pullman while it rocketed down the Concourse toward the grandstands. The car's left rear wheel flew into the air and landed on a spectator's car, leaving a dent in the roof. La Roche kept the car under control, traveling another 200 yards before bringing the car to a stop on the right hand side of the road, near the intersection with Belmont Avenue. The mechanician ran to retrieve the stray tire, but upon returning to the car, he discovered that it would not be possible to reattach it. The crowd in the grandstand rose to its feet to see what happened to the Pullman, and in the commotion, a boy seated near the edge of the grandstand fell to the ground. Doctors whisked him away to Presbyterian Hospital, and found that he suffered a contused jaw and a few scrapes to his face, but nothing more serious. The Stoddard-Dayton encountered tire trouble as well, but Ireland and his mechanician, Frank Harris, fixed the tire and got going again. Wallace took over the lead in the Palmer-Singer when Salzman's Thomas became the third car to have a tire problem on lap four. Salzman's trouble erased the incredible lead he had built and dropped him to fifth place. Meanwhile, the two Locomobiles dueled with the Apperson. Robertson came into second, with the Apperson a close third and Florida's Locomobile fourth at the completion of the fourth lap.

Salzman made a quick recovery and stormed back up to second on the fifth lap, followed by Robertson and Davis. On the sixth lap, Florida overtook Davis for fourth place, but it suddenly became third place when the Thomas dropped out on the next lap. The car's crankshaft broke while descending Sweet Briar Hill. The crowds initially thought that Salzman might have taken the turn too fast, but the driver actually heard a strange sound as he reached the end of the Concourse that led him to believe that the car had a mechanical problem. It just happened that the problem became terminal at Sweet Briar. The crowd urged the driver to fix the car and continue on, but the severity of the damage prevented any attempt to repair it and Salzman was out of the race. Salzman had predicted that the average speed of the race would be 60 mph. His car probably could not withstand the pace that he attempted to keep up. The Stoddard-Dayton, which had just had tire trouble on lap four, encountered valve trouble on this lap as well. Luckily for the driver, this problem made itself known on Belmont Avenue, so Ireland conveniently brought the car into camp. It turned out that the team did not have the spare parts to make the repair, but Ireland wanted so much to get back in the race, that he hopped in a car and drove into town to buy the parts he needed. In fifty-five minutes, he returned and repaired the car, but on his very next lap he stripped the pump gear and once again found himself on the side of the road. This time he called it quits for good.

On the eighth lap, the #10 Locomobile took the lead with Robertson at the wheel, followed by his teammate Florida in second, and Louis Bergdoll's American Locomotive in third. The Lozier of Ralph Mulford ran in fourth, with the Apperson and the Acme not too far behind. An unfortunate tire puncture caused the Palmer-Singer to lose the lead and drop all the way back to seventh place. Wallace and his mechanician, Charles Nauber, hurriedly attempted to change the tire but lost a lot of time, and the lead in the process. They would have to work hard if they wanted to make their way back up to the front.

The ninth lap saw the Apperson take over third place from the American Locomotive. Mulford also gave up his fourth place position and fell back to sixth. At this point, a one minute gap separated Robertson from his teammate Florida, who had a three minute lead on the Apperson. On the tenth lap, Bergdoll fell back two more spots to sixth, Mulford moved up to fifth, and the Palmer-Singer moved into fourth. In his attempt to overcome his earlier tire trouble, Mulford turned the fastest lap of the race of 8:32 on his tenth lap. He had racked up a new record for the course. The leaders held the same positions through lap eleven.

3. The Founders' Week Cup 45

The spectators get a good look at the No. 5 Thomas car as it sits abandoned along the side of the road. Salzman was running in second place when the car's crankshaft broke and put him out of the race. (1908). Photograph by Nathan Lazarnick, courtesy of the Detroit Public Library, National Automotive History Collection.

On the twelfth lap, the Apperson of George Davis came up to challenge the Locomobiles, passing Florida's #9 Locomobile on the track. A quarter mile ahead of Davis, Robertson circulated comfortably with a lead of 4:11. Florida ended up a half mile behind the Apperson, but in terms of overall time, Davis' move on Florida did not matter at all. The #9 Locomobile retained second place at the conclusion of the lap. Davis' Apperson and Wallace's Palmer-Singer shared third place. A few seconds back, Mulford hung onto the leaders in fourth position.

With the Locomobiles dominating the race with an undisputed lead, the focus shifted to the battle for third. On lap thirteen, the Palmer-Singer retook third place from the Apperson, but on the next lap, dropped to seventh on a particularly long lap, most likely caused by more tire trouble. The Apperson once again took third place, followed by Mulford's Lozier and Louis Bergdoll in the American Locomotive.

It was around this time that the Chadwick and the Pennsylvania dropped out of the race. The Pennsylvania had lost a few laps due to spark plug trouble. Zengle had to bring the car into camp to repair the problem. Then on his twelfth lap, after he just got going again, the engine expired near the Philadelphia & Reading Railroad Bridge on the approach to Neill Drive. Then the Chadwick suffered tire trou-

Race leader William Wallace and his mechanician hurriedly try to replace a tire on the Palmer-Singer during their eighth lap. The delay caused them to lose the lead and dropped them back to seventh place. (1908). Photograph by Nathan Lazarnick, courtesy of the Detroit Public Library, National Automotive History Collection.

bles on its thirteenth lap, and Harkins didn't feel it was worthwhile to continue on since he strayed so far behind. About seven minutes separated the top four cars of Robertson, Florida, Davis and Bergdoll on lap fifteen, and eight of the remaining nine cars in the race were on the lead lap. Only the Studebaker fell approximately four laps behind the leaders, and it ran into more trouble on its thirteenth lap. While making the turn at the Catholic Fountain, the car lost a tire, causing it to swerve, but Yerger brought it to a stop without anyone getting hurt. He put on a new tire and continued on. The order remained the same on lap sixteen, but this time around, Robertson signaled to his crew that he would be stopping for fuel and tires the next time by. On lap seventeen, Robertson made his only stop of the day. According to *The Automobile*, "All hands were ready, and the car had hardly come to a standstill before the Loco helpers were all over it like a colony of ants."[9] The crew changed four tires and added gasoline, oil, and water to the car. The stop took less than three minutes, a very good stop in those days. Robertson's lap was 14:20. Florida's #9 Locomobile took over the lead for the duration of the lap. At the end of lap seventeen, Florida led Robertson by a mere ten seconds, and Davis fell about two minutes behind. Robertson quickly overtook Florida. On the eighteenth lap, Robertson re-took the lead and put a full minute between himself and his teammate, but because of the interval, only thirty seconds separated the two cars on the track. Davis' Apperson trailed Florida by 1:24, but in terms of track position, Davis actually ran about two minutes ahead of Florida, or a minute and a half ahead of Robertson on the track. Throughout the race, these three cars came around in nine to ten minutes every lap, and they were very close together on the track. Although the lap times do not really show it, they dueled for position on the track as well as in overall time, and they raced very near each other at different areas of the course. Lap nineteen saw no changes in position, although Florida gained time on Robertson. He cut the gap between them in half, to only thirty seconds, during the space of a single lap.

On lap twenty, nine cars remained in the race, with seven of them on the lead lap. This was very unusual at this point in the race, and the announcer proclaimed that it was a record for stock car racing.[10] More cars began to have trouble on the next lap though. The American Locomotive of Louis Bergdoll broke down near Wynnewood Avenue due to a burst cylinder. Bergdoll ran in fourth place at the time of the incident. On the same lap, Wallace, in the Palmer-Singer, experienced one of the more hair-raising events of the day. A broken steering gear caused the car to skid on the upper turn of the "S" curve on Neill Drive. According to the *Philadelphia Evening Bulletin*, the car "left the road and ran broadside into a fence, sending a crowd of spectators tumbling into a ravine to escape it."[11] Wallace, his mechanician, and the spectators who were in the vicinity, all escaped injury.

On lap twenty-two the only real threat to the Locomobile dominance fell out of the race. The Apperson car had been running well, keeping pace with the Locos, so it surprised everyone when the two Locomobiles passed the grandstand with the Apperson nowhere in sight. The car suffered an expired engine, which took Davis out of the race. Davis appeared very distraught. He ran in third for quite a while, and had a good shot at winning before this misfortune occurred. Six cars remained in the race. The two Locomobiles occupied first and second. Robertson had a four minute lead on his teammate. Florida's Locomobile then experienced a series of mechanical problems, and he fell steadily back through the field to fifth place. The Acme held second place on lap twenty-three, but trailed eleven minutes behind Robertson, who had such a comfortable lead that he reportedly smoked a cigar for the last three laps.[12] Mulford was not content with his third place position. He gained on Patchke, cutting the gap between them to 1:21. The order did not change, although Robertson extended his lead even further. As he flew down the front straightaway to start his twenty-fifth lap cheers went up from the crowd, which began to surge toward the finish line to await the winner.

Robertson completed his final lap, and won the race in 4:02:30. Patchke came in second in the Acme with a time of 4:14:54, followed by Ralph Mulford in the Lozier at 4:17:26, and the fourth place car of Bert Maucher at 4:21:26, and then the officials stopped the race. Jim Florida's Locomobile and Frank Yerger's Studebaker did not complete the full twenty-five laps before the race ended. Florida completed twenty-four laps, and Yerger completed nineteen laps. They could not finish, because by this time, thousands of spectators streamed onto the course, despite the best efforts of the police to keep them back.

Robertson drove to the end of the straight, then turned the car around and stopped in front of the Mayor's box to receive his awards. Robertson and his mechanician, Glenn Etheridge, stood up in the car and received the congratulations

Louis Bergdoll makes the right hand turn that leads into Sweet Briar Curve, a sharp downhill left hander that is just out of the frame of this photograph. Behind Bergdoll's American Locomotive, spectators can be seen on the porch roof of Sweet Briar Mansion. From *Motor* (November 1908), courtesy Automobile Reference Collection, Free Library of Philadelphia.

of Mayor Reyburn. They bowed to acknowledge Mrs. Reyburn and the ladies with her, at which point she jumped up, exclaiming, "Oh, it was fine, fine," and thrust a bouquet of roses at the duo.[13] The cheers from the crowd were so loud that Robertson could barely hear what the mayor said to him. He had won races before, but never had he received such praise. Stunned by this reception, and quite abashed by

George Robertson in Locomobile No. 10 and teammate Jim Florida in Locomobile No. 9, run side by side on Neill Drive in this advertisement for the Locomobile Company. The Locomobile Company ran quite a few advertisements featuring Robertson and his victory in Fairmount Park. Good performances in racing events meant increased sales for automobile manufacturers. From *Everybody's Magazine* (1909).

Table 3. 1908—Top Three Finishers

No.	Car	Driver	Time
10	Locomobile	Robertson	4:02:30
14	Acme	Patchke	4:14:54
17	Lozier	Mulford	4:17:26

it all, Robertson received the first of his awards from the mayor. The mayor handed him a Quaker City Motor Club pennant. Robertson accepted the pennant, "and after looking at it a minute or two with a comical expression of helplessness, hastily handed it back to the Mayor."[14] The crowd roared with laughter at this expression of bashfulness, as the announcer declared that another car was coming, and to clear the track. The crowd withdrew, and the police roped off the course again, but no car approached the line. The announcement was made as a ploy to encourage the crowd to recede. This gave Robertson some breathing room for the rest of the presentation. He received the *Evening Times* Fob Medal, and then the Founders' Week Cup. The mayor's assistants passed the large trophy down the grandstand to the mayor, who presented it to Robertson. As he handed him the trophy, the mayor said:

> This was one of the greatest races the City has ever seen, and you, Mr. Robertson, richly deserve your victory. I wish you a long life and prosperity, both you and your able assistant Mr. Etheridge. May your shadows never grow less and may you cherish this cup as long as you live and hand it down to posterity as a valued trophy of a great event.[15]

As Robertson held the cup, the crowd urged him to make a speech. He almost dropped it due to his nervousness. All of the attention had made him very uncomfortable and he begged Etheridge, "crank 'er up and let's get out of this."[16] With so many people surrounding his car, there was no way he was going anywhere, at least not without shaking thousands of hands, and being interviewed by dozens of reporters. The mayor continued to pat Robertson on the back, saying, "Your children and grandchildren will honor you for this day's victory."[17]

Robertson also received the *Philadelphia Record* Trophy, for making the fastest time in the first one hundred miles of the race. The mayor then distributed the other prizes earned during the race. The MacDonald & Campbell Trophy was awarded to Cyrus R. Patchke for second place, who had this to say after the race:

> It was a great contest, and I am glad to have been in it. I had no trouble worth mentioning and am only sore at myself because I didn't win.[18]

Tires caused most of Patchke's troubles during the race. His four stops for tire changes, plus one for fuel, are what kept him from challenging for the lead. The same went for Ralph Mulford, who received the Bailey Cup for third place and the *North American* Trophy for turning the fastest lap. While he may have had the fastest car, he explained that tires were his downfall:

3. *The Founders' Week Cup* 51

Mayor Reyburn hands the heavy Founders' Week Cup to George Robertson with the assistance of one of his aides, as an interested spectator climbs out from under the grandstand to get a better view of the festivities. (1908). From *American Review of Reviews* (1909).

> Why it was a joyride and I feel fit to do it all over again. I had the hardest kind of luck or I think I would have won. Why I had to change tires five separate times and always at places far away from my repair camp. But I am not kicking, I made the fastest time for a lap anyhow.[19]

The top three cars carried three different brands of tires, and although Robertson won the race on Firestones, and had no tire trouble, this was mainly due to the manner in which he drove the car, and not the quality of the tires. Fairmount Park was considered a driver's course, which meant having the fastest car, or the best equipment, would not guarantee a victory. The fact is that Robertson's steady pace saved his car, while the others who attempted to catch him constantly had problems.

There were six brands of tires used on the cars. One car used Ajax, two were on Firestones, and three carried Continentals, including the third place car of Ralph Mulford. One car used Fisk tires, and seven were on Diamonds including the second place car of Patchke. Michelin tires were used on the Thomas and Michener's Lozier. All of the brands of tires were very equal, and although many of the cars had problems with tires, very few of them were due to punctures, but rather to wheels breaking or falling off due to the manner in which the driver piloted the car.

Firestone rightly ran an advertisement in the papers claiming victory because

This photograph of the Founders' Week Cup appeared in the program for the following year's park race. In this photograph, the trophy appears complete, with the etching of Robertson's No. 10 Locomobile that was added at the conclusion of the race. The artisans at Bailey, Banks & Biddle probably had Philadelphia City Hall in mind when they topped the trophy with a statue of William Penn that resembles the one that overlooks the city from that building's tower. (1908). Courtesy AACA Library & Research Center, Hershey, PA.

they had won the race, but so did Diamond. They claimed that more tires were changed on cars using other brands, than those on Diamonds. This was true, but many of the other cars made tire changes as a precaution. The Locomobiles may have been able to run the entire race on their original sets of Firestones, but they chose not to because they were doing so well and felt that they had the extra time to make a stop. Also since very few of the cars had tire punctures, Diamond really could not make a claim that their tires were better, unless they had actually won the race. The quality of the Locomobile team's Firestone tires impressed Robertson's mechanic, Glenn Etheridge. "We were particularly delighted with the rapidity with which we could change our Firestone demountable rims," he said. "To the racing man, to whom seconds look like hours if he is not on the go, such quick tire change[s] as these are eloquent."[20]

The same case can be made for the cars, as is made for the tires. The Locomobiles were in fine form, with the exception of Florida's late race problems, but most of the problems experienced by the other cars were due to crashes, or parts breaking because their drivers pushed them to the limit. It can not be said that Robertson won because he had the best car. The Fairmount Park Race demonstrated the true talent of George Robertson as a driver, probably more so than any other race he had competed in before. During the previous week of practice, many of the drivers agreed that the layout of the course would require a very careful drive, without unnecessary risk taking. Robertson drove exactly that type of race. He paced himself, took it easy through the turns,

"Firestone" Tires

"The tires of Sterling Quality."

AND

Firestone Demountable Rims

WERE ON

Winner of Park Auto Race

Giving another evidence of Firestone Superior Quality. An absolutely perfect tire score was shown by the two cars in the race equipped with Firestone Tires.

Philadelphia Branch: Firestone Tire and Rubber Company
256 NORTH BROAD STREET
General Offices and Factory at Akron, Ohio

This advertisement for the Philadelphia Branch off the Firestone Tire and Rubber Company ran in newspapers the day after the Fairmount Park Race. The benefits to local business from holding the race in the city extended beyond just automobile manufacturers. Notice that their address was on North Broad Street, or Automobile Row, as it was then known. From the *Philadelphia Inquirer*, 11 October 1908.

and went fast on the straight sections. As a result, he had no problems with the car, no accidents, and no tire problems. While well known for his mad dashes around the dirt ovals in endurance races, Robertson showed that he could just as easily adapt to a twisting park circuit, and drive a conservative race, if that's what was needed to win. Robertson explained his strategy in a post race interview:

> The course was not a fast one, and I early realized that anyone who attempted to "beat it" would come to grief. I figured it out that the Loco outfit could stand a 50-mile gait and win. I adhered to that schedule as nearly as I could.[21]

With this victory, George Robertson became a hero to many Philadelphia race fans, so it was probably with great interest that they followed the events of the 1908 Vanderbilt Cup Race, which took place two weeks later on Long Island. An American car and driver had not won the race in the previous three runnings of the event, and American automobile manufacturers were desperate to prove that their cars were better than their foreign competition. Those interested in automobile racing saw George Robertson as America's best chance for victory that year. His win at Fairmount Park surely contributed to his being the favorite. He went on to win the race in a Locomobile, and became the first American driver to win an international road race in an American car, forever cementing his place in auto racing history.

The mayor sought out the officers of the Quaker City Motor Club after the race and congratulated them for staging such a well run event. The inaugural Fairmount Park Race was such a great success that he wasted no time in doing so. After such a successful race, the Quaker City Motor Club immediately began discussing the possibility about having another one, even as soon as November. Motor club officials decided against the idea of a November race because they thought that the weather would not be good for a race, and that the cold temperatures would keep attendance down.[22] However, motor club officials did hope that the race would become an annual event, despite the Fairmount Park Commission's warning that the Founders' Week race should not be seen as a precedent. Bringing famous racing drivers to participate in a world class event would bring attention to the city, along with the revenue generated by out of town visitors who would come to see the race on an annual basis. Mayor Reyburn had thoroughly enjoyed the race. Reporters noticed that Reyburn leaned forward in his chair every time a car came past the grandstand so that he could get a better look. They held little doubt that he and his fellow government officials would be in favor of holding the race again. *The Automobile* reported that when asked about having another race, "every man-Jack of them acquiesced and said that it would be good to advertise the city."[23] Only two days after the race, the *Philadelphia Evening Times* also called for the race to become an annual event:

> Why not make the Founders' Week race an annual affair, with a valuable trophy as the prize. Automobile manufacturers consider this city one of the greatest motoring centers in the country and would gladly respond with entries to make the contest successful.[24]

The decision on whether to make the race an annual event would have to wait, as the Quaker City Motor Club would again have to approach the Fairmount Park Commission and ask for their permission. Although it seemed that the results of the race pleased the commissioners, there were no guarantees. The first order of business was to make any repairs to the park that were necessary. On the Monday and Tuesday following the race, the Quaker City Motor Club worked on repairing the roads that were damaged during the race. The Fairmount Park Commission inspected the work on Wednesday and discovered that the roads had not only been repaired, but that they were in better shape then they had been before the race.[25] This was especially true of the West River Drive, which was now a hard surface rather than a soft dusty road of cinders. More than $2,000 of the $2,500 given to the commission by the Quaker City Motor Club, to guarantee the condition of the roads, was returned. The city also refunded the club's $25,000 bond. So it turned out that any fears about damage to the park, or injuries, were unfounded. There were no serious injuries, and the park was returned in better condition than ever. On 13 November 1908, at a meeting of the Fairmount Park Commission, a letter was read from the Quaker City Motor Club, thanking the commission for the use of the park, and the commission's cooperation in organizing the event.

From the planning of the event, to the on-track action, the Fairmount Park Race was unique in many respects. This uniqueness made the race the great success that it was. The course itself was much different than other road courses in use at the time. For example, the Vanderbilt Cup race was run on a 13 mile course, while Fairmount Park was only 8 miles. Although criticized at first for being too short, the Fairmount Park circuit turned out to be great for the fans. In races with longer intervals, it was almost possible to win without passing another car, but not so here. The thirty second interval between the cars was made up in no time, allowing for close racing, with the cars frequently dueling side by side on the track. Though the race was decided by overall time, passing for position on the track often equaled passing for position in the race. Racing fans were not accustomed to seeing this type of action on a road course.

Another unique aspect was the twisting nature of the circuit. When looking at the course map today, it actually looks like there are more than enough fast sections, but this is because we are accustomed to seeing races on twisting road courses and tight street circuits. These days, the cars have become so fast that tight corners are added to tracks in an effort to slow the cars down. In the early days of racing it was exactly the opposite. Most courses were designed to be fast, with many long straightaways where the cars could run flat out. The turns at Fairmount Park added quite a bit of drama to the race as evidenced by the number of spectators who watched from the more dangerous corners.

Fairmount Park was also unequaled when it came to attendance. The 400,000-500,000 estimate was a record for attendance in this country. There are many reasons for the high attendance figures. This was the first major road race to take place in a large city. One and a half million people could reach the track in a half-hour or less. On Long Island, they did not have that many people within such a short distance of the track. Philadelphia also had a much better infrastructure than Long Island. For only a nickel, Philadelphians could take the trolley to Fairmount Park. They could then watch from one area of the track for a while, and then easily move to another vantage point by using the Fairmount Park Trolley system. The Strawberry Mansion Bridge also provided access to the interior of the course after the race started. This was something that could not be done at other venues. One spectator commented, "There isn't a finer all-round automobile racing course in this country, considering opportunity for spectators to see it and for drivers to speed."[26] Another reason was that Pennsylvania was a major market for automobile sales. In 1900, Pennsylvania was the state with the highest number of automobile registrations. In 1910, it was third behind New York and California.[27] This didn't just mean that there were plenty of automobile enthusiasts in the area who were interested in the race, but the fact that many Pennsylvanians owned cars meant that they could attend the race more easily, and could travel greater distances to get there. Finally, the race was the last event of the Founders' Week Celebration, and although Saturday was a workday in 1908, most Philadelphians took the week off to attend the parades and events scheduled for each day. This meant that there were no conflicts with work, and since there was no admission fee, anyone who wanted to see the race could easily attend.

The biggest difference between Fairmount Park, and other races was the city's involvement. Besides being the only road race to take place in a big city, the Fairmount Park Race was the first to have the full cooperation of a big city, or local government. The city allowed the use of a public park for the course, but even more importantly, they offered police protection. In the early days of racing, it was difficult to keep spectators off of the course. Masses of spectators would walk out onto the track to look for approaching cars, and then step back as the cars came through. This was incredibly dangerous, and race organizers often had a hard time keeping the spectators back. In Philadelphia, the entire course was roped off, and 1,500 police guarded the perimeter. That means there were 187 police per mile. Add the Quaker City Motor Club officials to that total, and you have a very well-protected course. This was the major reason why there were no serious injuries to spectators or drivers. When people stepped onto the course, the drivers were also put into danger. George Robertson unfortunately hit and killed a New York police detective during his victorious drive at Brighton Beach the week before the Fairmount Park Race. He was very vocal about the subject in the week following that accident:

> It is hard enough to drive a car and keep to the course in any automobile racing event, but nothing is more fearful from a driver's standpoint than to have a human being bobbing up on the course. Remember, the driver's life is at stake, and while we have a car opened up to her limit of speed, supposedly in the belief that the course is clear, it is beyond human power to prevent an accident should any one cross the path of the machine at a point entirely unexpected or unprepared for.[28]

With Fairmount Park, Robertson could not have been more pleased. "The course today was kept clear of spectators better than in any race I have ever seen. It was wonderful how well the people were kept back."[29] Superintendent of Police Taylor was applauded after the race for the fabulous job he and his men had done. In comparison, the crowd at the 1906 Vanderbilt Cup Race was approximately 300,000, about 200,000 less than Fairmount Park, and that crowd was uncontrollable, resulting in one spectator death, and numerous injuries. The uncontrollable crowd, not only put everyone in danger, but also interfered with the pace of the race. Drivers often had to slow down for fear of killing someone. It was protests about issues like these that led to the cancellation of the 1907 Vanderbilt Cup Race. For the 1908 running, the Vanderbilt Cup was run on a new course designed to limit the crowd. It was comprised of the Long Island Parkway and roads which ran far out of town. The entire course was also fenced in to limit access.[30] Even with these precautions, and only 200,000 spectators, the Vanderbilt Cup would continue to have crowd control problems, and a disturbing safety record. In Philadelphia's case, cooperation between the city government, the Quaker City Motor Club, and the public, made for a safe event, despite the record crowds.

4

A Charitable Event

On 12 March 1908, the Quaker City Motor Club made their request to hold a second race in Fairmount Park. Club representatives stated that they wished to use the same course and follow the same rules as the previous year. "Although we wish it understood that such conditions as you may see proper to impose will be strictly complied with," they told the park commissioners.[1] They planned to hold the race on 7 October, leaving much more time to make preparations than they had the previous year. The date was later changed from the 7th to the 9th, which was a Saturday, rather than a Thursday. Someone must have made a mistake when they initially proposed the 7th. This time, there was no Founders' Week celebration to serve as a special occasion to hold the race, and as a result, the debate at the Fairmount Park Commission meeting was not as simple, nor as calm, as it was the previous year. After seeing how well run the race was in 1908, some members were very much in favor of making it an annual event, but others, who had only approved it because of the Founders' Week celebration, began to make their presence known.

What is surprising is that the commission member who seemed most supportive of the 1908 race suddenly became an obstacle. Upon the reading of the letter from the Quaker City Motor Club, James Pollock immediately moved "that the request be denied with thanks."[2] Mr. Pollock was the commission member who, just a year earlier, said that consideration must be given to the motor car, and that he was happy that the race should be held. It turns out that he must have also been behind the clause which said that the 1908 decision should not set a precedent. "You know how scared we were last year," Mr. Pollock reminded Col. Snowden.[3]

When Pollock moved that permission to hold the race be denied, Samuel Gustine Thompson broke in and offered that the Committee on Superintendence & Police should decide the matter. Eli Kirk Price Jr., whose father is recognized as a major figure in the founding of Fairmount Park, also stepped in and said, "I move that permission be granted on the same conditions as those of last year."[4] Mr. Thompson was opposed to the race, and must have felt that it would not have a chance if the smaller committee made the decision. The members did not let it get that far. A vote was taken on Mr. Price's motion, and it was passed, but the argument did not end there. "When the smash-up comes, I can say I told you so," Mr. Thompson exclaimed. "Well no accident occurred last year," responded Sidney W. Keith.[5] Thompson had reluctantly cast his vote in favor of the event. Only Mr. Pollock cast a dissenting vote, and he made sure that it was recorded in the minutes.

Although the race was approved for a second year, opposition was now very evident within the commission. The Quaker City Motor Club, if they wanted to have any chance of really making this an annual event, had to find a way to convince the opposing commissioners to support it. So, the motor club came up with a plan. They decided to turn the race into a charitable event. All of the money from entry fees and the sale of tickets would be given to charity, and the event itself would be promoted as a venue to solicit donations. Frank Hardart, one of the founders of the Horn & Hardart restaurant chain, and a prominent member of the Quaker City Motor Club, forwarded the first of these donations to the mayor on 31 July 1909. It was a total of $100, contributed by five Philadelphia citizens. Patricians loved to involve themselves in charitable causes, and this plan was directed at them. How could Philadelphia's high society consciously fight to ban an event that gave its proceeds to charity? They couldn't, and so the plan worked tremendously. This is not meant to take anything away from the Quaker City Motor Club. While this idea was hatched to engender support for the race, the club was truly interested in helping charity, and even in 1908, they were completely unconcerned about making a profit from the race. If the club members were, they could have worked out a deal with the city allowing them to charge everyone who came to the race, or they at least could have constructed a lot more grandstands so that they could charge for tickets, but they did not. Even now that it was guaranteed that they would make no profit, they put every effort and every resource of the Quaker City Motor Club into promoting it, and raising money for the charitable institutions that were chosen to receive the funds.

On 11 August 1909, the Quaker City Motor Club announced who those beneficiaries would be. They chose The Pennsylvania Society for the Prevention of Tuberculosis, The Rush Hospital, the White Haven Sanatorium, and the Children's Aid Society. These four institutions would split the profits from the race, which based on the previous year, were expected to be between $15,000 and $25,000. To ensure that the money would be properly distributed, the club, and representatives of the four institutions, decided that Doctor Joseph S. Neff, Director of the Department of Public Health & Charities would lead the Executive Committee in charge of the race. Mayor Reyburn would serve as its treasurer. Under this committee, were the Finance Committee, the Publicity Committee, and various other committees which would plan the event. These committees were made up of various representatives of the Quaker City Motor Club, municipal officials, and citizen appointees, to make sure that all of the money was accounted for. The Contest Committee, which would

4. A Charitable Event

take care of actual racing issues, would remain under the control of the Quaker City Motor Club. Philadelphians, especially prominent Philadelphians, began to support the race in earnest. The *Philadelphia Public Ledger* reported on its growing popularity among the upper class:

> Lifted from a sporting event to a civic enterprise, with its charitable side calculated to enlist sympathies and help of foremost philanthropic Philadelphians, the Fairmount Park automobile race of 200 miles, October 9, is assuming proportions that will make it eclipse anything of the kind ever held in this vicinity.[6]

In terms of making preparations for the race, the charitable side definitely helped, as individuals and organizations began to volunteer their services. The University of Pennsylvania promised to send student volunteers to act as grandstand ushers and to assist spectators in finding their seats. Philip Johnson, a respected Philadelphia architect, volunteered to design the grandstand for no cost. This grandstand would hold 3,965 people. It was set ten feet back from the road in order to allow the teams to set up their camps directly in front of it. Now the crowds in the stands would be able to see the cars being repaired when they made their stops, unlike the previous race when the camps were set up on Belmont Avenue. This would encourage the sale of grandstand seats and parking spaces on the Concourse, which would mean more money for charity.

Others contributed money or prizes rather than services. The Autolight Motor Supply Company donated a gold watch with nineteen jewels made by Bailey, Banks & Biddle, which was to be awarded to the driver who drove the most consistent race. George H. Stetson, of the Herkness & Stetson Real Estate Company, put up $100 cash to the driver who made the fastest lap, and MacDonald & Campbell donated the first place trophy. It was a $1,000 trophy, again designed by Bailey, Banks & Biddle. The trophy stood 40 inches tall. The figure of Victory stood on the top holding a laurel wreath skyward. The base had an enamel seal depicting the Quaker City Motor Club's logo on the front, with the seal of the City of Philadelphia on the rear. The inscription read, "The grand trophy for winning car of the second annual stock chassis road race, 200 miles, under the auspices of the Quaker City Motor Club and the municipal authorities of Philadelphia, Fairmount Park, Philadelphia, October 9, 1909." This time the city got billing on the trophy as one of the organizers along with the Quaker City Motor Club. Only the charitable aspect of the race made this possible. There was also an engraving of a racecar on the reverse side. Other prizes would be awarded in gold coin. According to *The Automobile*, the club would accommodate any winner who preferred to have a trophy or plaque of equal value to his winnings.[7]

On 29 September 1909, one hundred and five grandstand boxes were auctioned at the Samuel T. Freeman auction house on Chestnut Street. Frank Hardart suggested auctioning the boxes so that even more money would be earned for the charities. Individual grandstand seats were sold for $2 each. Some of the parking spaces were sold for $30 at auction, the rest were sold for $10 each from the Quaker City Motor Club's offices at the Hotel Walton. Five hundred and ten of the parking

The MacDonald & Campbell Trophy, presented to the winner of the Second Annual Fairmount Park Race. The silver trophy was manufactured by Bailey, Banks & Biddle. (1909). Courtesy AACA Library & Research Center, Hershey, PA.

spaces were on the Concourse, with the rest being at eight other locations around the track. Area automobile clubs were allowed to purchase blocks of parking spaces for their members before they went on sale at auction, so many of them were already spoken for. The Globe Printing Company donated the printing of the tickets.

The Quaker City Motor Club began making arrangements for the race almost immediately. As in the previous year, the course was wired for telephone at sixteen points around the track. At these points were to be stationed announcers with megaphones who would keep the spectators informed of events on other parts of the track. Dr. H. R. Owen was again to fill the role of director of medical preparations. For crowd control, there would be 1800 police and 70 park guards in addition to 200 men from Company B, Engineer Corps., of the Pennsylvania National Guard. The mayor put an army of city workers in the park to get the course back into shape. The West River Drive was still in good condition, and only needed patching in a few areas. The city also gave special attention to the hairpin curve on Sweet Briar Hill, as officials wanted to make that area better than it was the year before. The workers made it slightly banked, and applied a layer of stone over the dirt. The turn off of Belmont Avenue onto Parkside Avenue and the George's Hill turn, where the Lozier flipped over the previous year, were in pretty bad condition, and also required some special attention. A telephone pole and a fireplug were removed from the right side of the turn at Belmont and Parkside Avenues to make that turn wider. The Concourse was made smoother than ever, and was covered with finely crushed gravel. Although the 1908 course was not bad, the 1909 course would be much better, simply because there was much more time to work on it.

The mayor could justify using more city workers, and spending more city money on the improvements, since the race was now a charitable event. Chief William R. Benson of the Bureau of Highways was in charge of the roadwork. He was assisted by Jesse T. Vodges, the Chief Engineer and Park Superintendent. On 9 September 1909, there was a meeting of the various committees in the mayor's office. Chairman Robert E. Ross, of the Quaker City Motor Club Contest Committee, gave his report on the work that was being done. "The danger in automobile contests is bad roads, but Chief Benson of the Bureau of Highways, is going to make the roads so perfect that it will be impossible for an accident to occur."[8] He also made another comparison to the Vanderbilt Cup, showing the Quaker City Motor Club's desire to surpass that event:

> The contest will be worth going miles to see. In the Vanderbilt races, people go from California to Long Island and then only to get a fleeting glimpse of the contestants, whereas our event will show the contestants at close range 24 times.[9]

By the time they had finished their work, the course was in excellent condition. "Taken in its entirety, the course chosen for the second annual holding of this race is in 50 per cent better condition than it was last October," was the opinion of Frank Yerger, the Studebaker driver who had participated in the 1908 event.[10] Yerger was asked to make two test laps of the course a few days before practice officially began. The race was getting so big, both in terms of the racing, and the charitable effort, that the city invited President Taft to attend. It was reported at this meeting that the President had sent his regrets to the Executive Committee because he would be on a trip to the West at the time of the race, and would be unable to attend.

While the Quaker City Motor Club and the City of Philadelphia made these preparations, the patricians embraced the race in a way that was never expected. "Willingness to aid in every way has been expressed by many of those whose names figure in the Blue Book, the Assembly list and as subscribers to the two opera houses," reported the *Philadelphia Public Ledger*.[11] The Assembly was an annual dance, exclusive to the patrician families in which the sons and daughters of society, came out into the public eye for the first time. They also compared the race to another Philadelphia tradition, the Army-Navy football game, "as a great outdoor event, in which society will be on dress parade."[12] In those days, the Army-Navy game was played at the University of Pennsylvania's Franklin Field. Football was one of the sports that "society" enjoyed, mainly because it was played by college students, and therefore was acceptable to the patricians, who went to the games to see their sons play. For the Fairmount Park Race to be embraced by society, and compared to the biggest college sporting event in the area, shows just how "accepted" it became, and all because of the charitable side of the event. "There has probably never been an outdoor sporting event outside of the Army and Navy football game which has appealed so strongly to society as the Fairmount Park automobile race," pronounced the *Philadelphia Public Ledger*.[13]

Although charity had done much to make the race acceptable, some of the patricians still wavered. On 7 October 1909, the *Philadelphia Record*, a supporter of the race, ran a letter to the editor which attacked the papers for failing to protest the idea of auto racing in the park. This was a good show of the paper's impartiality, but the letter points out that the papers had refrained in the past from publishing anti-race letters. "It is a singular fact," the writer accusingly wrote, "that not a newspaper in this city has published any protest, either by itself or any of its correspondents, against the extraordinary violation of law that is to take place on Saturday next."[14] The letter claimed that it was a "criminal offense" to drive through the park above the speed limit, or to race on a public road. It did not just question the legality of the race, but also of automobiles in the park in general. "They now so completely dominate the Park that they have made not only driving, but walking along its roadways so difficult and dangerous as practically to exclude other persons than themselves from its free enjoyment by them."[15]

The person who wrote this did not like automobiles at all. When they say that cars make it difficult, it most likely means that they were still getting around on horses. "Where do the Mayor and Park Commissioners get the right to give certain favored persons the exclusive use of portions of the park," the writer asked.[16] It even went so far as to say that if anyone died in a racing accident that the mayor and Fairmount Park Commissioners would be guilty of manslaughter. The papers had not run any letters like this before because they knew that this was an attempt to bring the commissioners back into the patrician fold; to scare them into believing that if anything went wrong, they were responsible.

The letter was signed MISSOURI, so we will never know who wrote it, but it is very likely that MISSOURI was a patrician. This was a person who could not accept the changing times, a person who disliked automobiles because they were new. Karl Benz produced the first practical automobile in 1885, and it took years of development before consumers began to feel that motor cars were worth the expense. By 1900, automobile registrations totaled only 8,000 in the entire United States of America. When MISSOURI wrote his letter, registrations surpassed 300,000, but the automobile was still relatively new, and some were not ready to accept it.[17] MISSOURI also had a problem with the race because, for manufacturers, it was "a means of advertising their wares and business."[18] These two points are mentioned only briefly. Most of the letter deals with the issue of safety, even though nobody was seriously injured during the 1908 race. The argument about safety was unwarranted, but the letter writer used the issue to hide his true motives. This would not be the last time that the safety argument would appear as a cover.

On 6 October 1909, it was revealed that the Fairmount Park Commission had demanded over 100 seats and 50 parking spaces for the use of the commissioners and their friends, and that they did not pay for them. It was expected that since the race was now a charitable event, there would be no free seats. The Quaker City

Motor Club had purchased parking spaces for its members, and specifically told the race committee that "the spaces be left aside for the use of the members at the same price at which said parking spaces will be sold by your committee to other citizens."[19] Mayor Reyburn and Doctor Neff had also paid for their tickets. They said that the only seats that they had to reserve for free were those for the officials and the media. Dr. Neff handled the complaint about the free seats for the park commissioners, and he did not hold back his disappointment with them. "The Park Commissioners have a number of parking spaces and some seats which we wanted them to pay for," said the doctor. "They demanded a space this year. They got it."[20] The commissioners had built their own grandstand for the 1908 race, but this year, they said that since they were allowing the race to be held in the park, they should get free seats. The *Philadelphia Evening Bulletin* did not mention the issue again until 8 October, in their report on the monthly meeting of the Fairmount Park Commission. The paper noted that the commissioners did not mention the race at all, and that they did not comment on the charges that they had deprived the charitable institutions of revenue from the large block of seats which they had received for free. The total value of the seats and parking spaces was determined to be around $900.[21] It should also be noted that at this meeting, Dr. J. William White became a member of the Fairmount Park Commission, replacing Samuel Gustine Thompson who passed away in September. Thompson had fiercely opposed the holding of the race. What effect this replacement would have on the future of the event was uncertain at the time, but Dr. White was known to be an avid sports fan.

While all of these matters were being attended to, the Quaker City Motor Club also sought new entries. For the 1909 race, twenty cars would be permitted to run, although the length of the track was still the same as the previous year. The committee sent out notices that the race was on, and encouraged all American makers to enter their cars early, so that they would get a spot in the field. Early in July, *The Automobile* began to speculate that the club might allow foreign cars to be entered. Because of the agreement between the AAA and the ACA, foreign cars would have to be driven by American drivers, if they were allowed. *The Automobile* reported this because the Quaker City Motor Club did not receive many entries for a recent trial run to Pittsburgh and back. Chairman Ross, of the Contest Committee, admitted that the club preferred that the entire field be composed of American cars, but that they intended to tentatively take the entries of foreign cars in case they did not receive enough American entries.[22] By mid-July, *The Automobile* was reporting that this opinion was not necessarily the opinion of everyone on the Contest Committee. Some wanted it to be a race for American cars only, but others saw that view as being cowardly, when there was no reason to fear foreign competition any longer. *The Automobile* agreed, "Those who follow the racing game closely are of the opinion that in a stock chassis event American makers have now nothing to fear from their foreign rivals, whatever may have been the situation a few short years ago."[23] George Robertson had won the Vanderbilt Cup in an American car, proving that a foreign car would not automatically win an event that included foreign machines. Those on the committee who wanted to allow foreign cars felt that doing so would prove that point even further, and would add more credibility to an American victory.

On 2 August, the Contest Committee announced that foreign cars would be allowed, as long as American drivers were behind the wheel. Apparently, the accusation that keeping them out was seen by the public as cowardly was enough to raise the committee's confidence in American machines, and accept the challenge.[24]

Entry blanks were mailed to interested parties on 30 July, and one day later, the club had its first entry, the 60 horsepower Acme car, entered by Malin Leinau, who also intended to drive it. Leinau was a local who had competed in other Quaker City Motor Club events, mostly endurance runs. This would be his first road race. C. A. Schroeder became the second entrant when he entered a 60 horsepower Palmer-Singer, as he had the year before. William Wallace would also be returning as its driver.

The next entrant was the 90 horsepower Simplex entered by John F. Betz III, who like Louis Bergdoll, was another wealthy member of a local brewing firm. Betz was an amateur who had competed in a few minor races, but nothing like this. The next car entered was an Apperson, rated at 49.2 horsepower, which was entered by the Philadelphia Auto Company, making a return appearance after their good performance in the 1908 race. Herbert Lytle was designated as the driver for 1909. Lytle was a veteran racer who had competed for the Vanderbilt Cup several times, and drove in the 1905 Gordon Bennett Race.

On 18 August 1909, L. E. French, who had entered a Pullman the previous year, entered a Kline Kar, a product of the B. C. K. Motor Company, of York, Pennsylvania. He did not specify a driver at the time. While the entry was accepted, it was later found that the minimum of twenty-five production cars had not been produced, meaning that it did not meet the requirements of a stock chassis, and so the entry was held as an alternate. The Lozier Motor Company also did not specify a driver when entering one of its 50 horsepower cars. Next was Erwin R. Bergdoll, making another attempt at the race. This time he entered a 120 horsepower Benz, which was a very fast car. He also entered a second one, a 60 horsepower model, which would be driven by Charles Howard, the foreman of the Louis Bergdoll Motor Company. Then his brother-in-law, Al Hall entered a 70 horsepower Welch. Hall was a former chauffeur for the Bergdoll family, who had married Elizabeth Bergdoll, the millionaire sister of Erwin and Louis.

It was now the end of August, one month after the list had opened, and half of the spots were filled. The next two entries came from Louis Bergdoll. Since his Thomas was one of the fastest cars in the hands of George Salzman the previous year, he entered one for himself this time, as well as a second to be driven by Willie Haupt. Both Thomas cars were rated at 70 horsepower. B. B. Larzelere of the Chadwick Engineering Works entered two 60 horsepower Chadwick cars in the race. One would be driven by Len Zengle, who had driven for the Pennsylvania team in 1908. The company would choose the second driver at a later date. Larzelere had driven over the course before entering the cars, and found it to be much improved over the previous year. On 18 September 1909, the Quaker City Motor Club announced some big news. George Robertson's entry had arrived. The people of Philadelphia greeted the news that Robertson would be returning to defend his victory of the previous year, with great joy. The *Philadelphia Public Ledger* initially reported that he would be driving a Locomobile again, but they had only assumed it because he had driven one the year before. This time, Robertson would be driving with his full time team, Simplex. This was the team with which he had won so many races. The Simplex Automobile Company, based in New York, entered the car, which was a 90 horsepower model, like the one entered by Betz.

On 21 September, the Chalmers-Fanning Motor Car Company entered two 40 horsepower Chalmers-Detroit Bluebirds. The Bluebirds had a reputation for being fast, and they had won more than a couple of races. The drivers of the Bluebirds would be Bert Dingley and Lee Lorimer. The Chalmers-Fanning Motor Car Company was the local affiliate of Chalmers-Detroit, an automobile manufacturer, founded in Detroit in 1906. On 25 September, William C. Longstreth of the W. C. Longstreth Motor Car Company entered a 60 horsepower Alco car. The Alco was a product of the American Locomotive Company which was represented the previous year by Louis Bergdoll's entry of one of their machines. Longstreth's business was the distribution and sale of Pullman cars, but he had just recently signed a deal to sell the Alco car as well, from his showroom on Race Street. This was a great opportunity for Longstreth to advertise his new business venture. Harry Grant, who had recently led a race at Lowell in an Alco, was designated as the driver.

The Columbia Motor Car Company entered one of its 32.4 horsepower cars, and appointed John C. Coffey as its driver. Columbia was the renamed Electric Vehicle Company. At the time, Columbia owned the Selden Patent, which was the United States patent on gasoline powered vehicles awarded to George B. Selden in 1895. The Selden Patent was mired in controversy from the beginning, because Selden had not produced a car during his ownership of the patent. After purchasing the patent in 1900, the Electric Vehicle Company sold licenses to other companies through a trade association, the Association of Licensed Automobile Manufacturers (ALAM), which allowed the licensees to produce gasoline powered cars. Several hundred manufacturers produced automobiles in the United States, but only a handful joined the ALAM. Most manufacturers felt that they did not owe anything to Selden, or the Electric Vehicle Company, since they had designed and built their cars on their own, and had far surpassed the 1895 technology of the Selden Patent. Litigation ensued, especially with Henry Ford, who did not recognize the legality of the patent. Ford eventually won in court in 1911, and negated the patent. It would have expired in 1912, regardless of the court's decision.

There were now eighteen cars entered with three spots remaining. The next two cars were from the American Motor Car Company of Indianapolis. One car would be driven by Robert Drach, and the other by E. O. Hayes. Both cars were rated at 60 horsepower. Drach and Hayes were both experienced drivers who had competed in road races previously.

Then an entry came in from the country's most popular driver. Barney Oldfield had been racing since 1902. He was a showman who did most of his driving on oval tracks at fairs, either challenging other drivers in match races, or attempting to break speed records. Despite his lack of experience in major road races, he was the most popular driver of his time. He had retired in 1908, but decided to return, this time competing in more organized events as well as matches. He had always been associated with record-breaking cars like the Ford 999, and the Peerless Green Dragon. This time he entered his new car of choice, the 120 horsepower Benz. It was just like the one that Erwin Bergdoll had entered, although it is unknown where Bergdoll acquired his car. The 120 horsepower car had been built for the 1908 French Grand Prix. Two of the three cars that competed in that race were brought to the United States to compete in the 1908 Grand Prize in Savannah. They were then purchased by Barney Oldfield and David Bruce-Brown.[25]

On 28 September, Oldfield's entry was rejected on the grounds that the car was not a stock chassis. The Quaker City Motor Club said that this was because it did not appear in the manufacturer's catalog for 1909. Oldfield and Jesse Froelich of the Benz Import Company, claimed that the car was in the catalog, but actually it was not.[26] Erwin Bergdoll's car was also eliminated, so he entered a 70 horsepower Welch in its place. Oldfield was angry, and he threatened to go before the racing committee of the AAA to fight the decision, but the Quaker City Motor Club was not worried. The club mailed Oldfield his $500 entry fee. "They certainly have my dander up, and I am on the warpath," said Oldfield. "In the Philadelphia case they never examined my car to find whether it was stock or not. They were flattering enough to state that if I was allowed in the race with my big car it would be a procession and not a race."[27] That was exactly what the Quaker City Motor Club was afraid of. With his 120 horsepower car, Oldfield was guaranteed to win, but what is interesting is that they did not question Bergdoll's earlier entry of the same model. One possibility was that they did not feel that Bergdoll would gain much of an advantage since he was an amateur. The car would be much faster in the more capable hands of Oldfield. But the more likely scenario is that they did not notice that it wasn't a stock car until Oldfield tried to pass it off as a 59 horsepower car. Both Oldfield and Benz claimed that the ALAM rated the car at 59 horsepower. Many other cars that were entered had higher ratings, and the Quaker City Motor Club knew that Oldfield would not enter a car that would give him a disadvantage. The 120 horsepower Benz was a fast car, there was no denying it. Trying to pass it off as a less powerful car was an immediate red flag to the officials.

This was not Oldfield's first run-in with the AAA. His reputation preceded him. The AAA had banned him earlier in his career for competing in unsanctioned match races. More recently, a race at the Narrangansett Track in Providence, Rhode Island, in which Oldfield was the main attraction, was not granted a sanction at the last minute. "I am in the racing game to stay, but the AAA will have to play fair with me, or there will be someone going to the mat," he threatened.[28] What bothered Oldfield so much was that the entry was held for five days before it was rejected. Contest Committee Chairman Ross, and a Mr. Hower of the AAA, advised Secretary Harbach of the Quaker City Motor Club, to hold Oldfield's entry until he was sure that there would be enough entries.[29] It turned out that both sides were not playing fair when it came to Oldfield's entry. If the race had a less than full field, chances are that the Quaker City Motor Club would have kept Oldfield in.

The next two cars entered were 30 horsepower Buicks, entered by the Buick Motor Car Company. Their drivers were Robert Burman and Louis Chevrolet. Chevrolet was a Frenchman who had moved to the United States, and began racing in 1905. He had competed in the Vanderbilt Cup Race, as well as the first race at the Indianapolis Motor Speedway just a few months earlier. He was known for his daring and recklessness. Burman had been associated with Buick since 1903, and had competed in his first race for the team in 1906. He was best known for his drive in the 1908 Grand Prize Race in Savannah, and his victory in the first race held at the Indianapolis Motor Speedway, the 250 mile Prest-O-Lite Trophy Dash.

On 2 October, the Lozier Motor Company specified Joe Seymour as the driver of their car. The Lozier entry was very important because it was a popular car in Philadelphia, mainly due to Ralph Mulford's win at Point Breeze in 1907, and his third place at Fairmount Park in 1908.

On Monday, 4 October 1909 the crowds poured into the park at daybreak to see the first practice laps, but there was a problem. Officials from the Quaker City Motor Club thought that they had the necessary permits to hold practice, but they apparently did not. A permit to speed over the course on this day had not been issued. Captain Hayes H. Duncan and his Fairmount Park Guards stopped the drivers who went out on the course. All of the drivers who went out for the first day obeyed the officers' orders to stop, except for Al Hall in the Welch. He continued to go around the track at speed and the police promptly arrested him. Hall's wife suggested that Sergeant Harry Hahn of the Park Guard drive back with them to their home on North Wynnefield Avenue, so that Hall could retrieve money to pay the bail. The officer agreed, and so they boarded Hall's car and started for home. On the way to Hall's house, the driver attacked the officer with a blackjack and threw him out of the car. It wasn't long before he was caught and held under $1,500 bail. Hall's explanation for his attack on the officer was, "that he just didn't care for the sergeant riding around with him and that he didn't feel like being locked up."[30] Friends arrived at City Hall on Monday night to pay the bail, but Hall had to return on Tuesday morning. It was then that he pleaded guilty to seven of eight charges. Four involved speeding, and three were for using his wife's driver's license. The last charge of assault and battery would be decided by a grand jury at a later date.

On Monday night, while Hall was being bailed out of jail, a meeting was held at the Hotel Walton where the drivers drew numbers that would decide the order in which they would start the race. John F. Betz III picked the number one spot. Other important numbers were Louis Chevrolet who picked unlucky #13, which was not skipped like it had been in 1908. Al Hall's entry received #21, although the officials had an announcement to make regarding Hall. R. E. Ross announced that Hall would not be allowed to drive the Welch, although the car could still take part with another driver behind the wheel. "The reason for our action," said Mr. Ross, "was that Mr. Hall has persistently refused to obey the orders of the Park police and in violation of orders speeded over the course in nine minutes on Sunday, when there were no precautions to prevent accidents."[31] This was the first time that anyone had learned of Hall's speeding over the course on Sunday. Mr. Ross continued, "Then again he acted unreasonable yesterday morning by getting the authorities down on him, and he is now under $1,500 bail for speeding, for using another's license and for ejecting Park Guard Sergeant Hahn from his car when arrested."[32] Hall believed that he could do anything he wanted now that he was a member of a family of millionaires, and his reaction to Ross' statement demonstrates this. "I'll be on the course tomorrow morning all right. Oh yes, I'll drive, won't I dearie?" he said to his wife as they both laughed.[33] Hall did not realize that the Quaker City Motor Club did not care who he was, and they were completely serious about excluding him from the race. Hall threatened to sue the club for not having the necessary permits, but he really did not have a case. The motor club held the position that when the police told Hall not to speed, he should have obeyed, whether he thought he had permission or not.

Monday also brought the news that Herbert Lytle would not be driving in the race. Lytle had been involved in an accident at a race at Riverhead, Long Island on 30 September. Lytle skidded on a turn, and the car overturned, crushing his mechanician James Bates, killing him instantly. Lytle was thrown about 20 feet from his car. His injuries would prevent him from driving at Fairmount Park. When it was found that Lytle would be unable to drive, two of the 1908 contestants, Jim Florida, and Frank Yerger tried to take his spot in the Apperson, but Apperson adopted a new policy after Lytle's accident that they would no longer allow married men to act as drivers or mechanicians. Hugh L. Harding was announced as Lytle's replacement. He was a veteran, who had competed in the 1906 Vanderbilt Cup and the 1908 Grand Prize, among other events.

Another car was allowed to enter on Monday. It was the 40 horsepower Isotta-Fraschini, with Louis Strang as the driver. The J. M. Quinby Company of New York entered the car, which was manufactured in Milan, Italy. Strang had been racing since 1905, and was a very popular driver. He was just coming off of a good year. In 1908 he won major races at Savannah, Briarcliff, and Lowell, all three in an Isotta-Fraschini. Strang had more recently driven for Buick as a teammate of Burman and Chevrolet. He had just quit his job with Buick on the previous Wednesday to join the Isotta Import Company.

The issue of the permit was ironed out by Tuesday morning, and the drivers finally took their first practice laps. Before the sun was even up, Wallace was out on the course in the Palmer-Singer. Since it was so dark, his first lap was only 9:50. The American car of Hayes was next out on the course, followed by Coffey in the Columbia. Coffey made at least eight laps, his fastest being a 9:18. Bob Burman made a few rounds in his Buick, turning four laps between nine and ten minutes. Len Zengle took four laps, which averaged 9:12, and Erwin Bergdoll averaged 9:25. The Acme car was also out on the course, but none of the drivers mentioned so far seemed to be pushing their cars to the limit.

A few drivers did try to make fast laps. Dingley made a lap of 8:55 and his teammate Lorimer was close behind him at 8:57. Harry Grant went even faster in the Alco, making a quick lap of 8:51, but this day belonged to Louis Chevrolet, who made the fastest lap of the day of 8:40. This was only eight seconds behind the fastest lap of the 1908 race made by Ralph Mulford, and twenty-two seconds faster than the best practice time from the previous year. Chevrolet promised that by the end of the week, he would turn an 8:00 lap.[34] As he had the year before, William Wallace offered another *Philadelphia Evening Bulletin* reporter a ride around the course. Perhaps it was newsworthy that the reporter was a woman. At about seven o'clock

Spectators line the South Concourse in front of Memorial Hall. The safety precautions put in place for the Fairmount Park Races can be seen here. All of the spectators are behind a rope, and there are three Park Guards keeping watch over the small stretch of roadway that is visible. (1909). Photograph by Nathan Lazarnick, courtesy of the Detroit Public Library, National Automotive History Collection.

in the morning, they boarded the Palmer-Singer and were off for two hair-raising laps. When it was over, the young woman seemed less shaken than the male reporter who took a ride the year before. "The exhilaration of the ride made perception sharper, I caught glimpses of the Schuylkill River, noted the tops of the far away trees, and began to distinguish the people," she said, reflecting on her unique experience.[35] Although the headline, "Girl Dashes Round Park Motor Course," must have seemed a bit of a novelty at the time, the reporter proved herself up to the challenge. One interesting exchange during the ride dealt with the Neill Drive turn, and it is interesting to hear Wallace's feelings about it. "This is the most dangerous turn of all," he said. "You have to slow up so much at the others that they really don't count."[36] Drivers must have held their breath entering Neill Drive, because although it was twisty, it was also very fast, and the initial turn off of the West River Drive was made more dangerous by the presence of the railroad bridge wall looming around the corner.

The Selden Company was allowed to enter one of its 36 horsepower cars on Tuesday. It was assigned #23. Charles Young would drive the car. The entry was made by F. E. Dwyer. George Selden, who originally patented the use of the gasoline engine for vehicles, operated the Selden Motor Car Company. Selden had not

William Wallace re-enters the park at 52nd Street and Elm Avenue, passing under the gaze of the spectators on George's Hill on his way toward the Catholic Fountain. A Fairmount Park Guardhouse is partially visible behind the man in the foreground, and the tracks of the Fairmount Park Trolley can also be seen, as their path continues along Elm Avenue. (1909). Photograph by Nathan Lazarnick, courtesy of the Detroit Public Library, National Automotive History Collection.

manufactured cars himself until 1906, when he formed his own company. The car did not regularly compete in automobile races, so the entry of a Selden was looked at with great anticipation. With all of the popular drivers entered, the only one missing was Ralph DePalma. On Tuesday, 5 October 1909, word got out that the Quaker City Motor Club was trying to get him to enter, which meant that they intended to start twenty-four cars if necessary, but it ultimately would not happen. DePalma chose not to enter.

Wednesday's practice session was much more eventful. George Robertson made his first appearance, and he received a standing ovation when he started off on his first lap. Jim Florida, Robertson's former Locomobile teammate, who had driven well in the previous year's race, temporarily rode along as guest mechanician on these first laps. Although the papers said that Robertson did not make an attempt at a fast lap, he earned a very respectable time of 8:42. Other drivers taking their first laps on this day were Charles Young in the Selden, Willie Haupt in the Thomas, Louis Bergdoll in his Thomas, and Len Zengle, who turned in an 8:35 in his Chadwick. Harding, in the Apperson, also took a few slow laps around the course. Betz made a few rounds in his Simplex, and Louis Strang made his first appearance in

4. *A Charitable Event* 71

Rowhouses serve as the backdrop for the turn at 52nd Street and Parkside Avenue. In this photograph, Bob Burman's Buick is followed by Charles Young's Selden as they rumble over the brick paved street. (1909). Photograph by Nathan Lazarnick, courtesy of the Detroit Public Library, National Automotive History Collection.

the Isotta-Fraschini. Anyone who visited the practice session looking to see high speeds found the second day very encouraging. Grant made a lap in eight minutes in the Alco but the drivers of the Buick and Chalmers-Detroit cars really put on a show. Bob Burman turned a lap of 7:47 in his Buick. His teammate Louis Chevrolet trailed close behind him on this lap. His close proximity must have urged Burman to make such a fast time. Chevrolet had to fall back near the end of the lap though, because of a newly resurfaced section near Belmont and Wynnewood. Burman's car kicked up stones on this section which pelted Chevrolet and his mechanician Jack Grennan. Nevertheless, Chevrolet completed the lap in 8:25. The crowds cheered Burman upon the completion of his record-breaking lap and officials ran to the car to congratulate him. When Chevrolet and Grennan came around all of the attention switched to the two injured men. Blood streamed from cuts on their heads and faces, and they both appeared to be in obvious pain. Doctors escorted them to an ambulance and took them to the hospital to be patched up. Bert Dingley, in the Chalmers-Detroit, had the second fastest time of 7:58. His time made him the only driver besides Burman to run a lap in less than eight minutes.

William Wallace barely avoided death on one of his laps. He made the turn off of Sweet Briar onto the West River Drive and began accelerating down the straight,

The Smith Memorial looms over Lansdowne Drive as Bert Dingley makes his way toward the Sweet Briar Mansion in his Chalmers-Detroit Bluebird. (1909). Photograph by Nathan Lazarnick, courtesy of the Detroit Public Library, National Automotive History Collection.

when a small boy ventured out onto the track into the path of the speeding car. Wallace swerved to avoid the boy, missing him by a mere six inches, and then barely avoided a tree as he ran off the road. Wallace became a bit of a hero because he risked himself to save the boy.[37] An incident on the Concourse had an even greater chance of turning into tragedy. A grandstand railing collapsed, and dozens of people lost their balance and fell onto the course. Nobody in the grandstand suffered any injuries, since they did not fall a great distance, but had a car been coming by at the time, it could have been much worse. The Quaker City Motor Club saw the timing of the collapse as a blessing, since a similar occurrence during the race could have been much worse. Officials immediately set out to strengthen the grandstand, so that there would not be any similar accidents on raceday when the stand would be packed with thousands of people.

On Thursday, all eyes focused on the Chalmers-Detroit Bluebirds. First, Bert Dingley attracted some attention, when he took his wife around the course as his mechanician for four laps, the fastest of which was an 8:35. "There's a woman!" the crowds shouted. "Bet you she's a newspaper reporter looking for a sensation," one person said.[38] The people of Philadelphia were unaccustomed to seeing a woman in a racing car, but Mrs. Dingley was well acquainted with the sport. She always traveled with her husband and had even served as mechanician for him in a race at Portland. She would return on Friday to again act as mechanician, but would not

4. A Charitable Event

George Robertson pours oil into his Simplex before the start of the 1909 race. On the right is Columbia driver John Coffey, who has come over for a chat. Robertson's mechanician, Glenn Etheridge, faces the camera. (1909). From the Collections of Henry Ford Museum & Greenfield Village, Neg. No. 1774.FP.09.2.

be beside him in the race. "I'd love to ride to-morrow in the Bluebird," said Mrs. Dingley, "but if anything should go wrong a man would be of so much more use, and I couldn't bear to think that I had been the cause of my husband's losing a race."[39] When asked whether she was afraid for either herself or her husband she said that she was well aware of the dangers, but that she accepted them and did not worry. "I'm not worried about him at all and I know all the dangerous places as well as he does," she said. "My first ride in a racing car left me badly shaken up and frightened, but now I could ride without any sensation at all."[40] An attractive woman who knew quite a bit about the mechanics of automobiles and was not afraid to get a bit dirty driving around in racecars shocked the public. "Her appearance is strangely out of keeping with her character...Mrs. Dingley typifies femininity, and it seems a little incongruous to connect her with the rattle and hum of a racing automobile," commented one reporter.[41] Dingley's teammate, Lee Lorimer, drew attention to himself in another way, by becoming the third driver in three days to set a new track record. The timers clocked Lorimer at 7:43. His time remained the only real fast lap of the day. The other drivers made more casual laps around the course. George Robertson had not broken any records, but he still proved to be the city's favorite

Table 4. 1909—Fastest Time of Each Driver in Practice

Car	Driver	Time
American	Drach	9:58
Thomas	Haupt	8:36
Acme	Leinau	9:11
Selden	Young	10:02
Columbia	Coffey	9:18
Palmer-Singer	Wallace	8:17
Chalmers-Detroit	Dingley	7:58
Apperson	Harding	9:10
Chalmers-Detroit	Lorimer	7:43
Simplex	Robertson	8:33
American	Hayes	9:10
Simplex	Betz	8:30
Chadwick	Parkin	8:35
Buick	Chevrolet	8:23
Lozier	Seymour	8:48
Thomas	L. Bergdoll	9:00
Alco	Grant	8:00
Welch	E. Bergdoll	10:10
Benz	Howard	9:17
Buick	Burman	7:47
Chadwick	Zengle	8:20
Isotta	Strang	9:30

driver. "There he goes, look at him; that's Robertson!" members of the crowd often exclaimed.[42] Robert Drach in the American attended practice for the first time on Thursday, as did Seymour in the Lozier and Howard in the Benz. John F. Betz had the only accident of the day when a connecting rod broke and caused the car to flip over. Since both avoided injury, Betz and his mechanician, George Tompkins, hitched a ride on the next car that came by and returned to their camp.

The final practice session took place on Friday. As in 1908, the crowds increased with each day of practice, and on Friday the estimated attendance was 12,000 people. Since the session started at daylight, many Philadelphians awoke early and went to practice before going to work. A blanket of fog hung over the course, so the drivers did not make any fast laps, at least none under the 8 minute mark. The biggest spectacle of the day actually took place in the pits as Harding prepared to start the Apperson for a practice run. He flooded the carburetor and the car burst into flame. Members of the Apperson team attempted to put the fire out with no success, so they turned off the feed of gas to the engine and allowed the fire to burn itself out. The car would be ready for the race on Saturday. The fire caused minimal damage which the team repaired in just a few hours. Bert Dingley also got into some trouble, getting a flat tire as he traveled down Sweet Briar Hill. Mrs. Dingley occupied the mechanician's seat at the time. "I was out of the car before it stopped, and took the tire off, while Bert adjusted the new one. I'm not such a bad mechanic really," she laughed.[43]

At a meeting on Friday night, Quaker City Motor Club officials decided that since Al Hall's Welch had been disqualified, the Kline Kar would be allowed to take its place as #21. The Kline Kar team had the car prepared and ready to go, but they had no driver, so the entrant decided that the car would not compete anyway. In an unexpected development at the meeting, the drivers presented a petition to the Contest Committee which was signed by many of the participants. The petition requested that G. Hilton Gantert be replaced as the starter of the race due to the fact that he was too inexperienced. The drivers wanted a New Yorker, Fred J. Wagner, to fill that role. Wagner had been the starter of the 1908 Vanderbilt Cup Race, and acted as the official starter of the AAA. He was available to perform the job since he was in Philadelphia seeking entries for the 1909 Vanderbilt Cup Race. The Contest Committee made a compromise and kept Gantert as the starter, but appointed Wagner assistant referee, so that Gantert would have an experienced advisor beside him. They also decided that the cars would start one at a time, at 15 second intervals, rather than two at a time, at thirty second intervals, as had been planned. The drivers were not thrilled about starting two at a time, so the Quaker City Motor Club listened to their concerns and changed their plans.

With all of the preparations complete, the 1909 Fairmount Park Race appeared that it would be even more popular than the 1908 event. With the added support of Philadelphia society, greater city participation, an improved track surface, the addition of more famous drivers, and a twenty-two car field, the Quaker City Motor Club had assured an incredible Saturday race. The drivers received their final briefing on the rules at the Friday night meeting, and then readied themselves for the twelve o'clock start on Saturday afternoon.

5

The Second Annual Fairmount Park Race

By Saturday, 9 October, visitors to Philadelphia found it difficult to find a hotel room. Automobile racing fans had come from all over the country to see the race. The *Philadelphia Evening Times* even reported that there were Canadians and Parisians booked into the city's hotels.[1] In the vicinity of Philadelphia's major hotels, thousands of cars lined the streets and parking garages reached their capacity; evidence of automobile owners driving from near and far to see the race. Since the officials scheduled the start of the race for noon, there was no need for the spectators to camp in the park overnight. The first anxious fans began to wander into the park at about nine o'clock in the morning. Then, the cars that had been parked on the downtown streets began their procession into the park. Police directed the motorists to their parking spaces in the most orderly manner possible. Other spectators came by trolleys, which were running on special schedules to move the masses of people into the park; and what a mass of people it was. Police estimated the number at 500,000. Before the race began, officials made an announcement which pointed out that it was exactly thirty-three years ago on this very day, that 185,000 people visited the park for Pennsylvania Day, or the opening day, of the Centennial Exhibition.[2] This number must have seemed small in comparison to the multitude of spectators who heard the announcement as they awaited the start of the race.

Hotels did a booming business on the sale of box lunches for their guests to take with them to the race. Vendors were also on hand to sell sandwiches and pretzels to the huge lunchtime crowd. Those who brought their cars also brought hampers full of food and participated in an early form of "tailgating." This was not just a record crowd for an automobile race, but for any event in the city. "Probably never before in Philadelphia has such an army of onlookers ever gathered as which dotted the western part of Fairmount Park yesterday," the *Philadelphia Inquirer* would later observe.³ Spectators again chose Sweet Briar Hill and Neill Drive as their favorite places from which to view the race, and the crowds filled these areas and the main grandstand long before the rest of the track. In yet another example of the race taking on comparisons to the Army-Navy game, The *Philadelphia Evening Bulletin* compared the grandstand to Franklin Field, "Girls in their best gowns and newest fall hats added the colors that loomed up so brightly against the rough, unseasoned boards of the structure. The boxes…held a representative assemblage of Philadelphians."⁴

It was a beautiful day, the sun was out, and a light breeze blew. The temperature was higher than usual for October, a much different scene from the previous year's chilly early morning race. At ten o'clock, the competing cars began to arrive at their pits, welcomed by the cheers and applause of their respective fans. Mechanics got to work on the cars, making final adjustments, and inspecting the vehicles. It took about a half hour for the police to remove the spectators from the racing surface, but by 11:30 A.M. they had cleared the course. From that point on, nobody would be stepping onto the course. The police would make sure of it. There were many more police on duty than the previous year. 2,192 patrolmen on foot, 80 mounted police, 80 Fairmount Park Guards, along with 100 signalmen and 80 umpires surrounded the track to keep things in order. They had the course entirely under their control. They closed the Falls Bridge since it empties its traffic directly onto the West River Drive. Entrepreneurial members of the nearby Schuylkill River boat clubs started ferrying people across the river, charging them five cents per trip. One man unfortunately fell overboard on one of these trips, but rescuers quickly pulled him out, and he continued on his way to see the race.

A few minutes after eleven o'clock, the mayor and his wife arrived at their box in the grandstand. The mayor invited Governor Stuart to join him, but the governor had another commitment and did not attend. Instead, he would be laying the cornerstone of an addition to the Union League clubhouse that afternoon. Drivers began to arrive at their pits by 11:30 A.M., and when the crowd saw George Robertson they roared with applause. Robertson noticed that none of the other drivers had been greeted with such vigor, and he said that he perceived it as a "good omen."⁵ Just before noon, the drivers moved their cars to the pits, and lined them up in rows of two on the Concourse. As Grant's Alco approached the starting line, the brazing on the steering column gave way. When he turned his wheel the car's tires did not move. The crowd let out a collective sigh when the announcer made it known that one of the cars would not be able to compete, but the Alco team could not relieve their disappointment. The car had no steering, and there was not enough time for the mechanics to fix it before the start.

A flag went up to signal that the cars were about to start. Signalmen from the National Guard relayed the signal around the course. It took only three minutes to travel the eight mile distance.⁶ G. Hilton Gantert, the starter of the race, stepped up to John F. Betz's big yellow Simplex, and began counting down the seconds. At

5. The Second Annual Fairmount Park Race 79

A view of the scoring stand on the South Concourse. The wires that are connected to the stand were phone lines, used for gathering information from other parts of the track and for sending updates on the progress of the race to local news agencies. (1909). Photograph by Nathan Lazarnick, courtesy of the Detroit Public Library, National Automotive History Collection.

twelve o'clock noon, he let the car go, and the race started. Gantert then stepped over to Drach's #2 American car, as he counted down another fifteen seconds. Drach wore a protective mask of chamois over his face with holes cut out for his eyes and mouth. The crowd found it pretty amusing. Gantert slapped Drach on the back and shouted, "Go!"[7] Charles Howard sped away next in his #3 Benz, and then George Robertson approached the line in his #4 Simplex. He again received a special cheer from the crowd, who still saw him as their favorite, although he had not been one of the faster cars in practice. Bert Dingley moved up to the line next in the #5 Chalmers-Detroit Bluebird, and then came the #6 Thomas car of Willie Haupt. Haupt, the local, received a generous amount of applause as he sped away. Malin Leinau's Acme departed next, and then came Harding in the #8 Apperson, and Bob Burman in the #9 Buick. William Wallace was at the controls of the #10 Palmer-Singer as it dashed away. Since Grant's incapacitated Alco bore #11, the American car started next with Hayes at the wheel. The race favorite, Louis Chevrolet, approached the line next in the #13 Buick. The crowd cheered him on as he put the car in gear and started on his way. John Coffey's Columbia was the fourteenth car to start. He and his mechanician, John Kowalker, put their goggles on, and when they received the word, they darted away from the line. Behind the Columbia, Louis

George Robertson waits as Starter Gantert counts down the seconds before sending the Simplex on its way. The No. 5 car is Bert Dingley's Chalmers-Detroit. Behind Robertson, is Willie Haupt in the No. 6 Thomas. (1909). Courtesy of Jerry Helck.

Bergdoll followed in the #15 Thomas. Bergdoll, "took his position impassively, with that coolness for which he is noted," observed one of the reporters who witnessed his start.[8] Len Zengle drove #16, a Chadwick, and he was quickly followed by Louis Strang's #17 Isotta. Joe Parkin drove the #18 Chadwick. Beside him was his father, Joe Parkin Sr., who acted as mechanician for his son. Mr. Parkin had been accompanied to the pits by his pet monkey, which amused the crowd, as well as Mr. Parkin himself, before the start of the race. Next came Lorimer in the second Chalmers-Detroit entry, followed by Erwin Bergdoll in the #20 Welch. Bergdoll and his mechanician, Frank Johnson, wore long dark coats with matching hoods and goggles. Car #21 had been Al Hall's Welch, which would not start, so Joe Seymour's #22 Lozier approached the line next. Finally #23, the Selden, with Charles Young driving, became the last car to start at 12:05 P.M.

Despite the fuss that was made about the Quaker City Motor Club's starter, G. Hilton Gantert, did an excellent job. All of the cars started right on schedule, and there was not a semblance of a problem. The crowds did not have to wait long to see a car come by again, only about four minutes. Drach, in the American, completed the first lap before the others, passing the line nine minutes and fourteen seconds after the start. He passed Betz in the process, making the lap in 8:59. Betz came by next, after being slowed down by a brush with a fire hydrant. He took the left-hand turn off of City Avenue onto Belmont Avenue too fast. The rear of the

Table 5. 1909—Starting Lineup

No.	Car	Driver	HP	Cylinder	Mechanician	Tires
1	Simplex	Betz	90	4	George Tompkins	Michelin
2	American	Drach	60	4	Joe Kachline	Michelin
3	Benz	Howard	60	4	E. Stecker	Fisk
4	Simplex	Robertson	90	4	Glenn Etheridge	Michelin
5	Chalmers-Detroit	Dingley	40	4	H.E. Richard	Michelin
6	Thomas	Haupt	70	6	Thomas Wilkie	Fisk
7	Acme	Leinau	60	6	Robert Argue	Firestone
8	Apperson	Harding	49.2	4	W.W. Clifton	Michelin
9	Buick	Burman	30	4	J.J. Grennon	Michelin
10	Palmer-Singer	Wallace	60	6	Charles Nauber	Michelin
11	Alco	Grant	60	6	Not Available	Michelin
12	American	Hayes	60	4	Arthur H. Johnson	Michelin
13	Buick	Chevrolet	30	4	Joe Nelson	Michelin
14	Columbia	Coffey	32.4	4	John Kowalker	Michelin
15	Thomas	L. Bergdoll	70	6	Joe Turner	Fisk
16	Chadwick	Zengle	60	6	Paul Dunlap	Firestone
17	Isotta	Strang	40	4	Leo Anderson	Michelin
18	Chadwick	Parkin	60	6	Joe Parkin Sr.	Firestone
19	Chalmers-Detroit	Lorimer	40	4	Thomas Kirker	Michelin
20	Welch	E. Bergdoll	70	6	Frank Johnson	Fisk
22	Lozier	Seymour	50	6	Not Available	Diamond
23	Selden	Young	36	4	Joe Harrigan	Firestone

car swung around and smacked the hydrant. A signalman took a yellow flag onto the course to warn that Betz was stopped in a precarious position, but not before Drach came flying past in the American car, just barely missing the stopped car. Betz and his mechanician jumped out, inspected the damage, and finding nothing seriously wrong, they hopped back in the car and continued on. Robertson crossed the line in third place, followed by Howard in the Benz and then Dingley in the Chalmers-Detroit Bluebird. In terms of time, Louis Chevrolet held first position, completing the initial lap in 8:40. Len Zengle's Chadwick took second place, with a time of 8:49, and then came Drach in third, with his 8:59.

Less than two minutes after it started, the Selden lost some time on Sweet Briar Hill. It experienced a tire problem as the car descended the hill. Young and his mechanician, Joe Harrigan, replaced the tire, but it took them about thirty-five minutes. It must have been something more serious than just a simple puncture. Bob Burman also had trouble on the first lap, but his was engine related. He stopped at the completion of the lap to try to fix the problem. He changed the sparkplugs, and poured flaxseed into the radiator to try to stop it from leaking. It worked, and Burman continued on his way, albeit a lap behind the leader. His first lap of 20:20 was well off the pace.

Seymour's Lozier became the first car to drop out of the race when its water pump broke on Neill Drive. Seymour and his mechanician left the car there and walked back to camp. Three drivers, in addition to Young in the Selden, had tire trouble on the first lap. They were Haupt in the Thomas, Leinau in the Acme, and

Leinau's Acme is about to be passed by Parkin's Chadwick early in the race. The stone wall that lined Neill Drive is visible on the left. (1909). Photograph by Nathan Lazarnick, courtesy of the Detroit Public Library, National Automotive History Collection.

Harding in the Apperson. All three took more than twelve minutes to complete their first lap. The Acme's trouble came at the Sweet Briar Hill hairpin. Leinau took the turn too fast, and drove onto the grass when he came around onto the West River Drive. Leinau dodged a few trees and guided the car back onto the road. When he reached the end of the West River Drive, and passed under the railroad bridge, the car lost a tire. This turn served as a dangerous place to make a tire change, but there was no other choice. Leinau and his mechanician, Robert Argue, replaced the tire and carried on. These three cars all had to stop at the pits to pick up a new spare at the completion of their first lap.

Chevrolet still held the lead on lap two, with a six second advantage on the second place car of Len Zengle. Robertson and Drach battled their way around the course, sometimes side by side, in a real contest for third place. They crossed the line tied for third place, each with an overall time of 17:40 for their first two laps. As they charged down the Concourse, Robertson followed closely behind Drach, but he managed to find some extra speed and flew past the American car before the end of the straight. "Mr. Mayor, that's going some," the announcer, W. Ward Bean, exclaimed through his megaphone.[9] The mayor laughed at being singled out for a special broadcast of the action. Dingley had a great second lap, moving up from twelfth to fifth. Wallace had the opposite luck in dropping his Palmer-Singer from eighth to eleventh. Bob Burman recovered from his engine problems and turned a lap of 8:07, which moved him from nineteenth to seventeenth, and Bert Dingley made the fastest lap so far of 7:48.

Louis Chevrolet still led the field on lap three, but just barely. Robertson was tearing around the track. He reset the fastest lap to 7:44 his third time around. He lagged only three seconds behind Chevrolet. Drach continued to hang onto Robertson's coattails, as both of them went ahead of Zengle in their pursuit of the leader. Dingley remained in fifth while Burman continued to recover from his first lap engine trouble. He moved up three more places to fourteenth, but his mechanical problems put him hopelessly behind. Meanwhile, Parkin in the Chadwick fell from fifth place on lap one, to eleventh on lap three. A battle also took place between the two local brewing families, over eighth and ninth positions. Only five seconds separated the cars of Louis Bergdoll and John F. Betz. Charles Howard lost time on this lap because he had to bring the Benz into the pits to replace an exhaust valve.

Two cars dropped out on the third lap. The Columbia's exit was due to an accident on the previous lap. Coffey followed close behind Parkin's #18 Chadwick as they passed through the Neill Drive "S" turn. As Parkin attempted to turn the Chadwick onto City Avenue, he skidded and went wide. Coffey tried to avoid the sliding car by going around the outside. Unfortunately, a tree stood in his path, and he ended up smacking it with his right rear tire. He also ran into the Chadwick, despite his best efforts to avoid it. The Columbia's rear axle and the frame were bent. The car managed to limp back to the starting line to complete its second lap, but then Coffey parked it, knowing that he could not continue on. Parkin continued on, although his rear tire had been loosened. No injuries resulted from the collision. Erwin Bergdoll was also put out on the third lap by a bad engine, which expired in the worst place it could have happened, on Neill Drive.

Chevrolet was the next driver to encounter engine trouble, this time near Sweet Briar, and by the end of the fourth lap, he had fallen all the way back to fifteenth. Although disappointed by Chevrolet's problems, the crowd roared with approval as Robertson inherited the lead. Drach, Zengle and Dingley trailed close behind the new leader. Betz won the battle with fellow brewer Bergdoll by jumping from ninth to fifth and moving two positions ahead of the Thomas. Burman also continued his charge back to the front, moving another two spots to twelfth place. Chevrolet was not the only one to have engine trouble on this lap. Haupt's Thomas also expired. He had moved up four spots on lap three, putting him in fifteenth place when he dropped out.

Robertson continued to lead on the next lap, but Zengle wasn't about to let him relax. He made a lap of 7:41, the fastest lap of the race, and a new track record. This pushed him into second place, only 1:12 behind Robertson. Dingley followed Zengle into third place as Drach had to pull his American car into the pits to replace a rear auxiliary air valve. He spent four minutes there, and so dropped back to seventh position. His time for lap five was 13:12. The battle a little further back between Louis Bergdoll and John F. Betz had become a three way battle, with Strang's Isotta passing Bergdoll on lap four, and securing fourth place from Betz on lap five. He led Betz by only one second at the completion of the lap. The attrition rate was

Hugh Harding puts two wheels on the curb as he makes a turn on the West River Drive. The iron fence that separated the road from the bank of the Schuylkill River provided extra protection for the spectators. (1909). Photograph by Nathan Lazarnick, courtesy of the Detroit Public Library, National Automotive History Collection.

increasing as a sixth car dropped out of the race, and this was only the fifth lap. This time, Lee Lorimer was the target of bad luck when the chassis of his Chalmers-Detroit split in half underneath the engine compartment. The chassis sustained damage when Lorimer skid into a gutter when coming under the Chamounix Bridge. By the time he reached the filter plant on Belmont Avenue, the car was broken. Lorimer pulled over and managed to stop the car, but it could have been much worse. The police had their hands full at Sweet Briar Hill around this time, trying to capture a trespasser on the track. It was not a person, but a rabbit which had been frightened by all of the noise. It started to run up the track with the police in pursuit. The police were not able to catch it until a boy reached out and caught it in his hat.[10]

The leaders remained the same on lap six, in fact, the standings did not change at all, but Zengle continued to gain on Robertson. He shrunk the gap between them to forty-eight seconds. The cars in the middle of the field juggled their positions on lap seven. Louis Bergdoll fell two positions to eighth. Drach began to move back up, by taking over sixth position, and Parkin moved into seventh. On the next lap, Parkin moved past Drach into sixth. Louis Bergdoll continued to fall back, now finding himself in tenth place. Hayes got into more trouble on lap eight, again at

5. The Second Annual Fairmount Park Race

Moments before their accident, mechanician Arthur Johnson braces for impact, as Hayes attempts to avoid slamming into a telegraph pole on Sweet Briar Hill. The car was totaled, but Johnson and Hayes walked away. Notice how there was a safe distance between the road and the spectators in dangerous areas such as this one. (1909). From *The Automobile* (14 October 1909), courtesy Automobile Reference Collection, Free Library of Philadelphia.

Sweet Briar Hill, which was really turning out to be the most dangerous spot on the track. As Hayes guided the American through the turn, the car swerved to one side of the track. He tried to correct, but swung the car over to the other side of the track, and slammed into a telegraph pole. Hayes managed to hold on and stay in the car, while his mechanician, Arthur Johnson, was thrown out and landed on his head about 72 feet away. The crowds tried to get closer, and the police had a tough time holding them back. Many feared that he was surely dead. A horse drawn ambulance arrived on the scene and doctors placed the unconscious mechanician inside to be taken to the hospital. Suddenly, and to the surprise of everyone, Johnson opened his eyes. "Say, that was a pretty good spill," he said.[11] Realizing that he was unhurt, except for a sprained arm, Johnson got out of the ambulance and returned to the car. He and Hayes determined that it was smashed beyond repair, so they began to walk back to camp, receiving acknowledgments from the crowd along the way. Police, meanwhile, dragged the damaged car to a safer position.

The number of accidents at the Sweet Briar Curve was enough to drive one man crazy, even though no serious injuries occurred there. A police officer assigned to guard that section of the track had asked that he not be assigned to race duty because he said that he had a feeling that something bad would happen. According to the *Philadelphia Evening Times*, his superiors laughed at his perceived vision and ordered him to take his position at Sweet Briar Curve.[12] After witnessing six cars encounter some form of trouble in that area, a few of them being quite spectacular, he lost control of himself. He tore off his uniform and ran into the woods screaming.

Louis Strang negotiates the infamous Sweet Briar Curve, the scene of most of the accidents during the 1909 race. Because of the hair-raising action that took place there, the Curve was also a favorite location of the spectators. (1909). Photograph by Nathan Lazarnick, courtesy of the Detroit Public Library, National Automotive History Collection.

Police were sent after him, but they did not find him until later that night when he turned up at his home. Automobile racing certainly was not for everyone.

On lap nine, the only changes in position took place in the middle of the field. The amateur Betz continued to get urged on by the crowd as he passed the much more experienced Strang for fourth place. Right behind them, Drach followed in close pursuit. He took re-took sixth position from Parkin, who had just passed him on the previous lap. On the next lap, all of these positions reversed themselves again, Strang passing Betz, and Parkin once again getting past Drach.

Betz continued his charge on lap eleven, again moving into fourth place ahead of Strang. He made a time of 7:54 on this very quick lap. The other brewer, Louis Bergdoll fell three more places, back to thirteenth, after a 43:48 lap caused by engine problems. Water was not circulating properly through the engine of his Thomas.

About this time, Leinau's Acme sped down the Concourse to complete its sixth lap. Suddenly, a tire burst on the car, sending it out of control. Leinau kept control of the car, and brought it to a stop, preventing it from careening into a field of parked cars alongside the track. The burst tire flew from the car and into the grandstand where it struck thirteen year old Luke Tierney of Philadelphia, who had come to see the race with a group of friends. The tire knocked the boy unconscious.

5. The Second Annual Fairmount Park Race

Len Zengle attempts to repair the engine of his Chadwick on the West River Drive. Zengle was running in second place when the car began to overheat. (1909). Photograph by Nathan Lazarnick, courtesy of the Detroit Public Library, National Automotive History Collection.

Grandstand ushers grabbed him and took him to a waiting ambulance that transported him to the German Hospital, on Girard Avenue, just east of the park. When doctors deemed that he was all right, he returned to his seat in the grandstand, where he watched the rest of the race. Leinau repaired the car and continued on, but then began to experience engine trouble. It took him over an hour to complete another lap, and then he parked the car and dropped out. The Acme team later discovered that the car's many tire troubles were due to a mistake that they made. They used 4½ inch tubes inside of a 5 inch tire cover.

With the exception of Harding's Apperson getting ahead of Drach for seventh place, no cars changed position on laps twelve or thirteen. On lap fourteen, the positions of the leaders finally changed. Robertson still occupied first place, but his closest competition, Len Zengle, had some bad luck which slowed him down. His fourteenth lap took 43:19, thus eliminating him from contention. The Chadwick's water pipes became loose and began to leak. The engine began to overheat, forcing Zengle to pull off to the side of the road on the West River Drive. He ran down to the Schuylkill River to get water to pour into the hot engine. Dingley's Chalmers-Detroit Bluebird assumed second place, trailing 4:54 behind Robertson's Simplex. Robertson made consistent laps in the 8:30s compared to Dingley's average of about 9:00 per lap. Betz moved into third, about three minutes behind Dingley. It was at

Bert Dingley motors along a straightaway in his Chalmers-Detroit Bluebird. The white hats of the police can be seen all along this section of the course. (1909). Photograph by Nathan Lazarnick, courtesy of the Detroit Public Library, National Automotive History Collection.

this time that Chevrolet dropped out of the race, a broken inlet valve had punched a hole in a cylinder of his Buick. He had completed eleven laps.

Around this time, an incident occurred at 52nd Street and Parkside Avenue. A boy fell out of a tree and laid unconscious on the track. Police thought that they had gotten everyone out of the trees, but this youngster was well hidden on a branch that overhung the road. The limb broke and the boy fell to the ground. Dingley came through this area of the track at the same time, and just as he turned the corner, two police ran out onto the track and dragged the injured child to the side. Doctors from the Municipal Hospital rushed to the scene. They found him to be fine, although he did have a concussion from the fall. As doctors attempted to put him into an ambulance, he woke up and ran into the crowd to avoid getting into trouble for being in the tree.

At the completion of his fifteenth lap, Robertson came into the pits. Following the same strategy as last year, he planned to make only one stop. He took on fuel, oil, and a full set of tires and was on his way, without losing the lead, in about three minutes. Dingley lagged 3:07 behind him. The third place car of John F. Betz and the fourth place car of Parkin stopped on the next lap, but the lost time dropped them back to sixth and fifth respectively. Both remained in the pits for a long time, and only for routine work. Betz blamed his delay on the inexperience of his crew. Strang took over third, followed by Harding in fourth. On lap seventeen, Robertson, Dingley, Strang, Harding, and Parkin held the top five positions, but Betz ran strong and attempted to move back up. He made two laps under 9:00, but continued to be mired in sixth place. The battle for third had been a duel between Harding, Strang, and Parkin, but on lap nineteen, Harding made a move in the Apperson. He ran steadily in the middle of the field for most of the race, and now found himself among the leaders in fourth place, despite having just stopped in the pits on the previous lap.

While the leaders circulated on lap eighteen, Zengle took the Sweet Briar Curve too fast, and it appeared that the car would flip over. As he continued down the hill, the car slid toward the wall of the railroad bridge, as spectators jumped from its path. Zengle cut the power, hit the brakes, and brought the car to a safe stop without hitting anything. Also on lap eighteen, Dingley followed Strang closely as they went up the West River Drive and under the Strawberry Mansion Bridge. Just beyond the bridge, as Dingley attempted to go by Strang, the Isotta ran into a rut which caused the car to veer in front of Dingley. Dingley swerved his car to the left-hand side of the road, scratching his wheels against the brick gutter that lined the roadway, with Strang only a few inches to his right. Dirt and oil sprayed the spectators who lined the side of the road. They had a close call, but nothing worse than a few soiled spectators resulted from it.

Strang dropped to fifth when he made a stop at his pit, but on the next lap he began to move back up by taking fourth place away from Parkin. With five laps to go, Robertson was securely in the lead by 4:42 over Dingley. Barring any mechanical difficulties, or mistakes made by Robertson, it seemed that nobody could stop him. Since first place seemed out of reach, the remaining drivers worked for the other prize winning positions. Louis Bergdoll dropped out on the nineteenth lap due to the water circulation problem he had been experiencing with his engine. Twelve cars remained, although only three of them had any real chance of winning.

On lap twenty-one, one of those at the front dropped out. John F. Betz, the local driver who had been doing so well, began to suffer from mechanical problems. His car had a broken pump. The amateur Betz impressed the crowds in doing so well against a field of some of the best professional drivers, and his fans showed their disappointment when he dropped out due to an unfortunate mechanical problem which he had no control over. He had said before the race that he did not think he really had a chance of winning, but that since he had received over $500 in speeding tickets, he would enjoy driving his car over the speed limit in front of the police for about three hours.[13] When Betz dropped out, his wife appeared to be the happiest person in the park. She sat in the press stand during the race and worried about her husband throughout the entire affair.

Robertson and Dingley led the race, well ahead of the rest of the field. Over eight minutes separated Dingley from the third place car of Harding. The duel for fourth place was the only one left to be decided, and it was settled on lap twenty-two when Parkin passed Strang's Isotta. Then Bob Burman's Buick finally gave up due to a leaking radiator. He was seven laps behind the leaders when he retired his

Smoke and exhaust trail behind the No. 4 Simplex as George Robertson makes a turn. (1909). Courtesy of Jerry Helck.

car. No changes in position took place for the rest of the race. A blue flag flew as Robertson came around to start lap twenty-five. He finished his twenty-fifth lap in 3:38:58. "Robertson's won," the crowd screamed as he crossed the line.[14] He continued past the grandstands, and then pulled off onto the side of the course. He and Etheridge left the car and walked back to the start. He found his wife's seat in the grandstand and climbed up to see her. "It was wonderful George! It was wonderful," she said.[15] Dingley came around at 3:44:20 to take second place. At this point Drach's American finally gave up due to a problem with the auxiliary gas tank, which had become loose. The loose tank caused the pipes leading to the carburetor to crack and forced Drach to withdraw while on his twenty-first lap. Then Harding's Apperson crossed the line, with a flat tire no less, to take third place. His time was 3:52:17. Senator W. J. Morgan suggested to the Apperson team that they send a telegram to Herbert Lytle, to let him know how well the car had performed. Lytle had wanted to drive in the race so much that he had tried to escape from his hospital bed on Thursday to try to make it to Philadelphia. The Senator thought that the good news might cheer him up. After his near escape, doctors moved Lytle to a sanitarium to recover from the shock of his accident. Although his physical injuries had healed, the doctors wanted to keep an eye on him for a while, and they needed a location with more security to keep him from attempting to run off to another race.

Two more cars finished the race. Parkin's Chadwick took fourth place, and

Table 6. 1909—Top Three Finishers

No.	Car	Driver	Time
4	Simplex	Robertson	3:38:58
5	Chalmers-Detroit	Dingley	3:44:20
8	Apperson	Harding	3:52:17

Strang's Isotta came in fifth. Director of Public Safety Henry Clay then blew his whistle signaling the end of the race. Four cars were still running, but they were not permitted to finish. Wallace completed twenty-four laps in the Palmer-Singer. Howard's Benz was making its twenty-second lap, and Zengle's Chadwick and Young's Selden were only on lap seventeen. The police released the crowds, who surged onto the track and made their way to the starting line. Robertson and Etheridge posed for photographs with the MacDonald & Campbell Trophy, but the mayor could not distribute the awards in a formal presentation like he did the previous year.

Chalmers-Detroit decided to protest the results of the race, claiming that Robertson's car was not a stock chassis because twenty-five of them had not been produced. It seems that the company made this protest and that their driver Bert Dingley had nothing to do with it. Dingley congratulated Robertson after the race, and it did not seem that he thought there was anything unfair about the results. A post-race interview with Mrs. Dingley also shows her satisfaction with the race results. "It was a splendid contest," she said, "and Mr. Robertson is to be congratulated on his success."[16] Some also believed that the J. M. Quinby Company, the entrant of the Isotta, was going to protest the results, but Samuel Thorton, the Philadelphia manager, denied that the company ever had any intention to protest. The J. M. Quinby Company served as the local distributor of Simplex cars, "hence the absurdity of any of our interests protesting our own cars," Thorton explained.[17] Robertson brushed off the allegations made about his car, and was confident that he would be declared the winner. The car had already participated in other AAA races, which meant that the AAA already deemed it to be a stock car on numerous occasions, but there would be a hearing anyway. Chalmers-Detroit had a right to protest the results if they felt that they had a legitimate complaint.

The crowd certainly showed their approval of Robertson's win. If his victory in the inaugural race did not do enough to make him a hero in Philadelphia, there was no doubt that with this second win, he became the favorite driver of many Philadelphians. The people continued to shout and cheer. "Oh, you, Georgie," became a familiar refrain, until the officials ordered the police to clear the park.[18] Robertson had become trapped in the center of the tremendous crowd that had surged onto the track, and he could not escape the thousands who wanted to congratulate him. Director Clay had to call in the mounted police to disperse the crowd and extract Robertson. A horse knocked one woman to the ground in the process. The spectators who witnessed this then attacked the mounted officer, but Director Clay arrived on the scene and berated the officer for being so rough with the crowd. The people were calmed by the fact that the officer had gotten himself into trouble

George Robertson (center, front) and Glenn Etheridge (right) pose for photographs with the MacDonald & Campbell Trophy. Behind them is a representative of the MacDonald & Campbell Company. (1909). Courtesy of the Robertson Family.

and their anger quickly turned to cheers for Director Clay. In little time, the police succeeded in their efforts to disperse the crowds, and the last spectators made their way out of the park.

Once again George Robertson showed his skill on a difficult track. Although he had a fast 90 horsepower Simplex, nobody took anything away from his victory. Everyone knew that the Fairmount Park course differed from all others, and that a victory had nothing to do with speed alone. "Robertson's victory is a great personal triumph, inasmuch as the Fairmount Park 8-mile circuit is what might be termed a driver's course," submitted a writer for *Motor Age*. He said, "On no other of the courses where big national contests are run off does the human element enter so conspicuously."[19] The fact that he drove a different car than the previous year, and once again had no problems with the car, shows even more effectively that Robertson's smart driving style had more to do with the lack of mechanical problems, and the victory, than the car did. The *Philadelphia Inquirer* reported that most people believed that Robertson's abilities won the race, more so than the Simplex. "The crowds who lined the course looked upon the victory as Robertson's and the general opinion was that it would have been impossible without the presence of the young driver at the wheel of the speedy machine."[20]

After the race, drivers, officials and other guests proceeded to the banquet room

The winner, George Robertson (left), receives the congratulations of second place finisher Bert Dingley, after the race. (1909). Courtesy of Jerry Helck.

of the Hotel Walton where they had dinner and enjoyed a vaudeville show. After the show, the mayor had a few words to say about the race. "The auto has come to stay," he said. "Today work as well as pleasure are being done with it. We are all glad that we have demonstrated that we can give the people a safe spectacle and eliminate the awful catastrophes that are common in such events."[21] George Robertson made a brief speech, and he used his time to heap more praise on the city, and the motor club, for the fine job they had done.

> Gentlemen to-day has been the most pleasing of my life. I have been a repeater. And I want to say that I have never seen such a fine course, and I have never raced under such perfect management. We, from outside, have all had a square deal, and the praise is all due to the Philadelphians who have arranged the meet.[22]

The Quaker City Motor Club intended for this dinner party to serve as the award ceremony, but because of the protest, the club did not distribute any of the awards. Late Saturday night, H. E. Coffin, Vice-President of Chalmers-Detroit, met with officials from the Quaker City Motor Club and realized that he would not win in his appeal of the race results. The Quaker City Motor Club referred him to an amendment of the rules, which the club distributed to all of the drivers and entrants at their Friday night meeting. The club gave everyone a pink piece of paper which stated:

Although crowd control was excellent during the 1909 race, the sheer number of people who wanted to get a glimpse of George Robertson afterwards made exiting the park a difficult prospect. Here, a crowd gathers on the South Concourse in front of the scoring stand. (1909). Photograph by Nathan Lazarnick, courtesy of the Detroit Public Library, National Automotive History Collection.

> We understand that this event is open to any car which complies with the definition of stock chassis, and in addition, to any car whose manufacturer satisfied the contest board by a display of twenty-five complete sets of parts or otherwise that it is a stock model for the coming season.[23]

So by participating in the race they accepted the amendment, and by accepting it Chalmers-Detroit had agreed that the other competing cars were stock if the Contest Board was satisfied that they were. They also agreed that the twenty-five cars did not have to be produced, only that the company had the parts, and intended to manufacture the completed cars during the coming season. As a result, Chalmers-Detroit saw no reason to continue the protest. Robertson became the official winner. On Sunday he vacationed in Asbury Park, New Jersey, returning to the City of Philadelphia on Monday afternoon. The Quaker City Motor Club scheduled an awards ceremony for Thursday night at Keith's Theatre on the 1100 block of Chestnut Street.

The Quaker City Motor Club's blue and gold colors decorated the theater's auditorium. After the regular vaudeville program, the ceremony took place. Government officials, club members, drivers and their families filled the main level of the theater, while the general public filled the balcony levels. The theater was packed with people. They first watched moving pictures showing highlights of the race, and then Harry Jordan, the theater's manager, went up on stage and introduced G. Hilton Gantert, the starter of the race. Gantert then introduced R. E. Ross, Chairman of the Contest Committee and referee for the race. After saying a few words and thanking everyone involved for making the race, "the greatest event in motoring history," Mr. Ross introduced Secretary Harbach who presented the awards to the winning drivers.[24]

On the stage, glass frames displayed the gold coins which would be presented to each winning driver. The coins were arranged to spell the letters Q. C. M. C. within each frame. As Secretary Harbach announced the name of each of the four drivers, they rolled onto the stage behind the wheel of their car. Joe Parkin received $500 in $2.50 gold pieces for his fourth place finish. Hugh Harding received $750 in $5 gold pieces for third place, Bert Dingley received $1,250 in $10 gold pieces for second place, and George Robertson received $2,500 in $20 gold pieces, as well as the MacDonald & Campbell Trophy, for his victory. With the introduction of each driver came cheers from the audience. The attendees were all huge fans of automobile racing and they showed it. Each driver also made a brief speech upon receiving his prize. More than one reporter commented on the speeches as not being very good. "As automobile drivers they are successful; yes, the best that America produces, but as speech makers, never! They're too bashful."[25] Only Len Zengle, who received the $100 prize donated by G. H. Stetson for making the fastest lap, left any impression with his acceptance speech. Zengle amused the crowd with some self-deprecating humor, saying that he wished he had been able to make all of his laps that fast.[26] All of the drivers made a point of saying that Fairmount Park was the best race in which they had participated. Dingley received the gold watch donated by the Autolight Motor Supply Company for making the most consistent time. He received the award not only due to the consistency of his lap times, but also due to the fact that he did not make a single stop during the race, which *The Motor World* declared, "an unprecedented feat in the history of automobile road racing."[27] The Chalmers-Detroit Company considered it a great achievement, and they used it as a chance to promote their product. Mr. Fanning said:

> The car never stopped an instant in the whole 200 miles and that certainly shows that it can be depended on for any ordinary touring speed, as the speed shown in Saturday's race will never be asked of the car in any touring trip that a purchaser might make.[28]

After the presentation of the awards, representatives of the four institutions that would benefit from the charitable monies went up on stage and made some brief remarks. The amount of money that these institutions would receive had not yet been calculated, and would not be for some time. In December, the receipts were finally totaled, and Dr. Neff reported that the four institutions would divide $7,617.34. The money collected totaled $11,735.41, but $4,118.07 went to expenses incurred in staging the event.[29] While the figure given to charity was lower than the

$25,000 that was estimated when the idea was first introduced, $7,000 was still a lot of money in 1909, and the four charities were happy to get their share of it.

The Fairmount Park Race again proved to be second to none in terms of the course itself, and the amount of people that could attend. A half million spectators for a sporting event was unheard of at the time. For a second year, no serious injuries resulted. The medical teams responded quickly to everyone who needed medical attention, whether participant or bystander. The large number of police and park guards prevented any interference by the crowds, so the race did not suffer from the interruption of people entering onto the track like other events did. The police had some scuffles with a few rowdy spectators, and a handful of drivers and spectators received minor injuries. A few people also passed out due to heat exhaustion because of the unusually high October temperature, but it still proved to be the safest road race in the country, if not the world. In comparison, the 1909 Vanderbilt Cup, which took place a week later, was run on a 12.64 mile course, perhaps taking a cue from Fairmount Park, since it was much shorter than the usual Vanderbilt Cup course. Taking another example from Philadelphia, only stock chassis cars could compete in the 1909 Vanderbilt Cup. Despite these efforts to reform the Vanderbilt Cup Race, attendance turned out to be low. The Vanderbilt continued to lose attendance as Fairmount Park broke attendance records. While Fairmount Park had twenty-five entries, the Vanderbilt had only fifteen. Even George Robertson did not take part in the Vanderbilt to defend his 1908 victory. The race began to take on a second class status when compared to Fairmount Park. The only thing that it had, which the Philadelphia race did not, was the name Vanderbilt.

The Grand Prize Race was not held in Savannah, or at all, in 1909. Without a doubt, Fairmount Park held the position of the biggest race of the year in the United States. It should also be noted that in August, two months before the 1909 Fairmount Park Race, the first events took place at the Indianapolis Motor Speedway. Accidents killed one driver, two mechanicians, and two spectators during a weekend of preliminary races. High speeds and a dangerous track surface contributed to the accidents. There was much work to be done to make the speedway safer. But now, for a second year, a road course, supposedly a far more dangerous form of racing, had a great safety record despite the fact that a half million people surrounded the twisting park circuit. This was once again due to the excellent planning, and the cooperation of the Quaker City Motor Club and the City of Philadelphia.

Visitors from far and wide loved the Fairmount Park circuit. Mrs. Dingley, a Californian, commented on the event. "You have a beautiful park here, and all Philadelphians ought to be proud of it," she said. She also commented on the safety of the course:

> Your police system is perfect…and they can protect a track and handle a big crowd better than I have ever seen it done before, and I have attended the Vanderbilt Cup Race and all the other big motor racing events in recent years.[30]

Just as in 1908, the papers did not have the words to describe just how big the event had become. "A more ideal setting for an automobile race would be difficult to imagine," was the opinion of *The Motor World*.³¹

With the prizes awarded, talk immediately shifted to the prospects for a race the following year. Rumors began to leak out about those involved in the decision making process. Based on his opposition to the 1909 event, race supporters saw Commissioner James Pollock as the leader of the opposition. Members of the Quaker City Motor Club and the municipal government had already broached the idea to the Fairmount Park Commission, though unofficially. The mayor still supported the idea one hundred percent. "The people seem to want it, so there is no reason why the race should not be given every year," he said, in a somewhat pointed comment.³² He basically challenged the Fairmount Park Commission to come up with a reason why there should not be a race. But he was diplomatic about it, and made it known that he did not expect an objection from them. "So many thousands went to the race that it is proved that it is wanted. I have heard of no objection on the part of the Fairmount Park Commission."³³ Could it be that the Fairmount Park Commission would have to back down completely now that the race was a charitable event? Philadelphia would have to wait until the next year, and the official request, before they would know for sure. At this point, all of the rumors were just speculation. "I hope you make this race an annual event, for you certainly know how to conduct such affairs." said Mrs. Dingley.³⁴ She hoped to return in 1910, and promised that her husband would win it next time.

One thing was for sure, and that was that nobody was particularly happy with the Fairmount Park Commission since they had received free tickets and deprived the charities of money. Dr. Neff's resignation from his position as a planner of the race resulted from this action of the commission. Dr. Neff told the mayor and the Quaker City Motor Club that he would not have anything more to do with the event in the future once the 1909 race was completed, and the charitable monies distributed. He said this ten days before the race, and not because he had a problem with the event itself, but because of the ticket scandal. Neff did not agree with the commission's order, and he did not want to have to work with them again in the future. He must have also wanted to distance himself from something that could earn a reputation for not being totally charitable because of the commission's blatant impropriety. Dr. Neff had given much of his time to making the 1909 race such a huge success, and to lose his leadership due to the commission's greediness was unfortunate. But Neff still had a very favorable opinion of the event, and the following week he made the case for an annual race in his weekly health bulletin. Dr. Neff really wanted to see the race continue because it raised money for charity, and although other events took place in the city which benefited charity, he felt that the race had an added bonus of being beneficial to the public health. "The sport itself is of a more healthful character, as the spectators must breathe pure air in the open, instead of as is often the case, vitiate, heated air indoors," he wrote.³⁵ So, while many other charitable events took place indoors, Dr. Neff liked the idea of having one that benefited charity, but also encouraged people to go outside. He went on to say that unlike other cities, Philadelphia had proven that it could hold a safe race, with no danger to contestants or spectators. He also praised the Quaker City Motor Club for coming up with the idea, and assuming the financial responsibilities. "It is the hope of the Department in charge of the Public Charity of Philadelphia that they will have the support of the municipal authorities, the Fairmount Park Commission and the general public in making this race an annual event."[36] Dr. Neff made his opinion abundantly clear. Another seven months would pass before the results of his pleas would be known.

6

Surpassing Vanderbilt

The prospects for a race in 1910 looked good, despite the fact that some opposition had developed in 1909. The success of the race, especially its charitable side, left many believing that it should become an annual event. The race had also become so big and so important in the motor racing world that the thought of not having it was pretty much out of the question. Nevertheless, the Fairmount Park Commission still had the organizers worried. They were unpredictable, and the Quaker City Motor Club knew that if it were not for these reasons; if the commissioners were not backed into a corner by the mayor, and public opinion, that they would rather the race not take place.

On 13 May 1910, Secretary Harbach went to the meeting of the Fairmount Park Commission and presented the application in person. The request was the same as in previous years, for permission to hold a stock chassis race in the park on 8 October. Harbach, in a continuation of the cooperation with the city government, also made the rest of the club's intentions known. The club would ask the Department of Public Safety to arrange police and medical preparations, and the Department of Health & Charities to choose the institutions which would benefit from the charitable monies collected. Eli Kirk Price Jr., who had seemed supportive of the idea in the past, moved that the request be granted. The commission then voted to approve the race for another year and charged the Committee of Superintendence & Police with handling the details.

This vote was not made by the usual cast of characters. The only appointed members of the commission to attend the meeting were A. Louden Snowden, Thomas De Witt Cuyler, James Elverson, Sydney W. Keith, James Pollack, and Eli Kirk Price Jr. The other commissioners in attendance held ex-officio seats. They included the mayor, Commissioner of City Property A. S. Eisenhower, the President of the Select Council James Hazlett, and George S. Webster, the Chief Engineer & Surveyor. Four of the citizen appointees did not attend. There was no objection from any of the commissioners this time around. It is possible that commissioners like James Pollack had changed their minds about the race after seeing how safe and popular it was in 1909. Perhaps they liked the charitable idea, and decided that the positives of the race outweighed the negatives. Or maybe someone like Pollack believed that there was no sense in objecting since there was no way that he would win a vote with the mayor and other ex-officio office holders in attendance. Either way, the 1910 race was on.

When the Quaker City Motor Club first proposed the 1908 race to the Fairmount Park Commission, the mayor threatened to attend the commission meeting that year, if necessary, to get the race approved. After seeing the threat of non-approval in 1909, the mayor must have thought it would be best to attend the meeting in 1910. Not only was the race approved, but the commission made a point to commend the club on the success of the 1909 race. The Fairmount Park Race now seemed to have the commissioners' blessing. It's a good thing, because it was now considered to be one of the major East Coast races. "It is now one of the leading contests in the list of important outdoor events, ranking with the Vanderbilt Cup and the Grand Prize Race," declared the *Philadelphia Record*.[1] *The Evening Times* referred to them as the "three classics of Auto Racing," and in 1910 they were scheduled to take place on consecutive weekends.[2] The Vanderbilt Cup would take place on 1 October on Long Island. The Fairmount Park Race was scheduled for 8 October, and the Grand Prize would take place the following week on 16 October. The Grand Prize would take place on Long Island, rather than Savannah in 1910, so all of the important action would take place on these two circuits.

The Quaker City Motor Club distributed entry blanks for the Fairmount Park Race during the first week of August. Instead of being open to all stock chassis cars as in past years, the AAA now had multiple divisions and classes within the rules which governed racing events. The Quaker City Motor Club distributed Class B entry blanks and would allow stock chassis cars which fell into one of the following divisions: Division 4B for 301-450 cubic inch cars with a minimum weight of 2,000 pounds, Division 5B for 451-600 cubic inch cars with a minimum weight of 2,300 pounds, Division 6B for 601-750 cubic inch cars with a minimum weight of 2,500 pounds. The Quaker City Motor Club prizes would be $2,500 for first place, $1,250 for second, $750 for third, and $500 for fourth. There would also be an additional $500 for the winner of each division.

Unlike previous years, when entries began to come in immediately, the first entry for the 1910 race did not come in until 14 August. The entrant was the American Locomotive Company, and they entered one of their Alco cars. Harry Grant would be returning as the driver. Just a week after his appearance in the 1909 Fairmount Park Race, Grant had gone on to win the Vanderbilt Cup in his Alco machine. In fact, it was the same machine, and not just another of the same model. He would continue to drive the identical car throughout the 1910 racing season. He was entered in the Vanderbilt Cup, Fairmount Park, the Grand Prize, and Elgin races. Grant answered the critics who laughed at his driving the same car:

Some have told me it is cheeky to enter this same stock car in all the big races and expect it to pull through. It is not cheeky, it simply expresses my faith that the race is not always to the swiftest. Staying power is what counts in a long race. I proved this last fall and I am out to try it again, that's all.³

The next two entries came from the Chadwick Engineering Works. Len Zengle would drive one of the cars, making his third appearance at Fairmount Park. At the time, he was the track record holder for fastest lap. His teammate would be Al Mitchell. Mitchell was a twenty-two year old Philadelphian who was employed as a demonstration driver at the local Chadwick showroom. He participated in a few races previously, and so could not be considered an amateur. The *Philadelphia Evening Bulletin* described him as being "full of pluck and grit, and known...for his quick headwork and clean sportsmanship."⁴ On 8 September, two more entries arrived. They were from the Benz Import Company and held extra importance because George Robertson would serve as one of their drivers. The winner of both previous runnings of the Fairmount Park Race would return again to defend his title in his third make of car in as many years. Benz entered the second car for Eddie Hearne. Hearne was a twenty-five year old from Chicago, who ran the Benz operation there. He had raced before, beating the likes of Bob Burman and Ralph DePalma on several occasions.

By 9 September, the motor club received only five entries. The papers kept claiming that the entries would soon be pouring in, but there was no sign of it. Something was wrong. It seems that the lack of entries was due to the new rules and the distribution of prize money. For one thing, many makes of small cars could not enter because the Quaker City Motor Club set the minimum piston displacement at 301. The club had decided not to allow divisions one through three in the race, which covered the smaller cars. Many car manufacturers that wanted to enter could not. The second problem was the distribution of prize money. With only $500 for the winner of each division, most of the prize money would go to the top four overall winners. So, contestants who brought less powerful machines, who may have felt that they could not win one of the overall prizes, were really only competing for a $500 prize. They just felt that it was not worth the effort and expense. This line of argument really held no weight, since Bert Dingley had come in second place in 1909 in a car that was less powerful than many others in the field. The nature of the course really did not give much of an advantage to a very fast car, and many cars usually dropped out because of the grueling circuit. Since the prizes concerned possible entrants, the Quaker City Motor Club had to address it, and they did on 11 September 1910. They announced that the event would be taken out of Class B, and would be placed in Class C. Class C was a non-stock class, with divisions based on piston displacement only, and not weight. The piston displacement of divisions 4C to 6C were the same as 4B to 6B, but the club also decided to allow a 3C Division for cars with a displacement of 231-300, and a 2C Division for cars with a displacement of 131-260. This opened the race up to most interested parties. To make the race even more attractive, they rearranged the prize structure, raising the division prizes to $1,000. The overall winner would still receive an additional $2,500, but there would be no awards for second through fourth overall. With this plan, just about any car that wanted to enter could do so. Officials believed that the entries would now start to pour in as originally expected. For the first time, the race would be non-stock, allowing thoroughbred racing cars to speed through the park.

On the same day that the motor club announced the new rules, the mayor had a meeting with Quaker City Motor Club officials to make plans for the upcoming race. Mr. Ross reported that bids were already coming in for the construction of the grandstand. The mayor announced his choices for the membership of the Executive Committee, which would be made up of Quaker City Motor Club members and representatives of the five institutions which would be the beneficiaries of the charitable funds. In 1910, the institutions would be St. Mary's Hospital, Mt. Sinai Hospital, the Playgrounds Committee, the Home of the Merciful Savior for Crippled Children, and the Police Pension Fund. Two days later, the Executive Committee met to elect its officers. Mayor Reyburn was elected chairman, and his secretary, William F. Gleason, was elected secretary of the committee. The committee decided to send invitations to President Taft and Governor Stuart to attend the race. They asked Dr. Neff to supervise the roadwork to assure that the roads would be as safe as possible. They also asked that he take care of the medical arrangements. Although he had promised that he would not be involved in the planning of the race again, Dr. Neff returned to assist with the 1910 event. He must have thought so highly of the race, and its charitable benefits, that he could not withhold his assistance in making it a success. The Executive Committee also set prices for seats and parking spaces. Grandstand seats were priced at $2, eight-person boxes were set at $25, and parking spaces were $10. They instructed Chief McLaughlin of the electrical bureau to set up telephone wires, as in previous years, and they ordered Director Clay to prepare the police arrangements. After two years of planning the race successfully, everyone knew what needed to be done. This meeting just made it all official.

It was also at this meeting that the mayor decided it would be better to offer trophies in addition to the prize money which was already put up by the Quaker City Motor Club. In order to do this, the mayor would need to find $2,000 in order to have the trophies designed and produced. He planned to ask the city's two legislative bodies, the Common Council and the Select Council, to make a special appropriation. He sent them a message the next day. In it, he tried to convince the councilmen that the race was an important event which had tremendous benefits for the city. "There is perhaps no fixed yearly event which directs the eyes of the world to Philadelphia more than this race," the mayor said.[5] The mayor was not just requesting money for something that interested him personally. The race had reached a tremendous level of importance. Evidence of this can be found in the reaction of the press. The mayor had been under fire from the local papers over his "city beautiful" plans. They felt that the money the mayor wanted to spend on a tree lined parkway would be much better spent on the city's schools and its aging port facilities. But, when the mayor requested the money for the trophies, the newspapers did not mention the port or the schools—they instead supported him. They said that the mayor's request "ought to carry weight with councils."[6] They cited the charitable benefits, the great interest from the general public, as well as its growth as a competitor to the Vanderbilt Cup in terms of national importance. "Last year it was generally admitted that it was the blue ribbon racing event of the year, going even a little bit further in importance than the Vanderbilt, which did not maintain its prestige," noted the *Philadelphia Inquirer*.[7] The mayor held the opinion that the city councils would approve his request, but an answer was not immediately forthcoming. The councils may have wanted to wait on making a decision until they had a chance to gauge the public opinion of the 1910 race, and to see if it would be big enough to justify spending the money on. At the time, the race only had nine cars, which may have made the councils a bit wary.

The Apperson Brothers made the next entry, entering one of their cars with H. M. Hanshue as the driver. Hanshue was a twenty-nine year old driver from Los Angeles who had been driving for six years. He was a veteran road racer, who counted a first place finish at Santa Monica, "the Vanderbilt Cup of the West," amongst his achievements.[8] This would be his first trip to the East to participate in a big race. A car that had not been seen in previous runnings of the Fairmount Park Race was the Jackson, but one would participate in 1910. The Jackson Automobile Company, of Jackson, Michigan, entered the car, with E. F. Schleiffer as the driver. Another new participant in 1910 was the Cole car, two of which were entered by the Franklin Motor Company, their local affiliate. The Cole was produced in Indianapolis by the Cole Motor Company. Bill and Harry Endicott would pilot the cars. They were brothers and natives of Indianapolis. Both drivers had much experience but were not very well known in the Philadelphia area.

By this time, the Quaker City Motor Club blamed the low number of entries on the fact that the Vanderbilt Cup was going to precede the Fairmount Park Race. There were already thirty cars entered in the Long Island classic. "It is not to be expected that all will survive the New York contest in shape to start in immediately on practice for another grueling long-distance race," suggested the *Evening Times*.[9] The Vanderbilt's reputation was nothing like Fairmount Park's, and it certainly would be rough not only on the cars, but on the drivers. To counter the effects of the schedule, the Quaker City Motor Club decided to leave the entry list open until 3 October, two days after the Vanderbilt Cup. That way, teams and drivers could decide after that race whether they were up to the challenge of Fairmount Park.

Then the unthinkable happened, and the prediction that all of the Vanderbilt drivers would not be able to compete at Fairmount Park came true. On 27 September, George Robertson was practicing for the Vanderbilt Cup on the Long Island circuit. He had agreed to take a reporter, Stephen Reynolds, on a fast lap of the circuit, as was often done in order to allow the reporters to better convey the sensations, and the work of the drivers, to their readers. Robertson was approaching the Massapequa turn at approximately 70 mph, when the reporter became frightened and grabbed his arm. Robertson lost control of the car, which hit a telegraph pole and flipped over. The impact threw Robertson from the car. He crashed through a wooden fence and landed in a field at least twenty feet away.

Initial reports said that brake failure was the cause of the accident, but Robertson would later say that it was the reporter's fault. "Probably terrified at the speed the scribe grabbed me. In that second I lost control of the car," he said.[10] Both the driver and his passenger were knocked unconscious. Robertson woke up a few minutes later and saw that the reporter had not sustained any serious injuries. "It was hospital again for me but my adorable companion got his story, and his derby wasn't even dented," Robertson wryly noted.[11]

Robertson sustained injuries to his collarbone, and dislocated his right arm. The next day newspapers reported that his injuries were not too serious, and that he would be able to participate in the Vanderbilt Cup. The Benz team was busy repairing the car, but a few days later, Robertson changed his mind. Upon the urging of his friends and family, he felt that it was best not to aggravate his injuries by jumping back in the car so soon. He announced that he would not participate in the Vanderbilt Cup, or the Fairmount Park event. Since the entrance fee was nonrefundable, the Benz team would have to find someone else to drive the car.

Robertson's fans in Philadelphia were saddened when they learned of his decision not to race. Even though the field was nowhere near complete, Robertson was the favorite. The other drivers must have seen it as somewhat good news, because without Robertson, it was guaranteed that the Fairmount Park Race would have a new winner in its third year.

On 29 September, John F. Betz became the tenth entrant. He and his Simplex machine would make another attempt to win the Fairmount Park Race. The Contest Committee actually pursued Betz and encouraged him to enter. It probably didn't take much to secure his entry. After his great performance in the 1909 race, there's no doubt that Betz felt he had some unfinished business in his hometown race. If anyone needed convincing, it was probably his wife, who would now have to sit through another race while worrying about her husband's safety.

The Vanderbilt Cup Race was run on 1 October 1910. George Robertson made the correct decision when he chose not to take part. At the end of the day, two mechanicians, a manager of an auto company, and a spectator were dead. In addition, there were nineteen other injuries ranging from bruises and broken bones to life threatening head injuries for a number of participants and spectators. Harry Grant won the race in his Alco for the second year in a row, but the horrible accidents overshadowed his victory.

The speedy cup circuit contributed to the accidents, but poor crowd control was the main problem as it had been in previous runnings of the race. Too many obstacles stood in the way of the drivers. Spectators were not kept from parking their cars on the outside of the dangerous turns, and so when drivers left the course, their chances of hitting a car, a fence, or a group of people was fairly high. The Vanderbilt also did not have the same level of officiating and police protection that Fairmount Park had. When there was an accident in Fairmount Park, police, officials, and medical personnel were always on hand to react immediately. On Long Island, when the Columbia car crashed, it took over an hour for them to realize the car was no longer running, and police were dispatched to look for it. By the time they found it, its mechanician was dead, and the driver was not far from it.

The attention of the motor racing world switched to Fairmount Park once the Vanderbilt Cup was completed. The entries began to come in faster, as the officials had predicted. In just two days, 30 September to 1 October, four entries arrived at the offices of the Quaker City Motor Club. John Megraw, a private owner, entered a Simplex, which would be driven by his brother-in-law, W. C. Mullen. Mullen was an amateur and had never driven in a road race such as Fairmount Park before. The next entry was a Ford, entered by the Ford Motor Company, through their local salesman Lou Block. Their driver would be Frank Kulick. Kulick took over the driving of the Ford cars from his boss Henry Ford back in 1903. He had established a few speed records driving for Ford, but the Fairmount Park Race would serve as a return to racing for the company, which had not entered a car in a race since 1905.

The next two entries came from the Bergdoll family, who were beginning to make the Fairmount Park Race a family affair. Al Hall, who was barred from the 1909 contest due to his illegal antics on the track, and his assault on a police officer, was back. He entered a Benz, which he planned to drive. Charles A. Bergdoll, brother of Louis and Erwin, joined Hall as an entrant. He would be making his first appearance in the race. Charles was the Treasurer of the Louis Bergdoll Motor Car Company, and he was an amateur when it came to racing. This would be his first big contest. The entries of Hall and Bergdoll brought the total number of entries up to fourteen cars. Plans for the race were complete, with the officials determined that it would maintain its reputation for safety, and would not be anything like the Vanderbilt Cup Race.

On Monday, 4 October 1910, practice began with over 5,000 people on hand for the first day. Approximately 600 of those watched from the Concourse. The officials scheduled one hour of practice each day. The session would take place from 6:30 A.M. to 7:30 A.M. During the weekend, American Locomotive withdrew their entry for Harry Grant, claiming that their exit was due to the change in the rules, concerning the classification of the cars, since the time that they made their entry. This was really just an excuse from the company, since W. C. Longstreth admitted that it was because "Grant could not stand the strain of three nerve racking races of national importance within the short space of three weeks."[12] Having just won the Vanderbilt Cup, Grant wanted to take a week off so that he would be rested for the Grand Prize Race in two weeks.

W. C. Mullen took to the course first, in John Megraw's Simplex, or "Greyhound" as the owner called it because of its speed and grey color. Mullen broke the rules by speeding along the course at 5:30 A.M., an hour ahead of schedule, and a very angry Captain Duncan forced him to stop. John F. Betz also made some laps of the track in his Simplex once the official practice session began. Betz took a representative of the Simplex Company around with him on his practice laps rather than his regular mechanician. The scorers did not record any official times on the first day of practice, but some observers said that they had timed Betz at around the 8:15 to 8:30 mark.[13] Len Zengle held the course record of 7:41. He and his teammate, Al Mitchell, also practiced on Monday. Erwin Bergdoll sped around the track in the Benz. The local driver was named to replace George Robertson in the factory car. It must have been an honor for him to replace such a star as Robertson. His brother-in-law, Al Hall, also practiced, with his wife riding along in the passenger seat, and Erwin's brother Charles Bergdoll also took a few laps. Only these

Spectators are seen here, viewing the track from one of the hills along the West River Drive. This is one of the areas on the drive where parking was allowed. Even here, where the crowd is well away from the road, a rope is strung from the tree to keep them from getting any closer. Near the left, one eager fan can be seen on the roof of a car. (1909). Photograph by Nathan Lazarnick, courtesy of the Detroit Public Library, National Automotive History Collection.

six drivers made practice laps on Monday. More were expected to arrive in town on Tuesday.

The Quaker City Motor Club was pleased to see that their prediction came true concerning an increase in the number of entries following the Vanderbilt Cup. They received fourteen entries on Monday, bringing the total up to twenty-seven. The Nordyke & Marmon Company of Indianapolis entered two Marmon cars, one to be driven by Ray Harroun, and the other by Joe Dawson. The thirty-one year old Harroun, a Detroit native, had been racing since 1906, but 1910 was his big year. He had already won races at Los Angeles, Atlanta, and a 200 mile race at the Indianapolis Motor Speedway. Dawson was also from Detroit. He worked as Harroun's mechanician during the 1909 racing season, and was now a driver himself, and making a fine showing of it. He came in second behind Grant at the Vanderbilt Cup Race.

The Stoddard-Dayton Company entered two of its cars. One would be driven by Hugh Harding, who drove the Apperson in 1909, and the other would be driven by young Tobin De Hymel. De Hymel was a twenty year old from San Antonio, Texas, who had been racing in the west for five years. He was on his first trip east to participate in the Vanderbilt Cup and entered the Fairmount Park Race since he was in the area. De Hymel was always referred to as an Aztec Indian, but his parents were French and Spanish. Even though it was known that he was not an Aztec, the local reporters kept referring to him as such, just to add an exotic twist to the event. The next car entered was a Mercedes entered by "T. J. Wosser." It was later learned that there was no "T. J. Wosser," and that the name was an alias for a Philadelphian "who does not care to have his name mentioned in connection with the motor racing game."[14] While the Quaker City Motor Club admitted this, they did not reveal the true identity of the Philadelphian. "T. J. Wosser" was obviously someone who feared the reactions of certain people if they learned that he were associated with this entry. The driver, Joseph Jagersberger, was an international racing star who had participated in premier racing events on both sides of the Atlantic.

The National Motor Vehicle Company was the next company to get their entries in. The National cars would be driven by Johnny Aitken and H. S. Wilcox. Aitken had only been driving for a year, but he already won numerous races, and recently finished third in the Vanderbilt Cup. Wilcox was an Indianapolis native who was twenty-two years old, and had mainly competed in races in that area. The Fairmount Park Race was to be his first race in Philadelphia. The National Motor Vehicle Company was located in Indianapolis, and had been constructing vehicles there since 1900. The next car was entered by the Mercer Automobile Company, based in Trenton, New Jersey, and owned by the Roebling family. They entered a Mercer Mercury which would be driven by H. P. Frey. Frey was a thirty-five year old Easton, Pennsylvania native, now living in Philadelphia. He had competed in many local events, and had just broken a few ribs when he was thrown into a telegraph pole during the Vanderbilt Cup Race. This would surely be a painful race for Frey. He would be driving the same car he drove in New York, it having been repaired and ready to go again.

Robert E. Hitemayer, a private car owner from New York, entered another Simplex. He selected Ralph Beardsley to drive the car. Beardsley was an amateur out of Newark, New Jersey. Philadelphians knew him for his participation in races at Point Breeze. He had been making a good showing in the Vanderbilt Cup Race when he crashed into another car that was stopped on the track. The Corbin Vehicle Company entered one of their cars and named Joe Matson as their driver. Matson was a twenty-six year old from Boston, Massachusetts, who was an experienced racer, even beating Robertson and Florida at a race in Indianapolis in 1909. The Abbott-Detroit Company, the successor to Chalmers-Detroit, entered the last three cars. Their drivers would be the brothers, Mortimer and Montague Roberts, along with Vincent Padula. The twenty-six year old veteran, Montague Roberts was born in Pittsburgh, but now lived in New York. He was known as a competitor in both national and international races, having competed in the Vanderbilt Cup and the French Grand Prix. He was also one of the drivers of the winning Thomas in the 1908 New York–Paris Race. He was best known to Philadelphians for breaking the track record at Point Breeze back in 1905. His brother Mortimer was twenty-two years old, and was a Philadelphia native. He had just finished second at the Massapequa Race on Long Island, a preliminary event to the Vanderbilt Cup. Vincent

Padula worked as the eastern distributor of Abbott-Detroit cars. Originally from Massachusetts, he had lived in Philadelphia for twelve years and competed in many local events during that time. He was thirty-seven years old.

With these drivers entered, the Fairmount Park Race was assured to be the biggest yet. Although the entry list was supposed to close at midnight, the motor club decided that they would keep the list open, perhaps in an attempt to surpass the Vanderbilt Cup in the number of entries. One last announcement was made on Monday, and that was that Harry Cobe would replace Schleiffler as the driver of the Jackson car. Cobe was a famous driver. He was twenty-three years old and had begun to make a name for himself in 1907, when he finished second in a twenty-four hour race at Brighton Beach. He was better known out west, having competed in races at Indianapolis. Apparently, the local manager of the Jackson Company, S. Blockson, wanted to drive the car, but his family was afraid for him and urged him not to do it, so Cobe was brought in to drive.

George Robertson made a surprise announcement on Monday that he would retire from racing. "I will never again ride in a race," he said.[15] Robertson decided to follow the wishes of his wife, who feared that the next accident could be his last. To take care of his family, he thought it would be best to lead a normal life. "I have $35,000 in the bank earned in racing, and as I am but twenty-six years of age I think I can earn enough in less dangerous work to take care of myself and family."[16] It was now assured that Philadelphia's hero would not race at Fairmount Park again.

The cars returned to the track on Tuesday morning. John F. Betz continued to make fast laps. His best time of the day was 8:27. His 8:15 from Monday was unofficial, but this showed that if it was not correct, he was not that far from it. Len Zengle improved on his times from Monday with a lap of 8:24 in his Chadwick. Erwin Bergdoll made four laps of the course, his best time being a 9:04. Willie Haupt tried some fast laps in Al Hall's Benz and made a fast lap of 8:29. Haupt showed that the car had the speed to do well, but Hall still planned to drive it in the race. Mullen made the fastest lap of the day. He turned a lap of 8:20 in John Megraw's Simplex. None of the drivers approached the track record, since they first wanted to spend some time familiarizing themselves with the course. Other drivers to go out on the course on Tuesday were Hanshue in the Apperson, Jagersberger in the Mercedes, Beardsley in the Simplex, and Al Mitchell in the second Chadwick, who got into trouble on the exit of Sweet Briar Curve. Mitchell quickly approached the curve as the car lost a wheel. The car skidded to the side of the road, where Mitchell brought it to a stop without causing anymore destruction. This was not the car that would be used in the race, but a new Chadwick car that the company tested.

When police saw a car of a non-competitor racing around the course, Captain Duncan demonstrated how serious he was about stopping trespassers. He borrowed Megraw's "Greyhound" and sped around the course to apprehend the transgressor. Scorers timed Captain Duncan's lap at 9:20, which they considered good for an amateur.

Three more cars entered the race on Tuesday, bringing the total up to thirty. The Lozier Company entered a car for Ralph Mulford, who would make his second start in the park. George Davis would also be making a return appearance. He entered an Apperson, which he would drive himself. Davis dropped out of the 1908 race due to mechanical problems while driving an Apperson, and Mulford finished third that year in the Lozier. These two alumni from the 1908 race added much talent to an already exceptional field. The third entry of the day came from the Franklin Motor Car Company. They had already entered two Cole cars, but decided to enter a Wescott as well. The car would be driven by Harry Knight, a twenty-one year old from Indianapolis who had finished well in a few oval track races in the west. A good finish in a 100 mile race in Indianapolis a few months earlier brought him to the attention of Wescott, which then entered him at Fairmount Park, his first major road race.

The committees in charge of the race were also active on Tuesday, making sure that the race would not in any way resemble the Vanderbilt Cup. Members of the Quaker City Motor Club joined Director of Public Safety, Henry Clay, and Assistant Superintendent of Police, Timothy O'Leary, in a meeting to discuss improved safety. Although the race had been a safe one in the past, the organizers were not content, and they discussed a number of new rules and announced them at the conclusion of the meeting. First, the committee placed Sweet Briar Curve, one of the most popular spots for spectators, off limits. Nobody would be allowed within sixty-six yards of the turn. The committee also placed the east side of the West River Drive off limits. This area was located between the track and the river. Spectators would have to stand behind the ropes near turns, where they would be strung further away from the track, and would only be allowed to stand at the track's edge on the straight sections. The officials also decided that they would stop the race once each division had a winner. Cars still on the track would have to stop, and could not return to the start until all spectators were clear. This decision was in response to the previous year's incident where a car sped toward the gathering on the Concourse after the race. They would also not allow anyone to crowd around the mayor's box. "One of the cars sped down the Concourse after the race was over last year, and created a panic. I saw the great throngs around Mayor Reyburn last year, and decided to prevent such an incident again," said Assistant Superintendent O'Leary.[17] Spectators would also be asked to spread out more, so that they could get out of the way if something happened. O'Leary said that the racers feared the crowds at the Sweet Briar Curve in 1909, and would have been more willing to go through the turn faster if they did not have to worry about hitting someone. "We considered the accident at the curve last year and we also took into consideration the fact that a policeman, who had been ill, became demented in his efforts to drive the spectators from the curve," he said.[18] So the officials responded to both the Vanderbilt Cup, and concerns raised during the 1909 event, in an attempt to anticipate complications.

The mayor was also out on the course on Tuesday, with Referee Ross, inspecting the track surface. There had been some problems with soft spots in the track over the first two days of practice. He found three particularly bad areas; Neill Drive, Belmont Avenue, and City Avenue. By the afternoon, city road crews arrived in the park to repair them. Mr. Ross blamed the soft spots on contractors that the Quaker City Motor Club hired to do the work, but he assumed that the course would be

Referee R.E. Ross (center right) stands alongside a police officer as he watches the activities from the sidelines. Ross was heavily involved in the staging of the 1909 and 1910 Fairmount Park Races, serving as both referee and Chairman of the Contest Committee. (1910). Photograph by Nathan Lazarnick, courtesy of the Detroit Public Library, National Automotive History Collection.

perfect for the race on Saturday. "The Mayor has now taken the matter in his own hands and work has begun under my personal direction," he said.[19] Even with these problems, the drivers believed that the course was at least as good as the 1909 course.

The mayor's support of the race was as strong as ever. "The Fairmount Park course has been declared to be the safest and best in the country for automobile racing by the speediest drivers who have raced in every part of the world. We have already held two races there without a single accident, and we shall take even increased precautions this year to assure the safety both of spectators and racers."[20] The mayor wanted to prove that nobody could stage an affair like this better than the City of Philadelphia.

Twenty thousand spectators gathered in the park on Wednesday to see practice on a much improved track surface than just twenty-four hours earlier. "Except a little softness at some of the turns the track this morning was fine and no driver has a right to complain. The condition of the course is so much better than the Vanderbilt that there is no comparison. And as for protection, I was delighted this morning," said John Aitken.[21] Aitken had to stop his car to prevent hitting spectators during the Vanderbilt Cup Race, spoiling any chance he had of winning. "It was genuine relief this morning to see the track clear all the way around," he said.[22]

Betz and Cobe furnished the thrills for the spectators as they raced each other around the course lap after lap. Manager Blockson sat in the mechanician's seat of Cobe's machine. His family could not have been pleased with the risk he took. Cobe's wife also acted as mechanician during his practice runs and planned to be beside him on raceday if the AAA allowed it. Cobe officially entered a male mechanician, Jack Casey, but he felt that his wife was the best person for the job. He made a request of the AAA to set aside the rule that did not allow women to participate in races, so that she would be able to ride with him during the race, but he had not yet heard their reply.

The first big accident of the week stole the headlines on Wednesday. Dr. George F. Simmerman, a dentist by profession, but well known as a balloonist, asked Harry Endicott for a ride around the course. He climbed into the mechanician's seat and they darted away. They went through the Sweet Briar Curve safely and then onto the West River Drive. Traveling along the river at 70 mph they reached the Philadelphia & Reading Railroad Bridge and took the turn onto Neill Drive. As they negotiated the turn, a rear wheel flew off the car, which slid toward the stone wall on the opposite side of the road. The front tire dug in and broke off, flipping the car over and sending its driver and passenger flying through the air. Both occupants lay there on an embankment, unconscious. Dr. Simmerman woke up momentarily, but it took a spectator with a hat full of water, retrieved from the Schuylkill River, to wake up Endicott. Frey came around in his Mercer, and when he realized what occurred, he stopped, put Endicott in his car and sped back to the Concourse. The doctor hitched a ride on the next car that came around. Physicians examined both men and found that they had only minor injuries. Endicott had bruises on his arms, chest and legs. The doctor's injuries also consisted of bruises, and no broken bones. Neither driver nor passenger had any memory of the accident itself. "I know we were traveling mighty fast down the river driveway and I know I traveled a bit faster when I went out, that's all I can say," said the doctor. "Some say the car turned over, I don't know."[23] Police dispatched a boat to retrieve one of the Cole's tires, which floated in the river. Endicott was confident that he would be okay to drive on Saturday, and the team seemed to think that they could get the car repaired for him in time.

Wednesday was the first day at the track for Harry Endicott and his brother Bill. Ray Harroun and Joe Dawson of the Marmon team, also made their first laps, but did not show any real attempt at speed. The two National cars of Aitken and Wilcox, on the other hand, did not show any reservation. Aitken made an 8:54 on his new favorite track, and Wilcox turned a lap in 8:50.

Len Zengle posted the fastest lap of the day. The holder of the fastest lap record made a lap in 8:03. While Zengle did not set a new record, he did make the fastest lap of the week thus far. W. J. Coghlan, the Philadelphia manager of the Chadwick Company expressed delight at Zengle's fine performance and that of the Chadwick machine. "Judging from their speed, ability and power last year, we should have no trouble winning this year," he said.[24]

When practice ended for the day, four more entrants announced their participation in the race. The Longstreth Motor Company entered two Pullman cars which would be driven by Ernest Gellard and Harold Hardesty. Gellard hailed from

Switzerland. He held the position of chief engineer at the Pullman factory in York, Pennsylvania, and designed the two cars that the local distributor entered. Hardesty served as the superintendent of the factory in York. He had no real experience in road racing, but had run in a few endurance runs before. Another entry made on Wednesday was the Otto, entered by C. W. Hardwood Nash. Frank Yerger would drive the car. Next, William Oliver Jr. entered a Mercer which he intended to drive himself. The local driver was known for his appearances in races at Point Breeze.

On Wednesday night the drivers met at the Quaker City Motor Club headquarters at the Hotel Walton to draw numbers. Officials also announced a change concerning the drivers of the Benz cars. Al Hall would not be taking part in the race. Erwin Bergdoll would take over the seat in his Benz, and Bergdoll would be replaced in the factory Benz by Willie Haupt. A letter also arrived at the club's headquarters on Wednesday, addressed to Secretary Harbach. It was from George Robertson, who wrote to say how sorry he was that he would not be at the race. "My one regret, since the accident, has been that I will be unable to drive in the Fairmount Park Race," he said. He still had a broken arm and rib, and would not even be able to travel to Philadelphia to see the event as a spectator. "Philadelphia seems like home to me, and I want you all to feel that were I in a position to go, I would be there for the races."[25]

On Thursday, over 30,000 spectators gathered in the park, just to see practice. The two brewing families made the fastest times on Thursday. Betz had the best time of 8:08, just five seconds slower than Zengle's best lap of practice. Erwin Bergdoll was not far behind with a quick lap of 8:14. Matson took his first practice laps in the Corbin, as did the drivers of the two Pullman cars. The only accident during Thursday's session occurred when the Wescott of Harry Knight collided with Frey's Mercer. They raced down the Concourse and approached the turn near the Smith Memorial. Knight trailed Frey when his car began to skid. He could not regain control and the car hit the rear of the Mercer. Frey's mechanician, C. H. Kittrell, fell out of the car. He did not sustain any injuries except for a few bruises. The Mercer ran off the road and hit a tree, which smashed the car. Unfortunately, this was the Mercer that Oliver was supposed to drive in the race. Since Frey's Vanderbilt Cup car had not yet arrived in the city, he had been using Oliver's car for practice. The Mercer factory had to repair Frey's Vanderbilt Cup car before it could be sent on to Philadelphia. They figured that once they finished the repairs to Frey's car, the car that he used in practice would be available for Oliver, but now there was no extra car. Oliver had to withdraw his entry only one day after making it. A few of the city's papers claimed that Bill Endicott was involved in this collision, rather than Frey, but since the Mercer was withdrawn, the *Philadelphia Evening Times* most likely had the story correct when they reported Frey's involvement.

Cobe received the result of his request on Thursday, concerning whether his wife would be able to act as his mechanician in the race. He was informed by the AAA that the rule barring women from participating in races would not be put aside, and that his wife would not be able to act as his mechanician. He argued that "she [would] make him a better partner in the race than any man whom he could select," but unfortunately, she would not get the chance to prove him right.[26]

Table 7. 1910—Fastest Time of Each Driver in Practice

Car	Driver	Time
Chadwick	Zengle	8:03
Benz	E. Bergdoll	8:14
Chadwick	Mitchell	8:13
Simplex	Mullen	8:20
Simplex	Beardsley	9:15
Simplex	Betz	8:08
Lozier	Mulford	No Lap Recorded
Stoddard-Dayton	De Hymel	9:37
Mercedes	Jagersberger	8:33
Apperson	Davis	9:54
Apperson	Hanshue	9:11
Stoddard-Dayton	Harding	8:44
National	Aitken	8:54
Jackson	Cobe	No Lap Recorded
Wescott	Knight	9:08
Marmon	Harroun	9:13
Benz	Haupt	8:25
National	Wilcox	8:50
Benz	Hearne	No Lap Recorded
Benz	C. Bergdoll	8:10
Pullman	Gellard	9:43
Mercer	Frey	11:15
Otto	Yerger	No Lap Recorded
Marmon	Dawson	9:07
Corbin	Matson	9:30
Pullman	Hardesty	No Lap Recorded
Abbott-Detroit	Padula	No Lap Recorded
Abbott-Detroit	Mortimer Roberts	11:28
Ford	Kulick	No Lap Recorded
Cole	H. Endicott	9:57
Cole	B. Endicott	9:45
Abbott-Detroit	Montague Roberts	No Lap Recorded

On Thursday afternoon, the appropriations subcommittee of the city councils met to take action on the mayor's request for $2,000 for trophies. The committee could not find $2,000 in un-appropriated funds, so they put through a transfer bill which would take the money from the mayor's appropriation. So, in effect, the councils approved the amount, although the mayor's appropriation already showed a deficit, even before the councils took $2,000 from it. With this action taking place only two days before the race, it really did not matter much, since the trophies had already been ordered, regardless of the councils' actions.

On Friday, the crowds again began to fill the grandstand and line the course to see practice, but then it began to rain. Everyone ran under the grandstand for cover, but they did not go home. They planned to wait around to see the practice spins even if they might not take place. Many of the drivers also arrived at their normal time, as if they were unaware of the rain. They intended to drive on the wet track until they were told that practice was cancelled or that they were not allowed.

Referee Ross and P. D. Folwell of the AAA made the decision. They had driven around the course with Captain Duncan and determined that it was too slick for practice to be held safely. Hugh Harding and Joe Dawson each managed to make a full lap before the officials cancelled the session. Harding's time for the lap was 9:48; Dawson's was not recorded.

The officials decided that since a few drivers did not have a chance to make a single lap of the course, they would be allowed to practice for one hour, from 6:00 A.M. to 7:00 A.M. on Saturday. The officials felt that it would make for a safer race if all of the participants had some familiarity with the route and track conditions. They also decided that if the race could not be held on Saturday due to rain, it would be rescheduled for Monday. Ralph Mulford was one of those who had not made a single practice lap, but since he had raced in Fairmount Park before, he wasn't too worried about it. "I know the course like a book," he said.[27]

The rain on Friday actually made the officials and drivers pretty happy. As long as additional rain did not fall overnight, and the wet track had time to dry before the race, it would lay the dust and harden the dirt better than any road crew could accomplish. On Friday night, the drivers met at the Hotel Walton to go over the rules with the officials and receive their final instructions before the race. They then returned to their hotel rooms to rest and prepare themselves for the big day ahead of them.

7

The Third Annual Fairmount Park Race

Just as 1909, the 1910 Fairmount Park Race was scheduled to start at noon. Of course, the crowds could not wait that long to take their places in the park. The campfires of those who had stayed the night in the park were seen glowing first thing in the morning, as the overnighters prepared their breakfast. It was a cold morning, and the track was still wet from the previous day's rain. The track surface was not soft or muddy, but just damp enough to keep the dirt tightly packed. It was in ideal condition for a great race. Although the dew in the air suggested that more rain was on the way, it was not due to arrive until later in the evening, leaving a window for the afternoon contest.

Referee Ross was out early in the morning inspecting the course. He found it to be fine for racing, but he waited until the first of the drivers took a practice spin before he made his decision. Harry Jones, probably a mechanic for the Otto team, was the first out in Frank Yerger's machine, and he also found it to be in great shape. Ross returned to the Hotel Walton and informed the motor club and the AAA that the race would take place. By 9:00 A.M., crowds were pouring into the park in force. Trolleys were so packed with people that they could not make it up hills.[1] George's Hill alone was covered with over 20,000 spectators. At the Sweet Briar Curve people stood ten to twelve deep behind the ropes. There were spectators perched in the trees and on the bridges. A special train pulled onto the Pennsylvania Railroad track on Wynnefield Avenue where its passengers would watch the race through the windows of their train car. The city streets were choked with vehicles heading to the park from all directions. The newspapers all agreed that there were more people in

1910 than in previous years, so the estimate of 600,000 spectators made by Tim O'Leary, the Assistant Superintendent of Police, probably was not that far off.[2] As in previous years, the only way to describe the large number of spectators was in military terms. "By 8 o'clock spectators were coming to the Park by companies; two hours later they were advancing in regiments, and between 11 and 12 o'clock they swept into the Park in brigades," wrote a *Philadelphia Evening Bulletin* reporter.[3] The biggest race in the country was getting bigger and bigger every year. As the fans entered the park, they were greeted by employees from the Lit Brothers Department Store, who were holding glass bowls to collect money for charity.

Mayor Reyburn was still very involved, taking a trip around the course with Director Clay and Superintendent Taylor to inspect the safety situation. At Sweet Briar, he ordered 6,000 spectators moved from the outside of a turn, to the inside.[4] It was the attention to detail from the organizers that set Fairmount Park apart from other venues. The crowd was not happy, but they were safer in their new position. Spectators had once again come from all over the country, and many license plates from surrounding states such as New Jersey, New York, and Maryland were visible. There were many notables amongst the crowd. The list read like a who's who of Philadelphia's industrial and commercial community. Jack Coombs, a pitcher for the World Series-bound Philadelphia Athletics, was in the stands. There were merchants such as James D. Lit of the Lit Brothers Department Store, and architects William Hewitt, John T. Windrim, and William Price. Industry was represented by men such as Arthur Dorrance of the Campbell Soup Company, and Henry Albert Disston of the Disston Saw Works which was based in the Tacony section of the city. There was another surprise guest, George Robertson, who with his arm in a sling, and a scar on his face, greeted the participants and then took a seat in the grandstand to watch the race. Robertson received a standing ovation when he appeared on the scene. He acted a bit like an ambassador for the race, or elder statesman, if an elder statesman can be twenty-six years old. At eleven o'clock Mayor Reyburn and his party took their seats in the grandstand. Director Clay and Misses Reyburn accompanied the mayor. Senator McNichol sat with his family a few rows away.

Just before the race, the public discovered that the mysterious "T. J. Wosser," the entrant of the Mercedes, was in fact Edward Schroeder. Schroeder was a wealthy Philadelphian who did not make his identity known because he did not want anyone to know that he had obtained a foreign driver to pilot the car. When the Mercedes rolled to the starting line, the announcer broadcasted the owner's real name by mistake. Schroeder was embarrassed that his identity was revealed, but said that he chose Jagersberger because he felt that he was the best person to drive the car. "Jagersberger has won several big races in France and Germany. I am confident he will win this one," he said.[5]

Philadelphia society had again filled the grandstand. Men wore suits and women wore gowns. According to the *Philadelphia North American*, half of those in the grandstands were women.[6] Salesmen shuffled through the crowd selling cigars, sandwiches, peanuts, and beverages. In the parking areas, spectators were perched on the roofs and running boards of their cars. They commandeered park benches from all over the park and carried them to the ropes so that their occupants would not have to stand. By eleven o'clock the participants were all in their pits preparing the cars and fine-tuning them for the race ahead.

Police made a final check of the course, and gave the spectators gathered in their assigned areas a final warning not to step onto the course. At 11:45 A.M., the cars moved to the starting line. They lined up in rows of three. Ten minutes later, Starter Gantert announced to the drivers, "Start your motors, everybody ready in a few minutes."[7] Exhaust pipes emitted loud explosions, and the smoke of the thirty-two cars hung in the air. The grandstand crowds rose to their feet, anxiously awaiting the start. Starter Gantert, and his assistant, Joseph Keir, made sure that all of the cars were in position. To enable all of the cars to get away before the first car came back around, a car would have to leave the line every ten seconds. There was no room for mistakes.

At twelve o'clock noon, car #1 was let go to the roar of the crowd. Hanshue sped away in the Apperson Jack Rabbit. Mortimer Roberts followed him in car #2, the Abbott-Detroit. The big blue National of Aitken left the line next, and Ralph Mulford followed him in his ghostly white Lozier #4. Erwin Bergdoll received the cheers of the hometown crowd as he disappeared around the first corner. Montague Roberts approached the line next in the Abbott-Detroit, and then came Harding in the Stoddard-Dayton. Harold Hardesty drove away in the #8 Pullman, and then came Davis in the second Apperson entry. Gellard's Pullman started tenth, and then ten seconds later Ray Harroun sped off in the #11 Marmon, a bright yellow machine. There is little doubt that Ray Harroun's wife watched from the pits as her husband started the race. She always accompanied him to races, and frequently rode with him on practice laps. Because of her experience in the car, she understood just how dangerous automobile racing could be.

> I have always insisted upon having a place in the pits, though, of course, I make every effort to be inconspicuous. I have my medical necessities close at hand, a surgeon's miniature kit and every possible convenience. For if ever he should be hurt, I would want to be the first at his side. But so far I have never had any use for my little bag.[8]

Len Zengle's Chadwick car roared away when Gantert gave the word, and then Megraw's "Greyhound" Simplex, with Mullen at the wheel, followed suit. Harry Cobe dashed away next in the #14 Jackson. Frey started next in the #15 Mercer, and Wilcox followed him ten seconds later in the second National entry. Two minutes and thirty seconds had passed since the first car started and Gantert was doing an excellent job of getting the cars away on schedule, one after the other. It was like clockwork. As one car left, another moved up to the line to take its place. Next came Jagersberger, who, in a bit of showmanship, threw his hands in the air and allowed the car to accelerate down the straight without its driver's guidance. Willie Haupt's Benz started seventeenth, and Harry Endicott's Cole started eighteenth.

The local brewer, John F. Betz, motored down the Concourse in car #19, his big yellow Simplex. Betz also received a greater cheer from the crowd, like Bergdoll had, in acknowledgement of his being a Philadelphian. Next, Vincent Padula

Table 8. 1910—Starting Lineup

No.	Car	Driver	Piston Displacement	Mechanician	Tires
1	Apperson	Hansue	597	M.W. Ferguson	Michelin
2	Abbott-Detroit	Mortimer Roberts	213	H.A. Deguise	Michelin
3	National	Aitken	447	Ed Covington	Michelin
4	Lozier	Mulford	570	Joe Horan	Michelin
5	Benz	E. Bergdoll	731	Frank Johnson	Not Available
6	Abbott-Detroit	Montague Roberts	213	Ernest Thying	Michelin
7	Stoddard-Dayton	Harding	487	Clarence Mason	Michelin
8	Pullman	Hardesty	286	Robert Emmett	Michelin
9	Apperson	Davis	597	Arthur Jackson	Michelin
10	Pullman	Gellard	256	Fred Seyler	Michelin
11	Marmon	Harroun	318	Harry Goetz	Not Available
12	Chadwick	Zengle	707	Billie Manker	Firestone
13	Simplex	Mullen	672	J.C. Fleming	Not Available
14	Jackson	Cobe	354	Jack Casey	Michelin
15	Mercer	Frey	300	C.H. Kittrell	Michelin
16	National	Wilcox	447	Roy Vernon	Not Available
17	Benz	Haupt	448	H.W. Fehyl	Not Available
18	Cole	H. Endicott	201	Charles Smith	Not Available
19	Simplex	Betz	672	George Tompkins	Not Available
20	Mercedes	Jagersberger	557	William Nash	Michelin
21	Abbott-Detroit	Padula	213	Jack Harkins	Michelin
22	Simplex	Beardsley	672	Glenn Etheridge	Not Available
23	Westcott	Knight	354	John Dietrick	Michelin
24	Ford	Kulick	201	Mr. Ferguson	Not Available
25	Chadwick	Mitchell	707	Scott Malott	Firestone
26	Benz	Hearne	448	Mr. Radley	Not Available
27	Cole	B. Endicott	201	H.C. Stanton	Not Available
28	Marmon	Dawson	299	Bruce Keen	Not Available
29	Stoddard-Dayton	De Hymel	487	Mr. Hogan	Michelin
30	Benz	C. Bergdoll	493	Eugene Stecker	Not Available
31	Corbin	Matson	270	Harry Zabosso	Not Available
32	Otto	Yerger	253	Walter Siemons	Not Available

launched the third Abbott-Detroit entry. Ralph Beardsley started off in the other Simplex machine when he received the word, and Knight followed him in the #23 Wescott. Frank Kulick's little Ford entry started next, and then came Mitchell in car #25, the Chadwick. Ed Hearne drove the second factory Benz, and then Bill Endicott piloted the #27 Cole down the straightaway. Ray Harroun's teammate, Joe Dawson, made the start in his Marmon, and then the young Tobin De Hymel accelerated down the Concourse in car #29, the Stoddard-Dayton. Charles Bergdoll, the rookie, started thirtieth in his Benz, followed by the #31 Corbin of Joe Matson. Then the final car, the #32 Otto with Frank Yerger driving, left the starting line. Gantert's watch showed a time of 12:05:20 P.M. All of the cars were on their way five minutes and 20 seconds into the race. Starter Gantert had once again performed his job perfectly. Everyone had started safely and on time.

About three minutes passed, as the crowd awaited the first car to come back around. Then they heard the sound of an engine in the distance, and Ralph Mulford's

Announcer Proud speaks into his megaphone, as Starter Gantert shakes the hands of other officials, after the successful start of the 1910 Fairmount Park Race. (1910). Photograph by Nathan Lazarnick, courtesy of the Detroit Public Library, National Automotive History Collection.

Lozier appeared and roared down the straightaway. He had already passed the three cars that started before him. Erwin Bergdoll hung on the back of Mulford's Lozier, jockeying from side to side in an attempt to get around him. Aitken's National closed up behind Bergdoll to make it a three car struggle. The three cars continued their battle as they disappeared around the turn at the end of the Concourse. Faster cars crossed the line behind them. Al Mitchell led the field with a time of 8:10 for the first lap. De Hymel took second place in the Stoddard-Dayton, while Mulford actually stood in third place. Charles Bergdoll had a very short race. He lost his gas cap on the first lap and had to retire from the race. The car never came back around and it left everyone wondering what had happened for a while. The local favorite, John F. Betz, also did not finish a lap. His car's crankshaft broke as he passed the North Wynnefield Trolley Station. The car swerved, as Betz lost control for a moment, but he brought it to a safe stop. He and his mechanician, George Tompkins, inspected the damage and found that they could not repair it. They pushed the car to the side and walked back to the start. Betz angrily declared, "I wouldn't say a word if it had been almost any other kind of trouble, for I don't think I'm a quitter, but after running my car in the practice spins all week with no more than I had with my watch, to have it develop a fatal defect in the race itself, and so early in the game that I had no chance is certainly hard luck."[9]

The veteran Willie Haupt had a terrible first lap of 20:02. Reports of the race left his slow time unexplained, but he picked up the pace on the next lap. Ray

Harroun's Marmon also had a slow first lap due to tire trouble. One of the tires burst as he came through the turn at 52nd Street and Parkside Avenue. Harroun and his mechanician, Harry Goetz, changed the tire, and then stopped at their pits to pick up another spare. Harold Hardesty also had a slow first lap in the Pullman. He only made it to the top of Sweet Briar Hill before he encountered a problem. One of the car's tires burst, and Hardesty, and his mechnician, Fred Seyler, jumped out to change it. Hardesty's Pullman crossed the line to finish its first lap with a time of 14:49.

On lap two, Mitchell continued to lead, but Mulford's quick pace and the clear track ahead pushed him into second place. Behind him, the competition bunched up. Three cars tied for third place, driven by Tobin De Hymel, Len Zengle, and Erwin Bergdoll. Bergdoll tore up the track, making the best time for the second lap. A little further back Aitken's National came around in eighth position. His lap of 8:45 moved him up four places from twelfth. Davis also moved up through the field. He went from eighteenth to fifteenth in a single lap. The #8 Pullman's first lap troubles continued on the second lap. The car had a twisted pump shaft, which put Hardesty out of the race. Harding also experienced engine trouble in his Stoddard-Dayton. He had to stop on lap two to try to correct the problem, and then he continued on, although his second lap took 23:47 to complete.

The drivers treated the crowds to a busy third lap. Mitchell continued to lead, with Erwin Bergdoll now besting Ralph Mulford for second place. De Hymel and Zengle closed up behind them, putting the top five cars within striking distance of each other. Mullen continued his charge through the field, moving from seventeenth to twelfth in his Simplex. The rest of the positions held steady, but amazingly, five cars dropped out of the race on this lap. First, Hanshue stripped a steering gear and retired his Apperson on Parkside Avenue, near the Wynnefield Avenue intersection. He had been running in thirteenth when the car broke down. Bill Endicott ruined his chances by trying to be friendly to another driver. He was taking the turn at 52nd Street when a faster car came up behind him. Instead of holding his line, Endicott swung to the outside to let the faster car through, and in the process, he broke a steering pin which put him out of the race. Then Hugh Harding, who had been having engine trouble during his second lap, parked his car after being delayed for twenty-five minutes. Harding was in seventh place after his first lap, and certainly would have been in the thick of it had it not been for bad luck. Montague Roberts' race also came to an end on lap three, due to ignition problems with his engine.

The most spectacular of the retirements on lap three occurred at the perennial danger spot on the course, Sweet Briar Hill. Beardsley's Simplex began smoking as he reached the top of the hill. Glenn Etheridge, his mechanician, hung over the side of the car to see if he could locate the problem, but the thick smoke obscured Beardsley's view of the road ahead of him. He knew that the Reading Railroad Bridge loomed somewhere near the bottom of the hill, but he could not see it. With Etheridge still leaning out of the car, they hit the stone support of the bridge, and the front of the car climbed the wall. The impact threw Beardsley clear of the wreck, but Etheridge slammed against the stone abutment. The driver jumped up almost instantly, and in his half conscious state, with blood pouring down his face from a cut on his forehead, found his way to the car and his partner Etheridge, who lay there unconscious, bleeding from a number of injuries. Police and spectators carried Etheridge from the wreck and placed him in a nearby car, which took he and Beardsley to West Philadelphia Homeopathic Hospital.[10] Doctors found that Etheridge had a broken arm, a broken leg, and internal injuries, along with various cuts and bruises. While they considered the injuries to be serious, the doctors optimistically said that he would make a full recovery. The car had been running in fifth at the time of the accident.

This left twenty-four cars running, but the attrition would not stop there. Mullen's Simplex "Greyhound" had been running really well, and occupied thirteenth place at the end of lap three. On lap four, Mullen's race came to an end. One of his car's engine cylinders cracked, forcing Mullen to withdraw. Then Matson's Corbin developed magneto problems which put him out of the race. Twenty-two cars remained in the contest. Mitchell had a twenty-one second lead over the second place car of Bergdoll, who had managed to get ahead of the third place car of Ralph Mulford. Zengle and De Hymel engaged in a battle for fourth. Zengle had a ten second lead at the completion of the lap. Wilcox had a slow lap in his National which dropped him three spots to eleventh place. On the next lap, Bergdoll shaved a second off of Mitchell's lead, but no other changes took place near the front. Bergdoll led Mulford by eighteen seconds, though in track position, the gap equated to ten seconds. Bergdoll could feel the pressure from the Lozier right behind him. At the Sweet Briar Curve, Bergdoll pushed so hard that the rear of his car slid around as he went through the turn. He straightened the car out, but Mulford pulled up right behind him. By the conclusion of the lap, Bergdoll managed to pull out only slightly ahead of him.

In the divisional standings, Mitchell led Division 6C in addition to the overall race. Mulford led the 5C Division by forty-one seconds over De Hymel. In the 4C Division, Aitken held the top spot, with Cobe about two minutes back. Dawson's Marmon led in the 3C Division, with no real opposition, and in the 2C Division, Mortimer Roberts had a thirty second lead over Harry Endicott's Cole.

On lap six, the leader Mitchell had an accident on Neill Drive. He went through the "dip of death" under the Reading Railroad Bridge, and descended a hill on his way to City Avenue. As he when downhill, he lost control of the car. Witnesses on the scene seemed to think that he went too fast, or that he didn't make the previous turn properly. It was probably a little of both. He made the previous turn so fast that he did not exit the turn properly, and in his attempt to get back on line, upset the car and lost control.[11] Mitchell could not regain control of the car. It swerved back and forth wildly as it flew down the hill. It flipped over, hit an embankment, flipped over again and finally landed against a tree. The car pinned Mitchell and his mechanician, Scott Mallot, to the ground, and trapped a police officer, Charles Bates, against a tree. Police and doctors rushed to the scene, and quickly extracted the unconscious driver and mechanician from beneath the car. They treated Officer Bates on the scene for cuts to his neck and thigh, but miraculously, he had no other injuries. An ambulance transported Mitchell and Mallot to St. Timothy's Hospital.

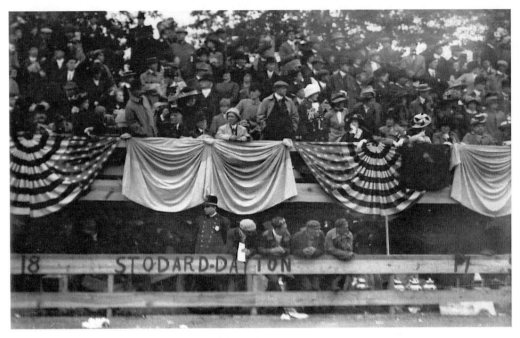

The grandstand incorporated room for the pits underneath. This allowed the spectators on the Concourse a close look at the teams preparing the cars prior to the race and working on them during stops. The well-dressed spectators in the grandstand contrast sharply with the grease covered mechanics in the pits below. (1910). Photograph by Nathan Lazarnick, courtesy of the Detroit Public Library, National Automotive History Collection.

The doctors quickly released Mallot because he had no serious injuries. Mitchell had cuts and bruises that would warrant an overnight stay. Given the violence of the accident, it is amazing that they did not receive more serious injuries. Some eyewitnesses reported that the front axle had broken, causing the accident. They must have been incorrect, since the Chadwick team later turned the car upright and drove it away.

The local, Erwin Bergdoll, assumed the lead due to Mitchell's misfortune. Although Mitchell's accident concerned and horrified the crowds, they cheered the new leader as he came by. Bergdoll led Mulford by forty-one seconds. The order did not change much on this lap, though Wilcox did have a slow round which dropped him down to fifteenth, and Yerger's Otto dropped two places to twentieth.

The order at the front did not change on lap seven. The only real movement involved Wilcox's National falling back to seventeenth after two slow laps. Kulick's Ford also contested Padula's Abbott-Detroit. Kulick had been making good time until lap five when he turned a lap of 16:07. This may have been due to a pit-stop, or an unscheduled tire change. Either way, he fell back to eighteenth, just ahead of Padula.

On lap eight, as Bergdoll came through the Sweet Briar Curve, a nineteen year old boy named William Frick, who was watching from a tree branch, got a little too enthusiastic, and in his attempt to see the leader come by, lost his grip on the branch and fell to the ground. An ambulance picked him up and took him to St. Joseph's Hospital with a concussion and a skull fracture. Almost immediately after doctors tended to Frick, Andrew Archer, a thirty year old, fell from another tree just a few yards away. He suffered two broken legs. These fans knew that they were not supposed to be in the trees. The police could not be faulted since the spectators hid themselves in the leaves, and the police had no way to know that they were up there.

Aitken, Zengle and Jagersberger careened up the West River Drive, in close proximity to each other on this lap, when Aitken's car started chugging and slowing down. His mechanician, Ed Covington, "gripped a spark plug in his teeth, and, while the machine continued to shoot forward, made his way out upon its shaking hood and tugged with one hand at the strap that bound it."[12] Covington changed the spark plug and the car continued on without losing position. In fact, Aitken's time for lap eight was faster than any of his times for the previous three laps.

Bergdoll set a quick pace, making laps of 8:02, 8:07, 8:15, and 8:09. With each lap he increased his lead over Ralph Mulford. By the end of the ninth round, he led the Lozier by fifty-five seconds. The third place car of Len Zengle fell even further back, with almost two full minutes between his car and the second place Lozier. On the ninth lap, he even lost his third place position to De Hymel's Stoddard-Dayton.

By lap ten, Bergdoll led both the race and the 6C Division. Mulford controlled the 5C Division, and Aitken led Division 4C by about three minutes. Dawson occupied first place in the 3C Division as well as fifth overall, which lent credence to the fact that you did not have to have the most powerful car to do well at Fairmount Park. In the 2C Division, Mortimer Roberts led Harry Endicott by a mere thirty-six seconds.

Laps ten and eleven proved to be uneventful, but on lap twelve, Ray Harroun stepped into the spotlight. "Number 11 has just broken the track record; his time was 7:38," exclaimed the announcer.[13] Harroun had been toiling in the middle of the field, but this time around, the timers recorded that he turned the fastest lap of the race, and also broke the track record. He cut three seconds off of Len Zengle's record of 7:41 made in 1909. De Hymel made a stop on lap twelve which dropped him from his third place position to sixth. Dawson and Aitken assumed fourth and fifth places respectively.

On the next lap, De Hymel made a good time of 8:05, which propelled him back up amongst the leaders, and into fourth place. The withdrawal of the #28 car assisted him. Dawson's Marmon suffered a broken axle which put it out of the race. The battle between Mulford and Bergdoll continued on, as strong as ever. Fifty-six seconds separated them in overall time, but only twenty-six seconds separated the cars on the track, and that varied at different parts of the course. At some points, the cars came so close together that the spectators held their breath or began to run for cover for fear that the cars would collide or run off of the course. They witnessed one such incident near the Belmont Pumping Station. The two cars just barely missed touching as they came around the corner, with Mulford's Lozier appearing to be on two wheels. Pumping station employees, who filled a grandstand built just for them, screamed as the two cars came toward them. One woman fainted, but the two drivers kept the cars on the course.[14]

Len Zengle dashes past Aitken's National near the 52nd Street turn that leads back into the park. In the rear, spectators watch the action from George's Hill. (1910). Photograph by Nathan Lazarnick, courtesy of the Detroit Public Library, National Automotive History Collection.

The next time around De Hymel had already given up his new position. Aitken moved up into fourth and Jagersberger followed him into fifth. Ray Harroun also had a continuation of his earlier bad luck when he had some sort of tire trouble on lap fourteen. The cause of his lap of 32:21 was not recorded, but this was much longer than a standard stop. This poor time took him all the way back to seventeenth position. He was probably trying a little too hard, and had to replace a tire as he did on his first lap. It may have also been some type of engine trouble or overheating. Whatever the problem, it made Harroun back off just a little, because he would not turn a lap below 9:30 for the remainder of the race. Some in the crowd believed that the same scenario could occur to Erwin Bergdoll. He consistently made laps of just over eight minutes and had not yet stopped for oil, water, or a tire change. According to the *Philadelphia Record*, "wiser ones who had been in races themselves, or who had studied the sensitive auto engine until they knew its every throb declared that Bergdoll was killing his own goose, that he was overtaxing his engines, and that his refusals to stop for water or oil would be his ruin."[15] Of course, Mulford and Zengle had to do the same just to keep up, but Bergdoll held the lead, and he set the pace. It seemed that whoever had the car that could withstand such hard running would win the race.

On lap fifteen, Bergdoll held the lead in the race, and the 6C Division. Mulford led the 5C Division over the Mercedes of Jagersberger. In the 4C Division, Aitken still held first, as well as fourth overall. In Division 3C, Gellard's Pullman opened up a ten minute lead over Frey's Mercer, and in Division 2C, Mortimer Roberts kept an advantage of about two minutes over Harry Endicott.

Laps fifteen and sixteen showed just how consistently the leaders kept pace. Mulford made both laps in exactly 8:15 each. Len Zengle turned both laps in exactly 8:08. So in those two laps, Zengle gained fourteen seconds on the Lozier. On lap sixteen Bergdoll finally got into trouble. Those who thought that he pushed his equipment too hard turned out to be correct. He came under the railroad bridge onto Neill Drive, when the car began to slow, and finally came to a complete stop.

Bergdoll and his mechanician, Frank Johnson, jumped out and took a look at the engine and found that an oil feed had broken. They pushed the car to the side, and Bergdoll's race ended. Ralph Mulford assumed the lead, running 1:47 ahead of Zengle, and then the real battle began. If the spectators considered the contest between Bergdoll and Mulford to be hair-raising, then the one that took place between Mulford and Zengle can only be described as epic.

On lap seventeen, the now second place Zengle, began his charge toward the front, making a lap in 7:57. This brought him to within 1:32 of Mulford, who for the moment felt content to maintain his steady pace. On the next lap, the lead decreased to 1:29. Zengle slowly gained on Mulford, but would he be able to catch him before the end of the race? On lap nineteen, attrition began to take its toll again. Wilcox's National went out due to problems with its radiator, and Harry Endicott's Cole had a broken spring leaf. Endicott had been tied for first place in his division at the end of the eighteenth lap, so the problem greatly disappointed him. This left sixteen cars running. De Hymel began to make another charge toward the front, getting past Jagersberger on the nineteenth lap, and then past Aitken and into third place on lap twenty. The battle at the front also heated up as Zengle sat ahead of Mulford by the end of lap twenty, but only by a mere three seconds! Zengle caught him so quickly because Mulford had to bring the Lozier into the pits. He took on oil, water and gasoline. Based on previous laps, the stop took about 1:20 to complete. It could have been even faster, but one of the members of Mulford's team forgot to fill the oil tank. Just as he prepared to leave the pits, he had to stop and wait for the oil to go in.[16] Nothing exciting happened down through the order, except that Willie Haupt and his Benz dropped out of the race. A stone became lodged in the shifting quadrant and Haupt could not change gears.

In the divisional races, Zengle drove the only remaining car in Division 6C, so as long as he finished the race, he would at least win his division. Mulford had the 5C Division well in hand with a ten minute lead over De Hymel. Aitken continued to control the 4C Division with about five minutes between himself and Cobe. Not to be left behind, Knight trailed Cobe by only two minutes. In Division 3C, Gellard opened a lead of fourteen minutes over the second place car of Frey, and in Division 2C, Roberts had a similar advantage over Padula. On the next lap, Padula got very lucky as both of his remaining rivals in his division dropped out of the race. Kulick stopped at his pits on lap twenty-one to change a tire, but he and his team must have been unaware of the rule which stated that only two men could work on changing a tire. Officials quickly realized that a rule had been broken and they disqualified the Ford.

Mortimer Roberts' car dropped out in a more dangerous fashion. He took the turn at 52nd Street and Parkside Avenue when the front axle broke. Roberts and his mechanician, H. A. Deguise, held on as the car slid to a safe stop, but one of the front tires flew through the air and into the crowd where it struck John Young. Spectators who saw the tire ran for cover. Young did not see the projectile until it was too late, and it knocked him to the ground. Doctors arrived on the scene and found him to be unconscious, so they put him in an ambulance and took him to West Philadelphia Homeopathic Hospital. This meant that Padula just had to finish the race to win the prize for first place in the 2C Division.

At the front, Zengle pulled out another five seconds on Mulford, making his lead over the Lozier eleven seconds. Because of the interval, this meant that the two cars were sixty-nine seconds apart relative to each other on the track. With this distance between them, they would not be dueling on the track, but dueling only on the scoreboard.

On lap twenty-two Mulford made a quick lap of 8:08, his fastest of the day thus far, cutting five seconds off of Zengle's lead. Then, on the next lap, he brought the gap down to only one second! Each time they came by they glanced at the scoreboard to see which one held the lead. Zengle nervously chewed on a cigar that he had been smoking since the race began. The crowds leapt to their feet, unconcerned with the other eleven cars on the course. Everyone watched Mulford and Zengle as they each turned blistering laps in an effort to outdo the other. Since they were only one second apart at the end of lap twenty-three, the race would be decided by the times they clocked on the last two laps.

On lap twenty-four, Zengle lost the lead to Mulford, who once again turned in an incredible lap of 7:59. Mulford now had a nine second advantage going into the final lap. The fans really did not have a favorite, so they cheered for both. Zengle hailed from Philadelphia, and drove a car that Chadwick produced close to home. Mulford was a popular driver in the area, who had become a favorite locally because he had treated the crowd to thrilling drives, much like this one, at Point Breeze and in the park on other occasions.

It appeared that Mulford only had to put in one more good lap to take the victory, but a race as exciting as this one could not end so simply, or so uneventfully. As Zengle neared the bottom of Sweet Briar Hill and came onto the West River Drive, a tire burst on his car. Zengle did not give up. He and his mechanician, Billie Manker, jumped out, repaired the tire very quickly, and continued their charge up the West River Drive. They lost about a minute and a half on the stop. While Zengle changed his tire, Mulford stormed up the West River Drive, unaware of the misfortune of his competitor, but gaining time on him nonetheless. He dashed under the railroad bridge at "the dip of death" and onto Neill Drive, and then, in amazing coincidence, Mulford also lost a tire. He jumped out of the car, and in equally fast time, changed the tire and carried on. He must have been surprised that Zengle did not pass him as he made the change. This had to clue him in to the fact that Zengle found trouble somewhere else on the course. The problem for Mulford was that Zengle did not have to pass him physically to win the race. Zengle started the race 1:20 after Mulford, and Mulford had a nine second lead at the beginning of the lap, which meant that the Chadwick could cross the line within 1:11 after the Lozier and still win.

Mulford crossed the line with a lap of 9:51. His total time for the race was 3:29:13. Mulford leaned over on the wheel of his car to rest, and anxiously waited to see if he would win, or whether Zengle could make the final lap fast enough to take it away from him. Zengle crossed the line 1:05 later. He completed the final lap in 9:36, for a total time of 3:29:07. Zengle won the race by six seconds over Ralph Mulford. The *Philadelphia Inquirer* reported that it was "the closest finish ever known in the history of automobile racing."[17] He averaged 58.05 mph during the race, com-

7. The Third Annual Fairmount Park Race 127

A close-up of Len Zengle's winning Chadwick as he motors along Parkside Avenue. (1910). Photograph by Nathan Lazarnick, courtesy of the Detroit Public Library, National Automotive History Collection.

pared to the 55.4 mph average made by Robertson in 1909. His total time amounted to a new course record. It took a few seconds for the scorers to confirm the result, then Announcer Proud declared, "The Chadwick wins; the Lozier is second."[18] The crowd roared with approval. For Zengle, the third try was the charm.

To counteract some of the difficulties that had occurred after the race in previous years, the organizers made some changes to the post-race ceremonies. When a car finished it had to pull off the track near the Soldiers and Sailors Monument at 42nd Street and wait there until the race was over. So Zengle did not drive back to the grandstand to immediately receive the mayor's congratulations as Robertson had. Unlike the previous year, the police kept the crowds in place. Nobody was allowed to step onto the course, or move toward the finish line until the officials stopped the race, and that did not happen until each division had a winner. About eight minutes after the leaders crossed the line, De Hymel finished in third, and then came Aitken in fourth. He also picked up first place in the 4C Division. Jagersberger came in fifth overall, but did not win his division since he was in the 5C Division with Mulford. Cobe finished sixth followed by Knight in seventh. Eighth place belonged to Gellard, who also won the 3C Division, and Davis earned a ninth place finish in his Apperson. When Davis crossed the line, approximately thirty-four minutes had passed since Zengle had won the race. Since Padula was the only car left

Second place finisher, Ralph Mulford, passes the grandstand on the Concourse. Mulford at least had the satisfaction of making Zengle's victory the narrowest win in road racing history up to that point. (1910). Photograph by Nathan Lazarnick, courtesy of the Detroit Public Library, National Automotive History Collection.

in the 2C Division, and all of the other divisions had already been decided, the officials declared the race finished and granted Padula the 2C Division victory, even though he was only on his twenty-third lap. Other cars still running when the race ended were those of Harroun, Yerger, and Frey. The decision not to let Zengle come back to the starting line for some post race festivities disappointed the crowds, but it made for a safer environment for the fans and the participants. As Davis crossed the line, a light rain began to fall. The race ended just in time. Once the race was declared finished, and the winners were known, the police began to move the crowds out of the park. They did this in an orderly manner, with no major incidents reported.

Zengle could not contain his excitement. He said, "I am tickled to death at my victory. I would rather win here in Fairmount Park than anywhere in the country, for this is my old home."[19] In a post race interview, he said that his strategy for winning was to take it easy for the first half of the race so that the car would be there in the end, but his lap times really do not prove this to be true. Zengle embroiled himself in the battle with Bergdoll and Mulford from the very beginning and made very fast laps throughout. *Horseless Age* described Zengle's race as being, "none too merciful with his car."[20] Zengle did not win because of strategy. He won because he drove a great race. He was fast, and he was consistent. The Chadwick was reliable enough to withstand the beating it had to take for 200 miles, and Zengle's Firestone tires held up pretty well, even though that last lap blowout almost cost him the race.

Table 9. 1910—Winner in Each Division

Division	No.	Car	Driver	Time
6C	12	Chadwick	Zengle	3:29:07
5C	4	Lozier	Mulford	3:29:13
4C	3	National	Aitken	3:42:20
3C	10	Pullman	Gellard	3:57:04
2C	21	Abbott-Detroit	Padula	Running-Lap 23

Zengle's victory was certainly a boost for Pennsylvania. With the driver a native Philadelphian, and the car a product of Pottstown, it helped to boost the city's and the state's position in the automotive world. This is exactly what the race was supposed to do, and in Zengle they found the perfect spokesman. "I am a Pennsylvanian," he proudly exclaimed. "The car I drove is a product of the Keystone State, which adds all the more to the luster and satisfaction of my victory."[21]

Ralph Mulford was disappointed with his second place finish, but could take solace in the fact that he lost to a more powerful car, and at least came out as the best in class. He almost won it, despite the odds. He blamed his final lap tire trouble for losing him the race. "Talk about the Stock Exchange being a gamble," he said. "Maybe it was because I ran out of candy, as I only took a couple of boxes along with me and they were gone long before I reached that last exciting lap. You can bet I'll take a bushel along next time if it is going to have any effects on the results."[22]

The Fairmount Park race was again a huge success and proved once again that the Quaker City Motor Club had organized the best race in the country. A few injuries occurred, but nothing too serious. Glenn Etheridge, who had the worst accident, was reported as doing better the next day. His doctors discovered that his injuries were not as bad as they had initially thought. He would recover, as would John Young, the spectator who was hit by a tire. Al Mitchell also spent some time in the hospital after his Neill Drive crash, but his doctors released him after a few days. Unlike at the Vanderbilt Cup, the drivers and mechanicians all received their money back from "death's pool"—a pool of money that they would give to the family of anyone who was killed during the race.[23]

On Sunday, the Chadwick Company put both of their participating cars on display. Team members drove Zengle's winning machine to the Bellevue-Stratford Hotel after the race, where they displayed it in the lobby. They also turned his teammate Mitchell's car upright after its somersaults on Neill Drive, and drove it to the company's showroom on North Broad Street, where it served as an example of the strength of their product. Both cars appeared in their post-race condition. They had not been dusted off, nor did the company make any repairs. Of course, crowds came out to see them, adding more to the economic benefits for the city.

On the Monday following the race, the *Philadelphia Evening Times* reported a story, which was almost exactly like one that appeared the previous year. The paper figured that the charitable institutions were deprived of $1,600, or $400 each, because the Fairmount Park Commission did not pay for 300 grandstand seats, and 100 parking spaces. "I paid for my box," said the mayor, "but I do not propose to criti-

More entries and multiple divisions meant a much larger scoreboard for the 1910 race. The Quaker City Motor Club also decided to use a white board with black paint rather than the chalkboards of previous years. This made the results much easier to read. (1910). Photograph by Nathan Lazarnick, courtesy of the Detroit Public Library, National Automotive History Collection.

cize them. It rests with them what they should do in a matter like this."[24] Apparently, the commission did not learn from their mistake the previous year, even after the mayor pointed out that it was inappropriate to accept free tickets when the proceeds were going to charity.

Thomas S. Martin, the Secretary of the Commission, said that the commission did not request the tickets in 1910. That may be so, but they did not have to accept them. The Quaker City Motor Club probably sent the tickets to the commission because they had requested them in 1909. It was most likely an attempt on the club's part, to appease the commission and stay in their good graces. Instead, it only served as an embarrassment for the commission, as its wealthy socialites were seen as stealing money from "the little crippled children," "the unfortunates," and the "worn out policeman," who would have been the beneficiaries of the funds.[25]

On Wednesday, the Quaker City Motor Club announced that there had been an error in the scoring, and that Ray Harroun did not actually make the fastest lap of the race. The scorers had accidentally posted his time as 7:38 for his twelfth lap, when in fact; his time was 8:38. His overall time for the race did not change since they had used the correct time when calculating his cumulative total. This meant that Len Zengle's lap of 7:57 was the fastest of the race, and that the course record would remain the time of 7:41 that he made in 1909.[26]

Honors for the hometown hero Zengle would take place all week. He had been the guest of honor at a dinner at the Bellevue-Stratford Hotel on Saturday night, just before he parked his car in the lobby. Zengle sat in the car while it was pushed up a wooden ramp and through the south door on the Broad Street entrance of the hotel. The Quaker City Motor Club also had a party on Saturday night. There were over five hundred in attendance including club officials, politicians, and the participants of the race. They were entertained by Vaudeville shows, and movies of the French Grand Prix.

On Wednesday, Zengle returned with his car to Pottstown where locals honored him with a parade. Crowds lined the streets to cheer the driver of the car who had brought their local company such fame. At the conclusion of the parade, speeches were made in front of the Chadwick factory, by city officials and representatives of the company. Then on Thursday, he returned to Philadelphia for the award ceremony which took place that night at the Chestnut Street Opera House.

Like the previous year, Quaker City Motor Club members, city officials, and interested persons packed the theatre. The #12 Chadwick was in the center of the stage. Zengle was behind the wheel, and his mechanician sat beside him. To Zengle's right was a table on which stood the various race trophies, and on his left stood officials of the motor club, along with Mayor Reyburn. Secretary Harbach was the first to speak, welcoming everyone to the ceremony and explaining the evening's program before introducing Leander D. Berger, President of the Quaker City Motor Club. Berger served as the master of ceremonies, and he introduced other speech makers such as Director Clay, who talked about how orderly the police and the fans made the race. Starter Gantert, Referee Ross, and Paul Huyette, the official timer, also spoke. Then it was time for Mayor Reyburn to present the awards. Zengle received the Philadelphia Trophy for his first place overall victory. The cup was bowl shaped, on top of a tall stem. The stem was surrounded by four winged wheels at the bottom of each pilaster. Each of the spaces between the wheels held an etching. Three etchings depicted City Hall, Independence Hall, and the race course with a racing car. In the fourth space was inscribed, "Philadelphia Trophy, 200 mile road race, under the auspices of the Quaker City Motor Club, Fairmount Park, 1910." Covering the bowl was a lid of wire mesh designed to hold flowers. It measured 19.5 inches tall and 15.5 inches in diameter.[27] He also received two checks, a $2,500 check for first place, and $1,000 for the divisional win. As the checks were presented, photos of them were projected onto the theatre's screen. The other four divisional winners, Ralph Mulford, J. D. Aitken, Ernest Gellard and V. P. Padula, each received $1,000 checks for winning their respective divisions as well as a trophy from the city, each valued at $400. Reports on the ceremony do not specify which class received which trophy, but the city had ordered five prizes, and it was up to the mayor to decide who would receive each one. Zengle had already received the trophy which was produced by Reed & Barton of Massachusetts. Two were produced by Maxwell & Berlet, Inc., Jewelers, who were located at 16th and Walnut Streets in Philadelphia. They were a silver cigar box, and a silver reproduction of a racecar on a pedestal. The cigar box measured 17 × 14 × 15 inches. A William Penn statue stood on each corner of the box. On each side was an etching. The four etchings depicted Independence Hall, City Hall, the park course, and William Penn's treaty with the Indians. On the lid, the city seal acted as the handle.

Designers based the car statue on John F. Betz's Simplex. It measured 16.5 inches long and 6 inches wide. On the ebony base, in silver, it read, "Philadelphia Trophy."[28] It also had a bronze liberty bell. It measured 13 inches tall, and 20 × 11 inches at the base. Two trophies were produced by Bailey, Banks & Biddle. One stood 30 inches tall, and had an engraving of the start of the 1909 race on the front, as well as a bas relief of William Penn. The other one also measured 30 inches tall, and had an engraving of another scene from the 1909 race and the city flag in colored enamel. Both had the seal of the city near the top, as well as winged wheels similar to those on Zengle's trophy. The prizes awarded in 1910 made it the richest race so far in motor racing. The Quaker City Motor Club prizes totaled $9500, and the city put up $2,000. In addition, various companies involved in the automobile trade had put up several thousand dollars in additional prizes. Mayor Reyburn gave a brief speech before presenting the awards. The award ceremony was not the end for Zengle. On Friday night, he was in Norristown for a dinner in his honor, given by the Norristown Automobile Club, of which he was a member. It was a long evening of entertainment. There were speeches, vaudeville acts, and even a brass band from Pottstown which performed parodies of popular tunes in Zengle's honor. The song "Has anyone here seen Kelly?" was changed to "Has anyone here seen Zengle?" and so on.[29]

Then, on Sunday, he returned to Philadelphia where his car was put on display in the main arcade of the Lit Brothers Department Store. Besides the car, his first place trophy was also on display, as well as Zengle himself, who would spend some time there throughout the week, greeting the public who came out to see the car.[30]

For the third straight year, the City of Philadelphia and the Quaker City Motor Club staged a safe and successful race. With each year, the event just became bigger and bigger. The number of spectators that attended the race was on the verge of being unbelievable, considering that it was the year 1910. There were simply too many people going to see it for anyone to consider the possibility of there not being another race the following year. Philadelphia society was still greatly in evidence at the race, if for no other reason than to support a good cause. The charitable side of the race had seemed to stop most controversy for the time being. But even more than that, those who attended the Fairmount Park Race, whether wealthy socialite, or middle class worker, seemed to truly enjoy the event. The victory of a local car and driver made it even more interesting. After three years, the race now seemed untouchable. It had become an annual event that people looked forward to, just like the Army-Navy Game. Prospects looked good for a continuation of the tradition the following year or possibly even sooner if the mayor and the Quaker City Motor Club had their way.

8

Controversy

The possibility existed that the city could host a race much sooner than the following October. In the aftermath of the tragic Vanderbilt Cup Race, William Vanderbilt declared that the events that took place would not interfere with the running of the Grand Prize, which was scheduled to take place on the same course. In fact, he called the Vanderbilt, "the greatest event in the history of the annual contest for the cup."[1] Despite Vanderbilt's feelings, others on Long Island, and across the country, felt much differently. The Vanderbilt Cup Race had given auto racing a black eye, especially road racing in particular. There were cries to end the sport all together. That would not happen, but the running of the Grand Prize on the Long Island course was less than certain. On 3 October, the Nassau County Board of Supervisors held a meeting to discuss the prospects for the Grand Prize Race. Some of the supervisors did not want the race to be held at all, but they decided not to cancel the permit for fear of a lawsuit against them, and because the promoters promised better course protection and a later starting time which would prevent late night travel to the course.[2]

Even with these changes, the entrants were not happy, and preferred that the race be held elsewhere. One who was more outspoken than any other was Jesse Froelich of the Benz Company. "Unless I am absolutely assured that the course will be properly guarded in the way that the races are guarded in Europe, as well as the way the public has been protected in Savannah, Lowell, Philadelphia, and Elgin, I positively will not permit our cars to start in the Grand Prize Race scheduled for October 15," he said.[3] The day after Froelich made his comments, William Vanderbilt informed him that the Benz cars would be banned from the race. "In view of…the criticism you make of the management of the race, which we consider to be absolutely uncalled for and unwarranted, we do not think it wise that the cars under your management should compete."⁴ Vanderbilt's shunning of the Benz team would not matter. The very next day, Vanderbilt announced that the Grand Prize would not take place on Long Island after all. The Motor Cups Holding Company, which oversaw the Vanderbilt Cup and the Grand Prize, could not secure the militia to protect the course as it had planned. That, combined with criticism from entrants and the public, made it impossible to stage another race on Long Island.

As soon as the announcement was made, other cities began to contact the Motor Cups Holding Company in an attempt to secure the race. Two names that surfaced immediately were Savannah and Indianapolis. Savannah staged the 1908 Grand Prize Race, so it was the first alternate site considered. Vanderbilt personally contacted the mayor of that city and asked him to make a proposal, to which the mayor responded by sending a delegation from the Savannah Automobile Club. The Indianapolis Motor Speedway also wanted the race and put up a $10,000 purse as an incentive. The speedway really did not have a chance since the track had proven that it could be just as dangerous as the Long Island circuit, and in addition, the Motor Cups Holding Company desired to keep the Grand Prize on a road course.⁵ According to the *Philadelphia Evening Times*, "the officials believe the race should be held on a road where the conditions of actual travel would have to be overcome by the flying drivers."⁶ This announcement, that the race would not take place on Long Island, was made only two days before the Fairmount Park Race. Drivers had already started to practice on the Fairmount Park course and had expressed how much better and safer they found it to be when compared to the Vanderbilt Cup, but it was not until Saturday, after the race, that Fairmount Park suddenly became the obvious choice of location to hold the Grand Prize Race.

George Robertson found the mayor after the race on Saturday and suggested to him that the city should try to secure the Grand Prize since it could not be held on Long Island. The mayor liked the idea, and so he tracked down Referee Ross and said, "I see they are looking for a place to hold the Grand Prize Race scheduled for next week and which has been abandoned so far as the Vanderbilt course is concerned. What is the matter with holding it right here?"⁷ The mayor felt that the city could hold the race as planned, the following week, and they would just have to leave the grandstands in place for that extra week. "Why not get the Grand Prize race over here and give the proceeds to charity?" the mayor continued.⁸ Of course, he would receive no argument from Mr. Ross, nor any member of the Quaker City Motor Club, who believed it was a great idea and immediately set to work on trying to secure the race. Many individuals in the racing world supported their efforts, including New York reporters, race organizers, and men involved in the automobile trade. "Doc" Percival, described as a veteran publicity man and automobile expert, who worked for the Abbott-Detroit Company, said prior to the 1910 Fairmount Park Race, "I have attended every Vanderbilt Cup event and all of the big races in the South and West, but I must confess that I have never in my experience in the automobile racing game seen a race of large magnitude handled as well as you Philadelphians have handled your last two events."⁹ Another New Yorker, who had attended the Vanderbilt Cup and the Fairmount Park Race said, "I, as an automobile enthusiast would like to see the race for the Grand Prize come off here. This is the sentiment of many of the motorists who were here from out-of-town today, and we are certainly going to boom Philadelphia for the Grand Prize race when we get back home."[10] "While the Savannah course has a first class circuit...it does not afford the same opportunity for testing motor cars and drivers that your tortuous Fairmount Park course, with its grades and twists and turns does," said another.[11] A former New York State Senator, Senator Brown, also pledged that he would help to bring the Grand Prize to Philadelphia. The rumor surfaced that the Motor Cups Holding Company had already assured Savannah the race, but nothing was official yet, and Philadelphia had certain advantages that made it a more obvious choice. The Philadelphia organizers wanted to hold the race in one week, on 15 October, as originally scheduled. In addition, many of the teams that entered the Grand Prize Race were already in Philadelphia. They decided to wait there until they knew where the Grand Prize would be held, and hence where they would be off to next. Other teams, who had not competed in Philadelphia, had already arrived in New York, and it would not be as difficult for them to get to Philadelphia, as it would be for them to get to Savannah. R. E. Ross talked to S. M. Butler of the AAA and came away believing that "Savannah will not be decided upon until Philadelphia has been heard from."[12]

A meeting was held on Monday in the mayor's office where all concerned parties talked about the staging of the Grand Prize. Since the mayor and the Quaker City Motor Club had already thrown their support behind it, the only obstacle that could arise would be the Fairmount Park Commission, and even they would not turn down the chance to steal the Grand Prize away from New York. Thomas S. Martin, Secretary of the Commission, said that requesting permission from the commissioners "would be a formality." "If the mayor wishes the Grand Prize held here he has only to say so and the Commission, I am sure, would do as he asked," he said.[13]

But on the very next day, 10 October 1910, the Motor Cups Holding Company announced that the Grand Prize would be held on 12 November in Savannah. Savannah sent their delegation to New York as soon as they heard that the race was up for grabs. By the time Philadelphia officials informed the Motor Cups Holding Company that they wanted to host the race, they were told that the contest had already been given to Savannah. This should not be viewed as a case of one site being chosen over the other. The Quaker City Motor Club did not get their bid in early enough to be considered and the club did not have the support from William Vanderbilt that Savannah had. The motor club instead set their sights on the 1911 Fairmount Park Race.

One member of the Quaker City Motor Club would not be involved in those plans. R. E. Ross, Chairman of the Contest Committee and race referee, resigned from the Quaker City Motor Club in November 1910. His official reason for leaving was "the pressure of other business," but there were rumors that a rift had developed between Ross and the club, possibly over the Fairmount Park Race.[14] "Pressure of personal business was entirely responsible for my withdrawal and there was no disagreement between the club and myself," Ross insisted.[15] Although Ross vehemently denied the rumors, and claimed that his departure from the club was amicable, there was some controversy brewing about the way that the Quaker City Motor Club handled the race, more specifically, the way the club handled the money. The newspaper and trade journals reported that the Quaker City Motor Club intended to make a $5,000 profit from the race, even though all of the money was supposed to go to charity.[16] They also reported that the Philadelphia Automobile Trade Association was displeased with the way the club handled the race, and that they intended to form their own contest committee to control racing in the Philadelphia area. The races were so successful, and had done so much to promote the trade in the city, that the trade association really had nothing to complain about, other than the fact that they thought they entered their cars in a charity race, when it was now being said that the motor club would make a profit. The problem of control over the race was not a new one. An event as successful as the Fairmount Park Race could obviously make money. The problem, at least from the trade association's viewpoint, was that all of the money went to charity and none of it went directly into the pockets of the auto companies. The Philadelphia Automobile Trade Association was not the only group that sought control of the race. The AAA had also made attempts, such as insisting that their officials run the event, rather than those of the Quaker City Motor Club. So far, the motor club had been very good at resisting these overtures, and it was probably their resistance that led to William Vanderbilt's choice of Savannah for the Grand Prize. Now that it appeared that a profit would be made, the Automobile Trade Association was quick to jump into the fray.

Newspaper reporters offered the idea that Ross agreed with the trade association about the control of racing in the city, so it is likely that he and the trade association were both angered by the fact that the club would make a profit. Ross himself intimated that this was the case by saying, "As far as the management of the Park race goes, it is a question whether the club should benefit by the same."[17] To avoid a confrontation with his former organization, he went on to say that its members had spent a lot of money on the races, so perhaps they were entitled to some profit now that the race was so successful.[18] But what it really comes down to is that both Ross and the trade association must have felt that by taking a private club out of the mix, issues such as this could be avoided, and if anyone was to benefit from the races, it should be the trade association or the manufacturers of the cars that competed.

At this point, the total receipts of the race had not yet been reported to the mayor, or the charitable institutions, so how the Quaker City Motor Club's intentions with the money leaked out is unknown. It may have been through Ross, who did not try to hide it, and in fact confirmed it when interviewed about his resignation. Secretary Harbach denied Ross' $5,000 figure, and stated that the profit for the club would actually be around $2,000.[19] All of the profits were supposed to go to charity, so this admission of profit taking by the club did not sit well with the mayor, who had spent a lot of time promoting and planning the race for three years, first as an event for Founder's Week, and then as a charitable event. He did not take any immediate action, as the receipts had not yet been totaled, but when the club totaled the receipts and distributed the money to the charities in January 1911, the mayor took action, demanding a full report on where all of the money went. The club reported that the receipts from the grandstand seats, parking spaces, and entry fees totaled $10,309. Expenses for the race totaled $3,686, which meant that $6,623 remained to be divided amongst the five charities.[20] This was all well and good, but if this was a full accounting of the race income, where was the money that the club intended to keep?

The money in question came from the sale of advertisements in a program that the club distributed at the race, and supposedly totaled somewhere between $6,000-$7,000. "The program which the club issued contained many advertisements from merchants all over the city who, I understand, made substantial payments therefore, in the belief that the money was to go to charity," the mayor said in a meeting with the club on 20 January 1911.[21] This meeting was also attended by the citizen's committee in charge of the race, of which R. E. Ross was still a member. Officials from the Quaker City Motor Club denied that they were at fault for failing to turn over the money from the program, offering several reasons why they were entitled to it. First, L. D. Berger, the club's president, stated that the program was not a program for the race, but an annual program for the club, that included all of their events. "None of our solicitors ever told a merchant that the 'ads' in it were to go to charity," he said.[22] Another reason why they did not turn over these supposed profits from advertising, was because there was not much of a profit. The club had distributed the program at the Fairmount Park Race for free. The *Philadelphia Public Ledger* quoted an official as saying that the profit did not exceed $2,000 once expenses were factored in. He believed that the club deserved to keep that money "because of the entertainment afforded more than half a million people who witnessed the race."[23]

This money produced by advertising in the program was the only money in question. The club stated that Dr. Neff was in charge of the $10,309 and that he had taken the expenses out of that. The club kept the entrance fees, which covered the cost of prizes and the printing of entry blanks. There was nothing the mayor could do about the money from the program. "It was news to me about this advertising money, but what could I do or what can you do?" he asked. "There was no hard and fast agreement."[24] He was right about that. Money from the sale of advertisements in the program was never discussed, and in its petition to the park commissioners, the Quaker City Motor Club had only promised to turn over money, "from the sale of grandstand seats, parking spaces, donations, sale of programs and contributions of our club and others."[25] The program had not been sold, so the Quaker City Motor Club was technically correct in keeping the money. Yet, it seemed to be splitting hairs, and the mayor did not appreciate it. "It will never occur again," he said. "Next fall we shall take better precautions, and the entire proceeds of that race, after deducting legitimate expenses, will go to the last penny to charity."[26]

Motor club officials said that they would prepare a more detailed accounting of where every penny went, in relation to the race, and this must have appeased the mayor, who took back some of his harsh words when the race came up for approval again in March. On 10 March 1911, the Quaker City Motor Club made their annual petition to the Fairmount Park Commission. The club requested permission to hold the race on 7 October, with fifty percent of the profits going to the Children's Playgrounds, and the other fifty percent to be split between the Park Guard Pension

This is the controversial program that was distributed at the 1910 Fairmount Park Race. Although the Quaker City Motor Club claimed that it served as their annual program, and not a program for the race, the program itself seems to state otherwise. The fact that the motor club mentioned the city's cooperation on the cover is enough to justify the mayor's position concerning the distribution of advertising revenue. (1910). Courtesy Automobile Reference Collection, Free Library of Philadelphia.

Fund and the Police Pension Fund. Fred Dunlap, a member of the Quaker City Motor Club, who held a seat on the commission due to his position as Chief of the Waterworks, moved that the permit be approved. The commissioners voted and granted their permission.[27] Permission to hold the race passed through the Fairmount Park Commission with no problems in 1911, a surprise, considering the question of whether the Quaker City Motor Club was the right group to run the race. But for the commission, there really was no other choice. The Quaker City Motor Club organized the race for three years, with no serious accidents and no deaths. If the race was to be held, who else could the commissioners trust to do it and produce the same results?

The press believed that the Quaker City Motor Club might still not be able to hold the race, since the mayor might not approve of their running the show in 1911. This led the Philadelphia Automobile Trade Association, which preferred to have the Quaker City Motor Club hold the race rather than have no race at all, to approach the mayor and make sure that he would give his approval. The mayor responded that he was all for it. "It may be that my criticism regarding the race held last October created the impression that I was opposed to a renewal of this race. This is not so. What I said was that there should not be any misunderstanding as to the disposition of the funds of such race in the future."[28] The mayor still favored the race, but he did not particularly care for the Quaker City Motor Club anymore. Before the mayor actually gave his approval to the 1911 race, he discussed the issue with the Automobile Trade Association, the Fairmount Park Commission, and the AAA. The Fairmount Park Commission obviously wanted to stay with the Quaker City Motor Club, because the commissioners knew that the club could run the race safely. The AAA felt the same way, and S. M. Butler suggested to the mayor that the Quaker City Motor Club should once again be allowed to conduct the race. Since the Automobile Trade Association was not the best group to run a charity race, and really had no experience running a large race of this kind, the mayor had to go with the Quaker City Motor Club. It would take almost six months before he would give his approval, and the race was officially announced. During this time, the mayor sat down with the club officials and worked out the specifics about how the money would be handled. The new agreement was basically same as the old agreement. Money from the sale of grandstand seats and parking spaces would go to charity. The only difference was a promise from the motor club that there would be no program issued.

The motor club chose Fred Dunlap to replace R. E. Ross in the important position of race referee. On 18 August 1911, he mailed the entry blanks to the automobile manufacturers. The race would be in Class C as it was the previous year. Class C had six divisions and was for non-stock cars. This race would only allow four of those divisions, thus eliminating the very small cars. Division 3C was for cars with a piston displacement of 231-300 cubic inches. Division 4C was for 301-450 cubic inch cars. Division 5C was for 451-600 cubic inch cars, and Division 6C was for 601-700 cubic inch cars. There were no weight restrictions. There would be no official race trophies awarded in 1911, perhaps because the mayor did not want to ask the city councils for money to pay for them after the controversy caused by

A steamroller traverses the course in preparation for the 1911 Fairmount Park Race. Dirt roads needed plenty of maintenance, even under normal driving conditions. For an automobile race, constant rolling and oiling was necessary to pack down the dirt and create a hard surface for the cars to safely race on. (1911). From *Motor* (October 1911), courtesy AACA Library & Research Center, Hershey, PA.

the Quaker City Motor Club keeping some of the 1910 profits. The club did offer its normal monetary prizes. The overall winner would receive $2,500, and each division winner would receive $1,000 each. Additional prizes would be offered by automotive companies in the weeks leading up to the race. Rayfield Carburetor offered prizes of $200 to the driver who won his class while using one of their carburetors, and $300 for the fastest overall driver using a Rayfield carburetor. The Remy Company offered $250 for first place, $100 for second place, and $50 for third place in each division, if the car had a Remy ignition. The Remy prize money would be awarded to the driver rather than the entrant.

The first entry came back to the club on 2 September, when the Lozier Company entered Ralph Mulford in the race. After coming so close in 1910, Mulford had to give it another try. He would drive the same car he drove in the first Indianapolis 500 in May. It is still a subject of much debate, whether Mulford's Lozier actually won the 500, but the victory went to Ray Harroun, possibly because of a scoring error. The car would be entered in the 5C Division.

Within two weeks, the club received six entries. Two had come in from George G. Brownlee of the Tioga Automobile Company, who entered two National cars. As the local distributor of the National car, Mr. Brownlee convinced the company to enter the two cars in the race. The National Motor Vehicle Company did not feel that their car needed to prove itself in competition any further, after winning the Elgin and Illinois Trophy Races, but they agreed to enter one car in their name if Mr. Brownlee entered the other.[29] One of the cars would be driven by Len Zengle, winner of the 1910 race, now appearing in his third brand of car in four Fairmount Park Races. He would drive a National 50, while Don Herr would drive the National 40. Both cars would be in the 4C Division. Indianapolis native, Don Herr, had been racing for National for about five years, and had recently piloted the car to victory in the Illinois Trophy Run.

The Ideal Motor Company of Indianapolis entered one of their Stutz cars for Gil Anderson to drive. Anderson became popular while serving as a mechanician for Adolph Monson in a race at Crown Point, Indiana. When their Marmon car's radiator became loose, Anderson climbed onto the hood to hold it on. This amazing feat got him a ride in a Stutz in the first Indianapolis 500. The Stutz would be in Division 4C. Frank Hodson, a private owner, entered a Fiat. He purchased the car just so that he could compete in the Fairmount Park Race. He also hired a Fiat mechanic to prepare the car, and contracted Lee Oldfield to drive it, because his wife would not let him drive it himself. The car would be in the 6C Division. The J. I. Case Threshing Machine Company of Racine, Wisconsin, entered one of their cars, which would be driven by Joe Jagersberger, the fifth place finisher in 1910. The Case Company was mainly known for their agricultural equipment, but they had just started manufacturing cars after purchasing the factory of a motor car company that had recently gone out of business. The Case would be in Division 3C.

Entries were not coming in as fast as expected. By 24 September, these were the only six entries, but this did not deter the Quaker City Motor Club, which continued to make plans, and got to work on the course, rolling, oiling and banking turns, just as they did for the previous three years. The lack of entries did not overly concern the motor club, because just as in 1910, they expected many entries to come in at the last minute. It also did not deter spectators who rushed for tickets when they went on sale on the 27th. The Long Island Motor Club even bought 200 seats and hired a special train in order to take its members to the race—not a surprise since there was to be no Vanderbilt Cup on Long Island in 1911. New Yorkers would have to go to Philadelphia to satisfy their need for road racing.

Charles Howard, who drove a Benz in the 1909 race, made the next entry. This year he would not be participating himself, but instead entered a Mercedes on behalf of the Boulevard Garage, where he currently worked. The car would be driven by Spencer Wishart, and would be in the 5C Division. Wishart was a twenty-one year old member of a wealthy family who had been racing since he turned eighteen, when his father bought him a Mercedes. He finished fourth in the 1909 Vanderbilt Cup Race and also in the first Indianapolis 500. Weldon & Bauer of Newark, New Jersey, entered a third National car in the race. The company designated Harry Koopman as the driver. The car would be in the 4C Division. The spots began to fill up more quickly with only a few days remaining before practice was to begin. It was only a matter of time before a member of the Bergdoll family entered the race, and Erwin came forward first with his 90 horsepower Benz. It was the second car to be entered in the 6C Division. In the 1910 race, Bergdoll proved how fast he could run. When he made his 1911 entry, he was just coming off of a great drive against Ralph DePalma at Point Breeze that was called off due to rain before it could be decided.

The Mercer factory in Trenton, New Jersey entered two Mercer cars. One would be driven by Hughie Hughes, and the other by Harvey Ringler. The cars would

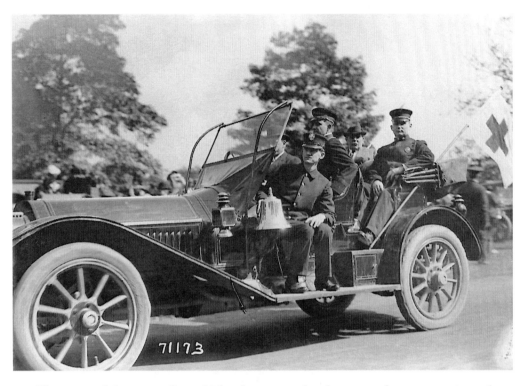

This is one of the many safety vehicles that were on hand to respond to emergencies at the Fairmount Park Races. In this photograph we see a crew composed of a driver, three police officers and a fifth man in the rear, who is probably a doctor, since the car bears a Red Cross flag. (1911). Photograph by Nathan Lazarnick, courtesy of the Detroit Public Library, National Automotive History Collection.

be in the 3C Division. Hughes was an Englishman who had been racing for a long time, even having driven in the 1904 Gordon Bennett Race. Ringler was a local track racing star for the Mercer team who had not been racing for very long, but he had won quite a few races in his short career. He also ran a café at 7th and Market Streets in Philadelphia. While Ringler was new to the Fairmount Park Race, another local favorite would be returning for his third try at victory. John F. Betz went out and bought a Fiat to drive in the race, after two disappointing tries with his Simplex. The new car had 110 horsepower, making it the third car in the 6C Division, along with Erwin Bergdoll's Benz and Lee Oldfield's Fiat. The two brewing families would once again be going head to head.

Next to enter was Harry Grant, the winner of the 1909 and 1910 Vanderbilt Cup Races, who had entered the Fairmount Park Race a year ago, but decided to withdraw at the last minute. Grant would drive a Lozier in 1911, instead of his familiar Alco. Grant's Lozier was the same model as Mulford's. Charles Basle entered next. He would drive a Cole entered by the Philadelphia Motor Company. Basle was a twenty-six year old from Paris, France, who came to the United States when he was eighteen and began driving for Mercedes and working as a mechanic. He set a speed record at Ormond Beach, Florida in 1905, when he was only twenty.

8. Controversy

The Quaker City Motor Club had set the maximum number of entries at thirty, but on 1 October 1911, the day before the scheduled start of practice, the club had only received thirteen entries. Entries would be accepted until the fifth, but certainly this must have been a bit of a disappointment when compared to the number of entries in 1910. It seems as though the death of automobile racing on Long Island affected the Fairmount Park Race. Drivers used to travel to New York to compete in the Vanderbilt Cup, and then would head straight to Fairmount Park. Without a race on Long Island, drivers and teams did not travel to the area as they had before.

On Monday morning, drivers began to arrive at the track to take their first practice spins. Sunday had been a horrible day, with lots of rain, so before anyone went out on the course, Captain Duncan rode along on an inspection tour of the track. When he returned to the start, he announced that the track surface was too soft, and that practice would have to be cancelled. A thick coating of mud covered the course, and those who had come out to practice, such as Harvey Ringler, John F. Betz, Hughie Hughes, Ralph Mulford and Harry Grant, all agreed that the cancellation was for the best, not just because the track was too dangerous, but because driving on the wet surface would tear up the track and make the rest of the week more dangerous as well. As everyone was packing up and going home, someone shouted, "Here comes Bergdoll in his Benz."[30] Bergdoll came flying down the Concourse, and continued on, as if there was no problem. Although nothing happened on the course on Monday, the race did benefit from the entrance of a few more cars. Grover and Charles Bergdoll each entered a Bergdoll 40 in the race, a product of the Louis J. Bergdoll Motor Company. Charles had competed in 1910, but the 1911 race would be Grover's first attempt. He was the brother of Charles, Erwin and Louis. Although the Bergdoll family took part in all of the Fairmount Park races, this was the first time that they entered a car bearing their name. The two Bergdoll cars would be in the 3C Division.

Two Ohio cars were also entered in the 3C Division. They were produced by the Ohio Motor Company of Carthage, Ohio. One would be driven by Harry S. Matthews, and the other by George P. Parker. Matthews was a twenty-three year old from Cincinnati. He had been racing for two years, always driving an Ohio, but had never won a race. Parker was the local dealer of Ohio cars. He had started his career in racing a few years earlier by serving as Louis Bergdoll's mechanician in a few events, but soon became a driver himself. Edward Schroeder, who had been embarrassed when he hired a foreign driver to pilot his Mercedes in 1910, entered his car again, but this time he hired a fan favorite, William Wallace, as the driver. The Mercedes would be in Division 5C. This brought the total number of drivers up to nineteen.

On Tuesday, fourteen of them arrived at the track for what would now be the first day of practice. The rain had the same effect in 1910. It packed down the dirt even better than it would have been without the rain. Captain Duncan and the park guards arrived at the track early and roped off the course. Hughie Hughes had the honor of being the first driver to take to the track. Harvey Ringler rode along as mechanician to see the course which he had never driven on before. Close behind Hughes, Donald Herr motored along in his National. Herr's lap was 7:56, not bad

Jim Nasium Takes Bird's-Eye View of Auto Course in Fairmount Park and Sees Practice Stunts

This cartoon, by *Philadelphia Inquirer* cartoonist Jim Nasium, pokes fun at the Fairmount Park Race. Jim Nasium was the pseudonym of Edgar F. Wolfe, the cartoonist for the paper's sports section. From the *Philadelphia Inquirer*, 6 October 1911.

at all for his first try. But even though Herr's lap seemed fast, Erwin Bergdoll came by next with a lap of 7:42, just one second shy of the record. Not one to hold back, Bergdoll wanted to show that he was the one to beat. He would take that time home as the best lap of the day, with Herr's time coming in second best. Jagersberger turned in the next quickest time with a lap of 7:58. These were the only three cars under the eight minute mark. Other drivers were more content to take a day to feel out the course before turning a really fast lap. John F. Betz caused some puzzlement when he made a few laps in his Simplex. Of course, he had entered a Fiat, so everyone wondered what was going on. When someone asked him why he was not driving the car he had entered, Betz said that he "was saving the best for last."[31] After practice, Quaker City Motor Club officials asked the drivers whether there were any bad spots on the course. The drivers replied that there were some soft spots on City Avenue and near Wynnefield Avenue, so a work crew was immediately dispatched to repair those spots before the next day's practice.

Later in the afternoon, after practice ended, some of the mechanics from the Louis Bergdoll Motor Car Company took Grover's car out for a test drive and had a collision with a trolley at the intersection of 18th and Callowhill Streets. The accident severely damaged the car, and the mechanics determined that they could not repair it before the race. The company also decided that Charles' car was not strong enough to make it through the race, and so they withdrew that car as well. This left seventeen cars in the race, but then another entry arrived. The Studebaker Company entered an E. M. F. car, which would be driver by Jack Tower. E. M. F. stood for Everitt-Metzger-Flanders, a Detroit company which produced the cars for Studebaker. Tower had driven the car at a recent meet at Point Breeze, and had won two of the events. Although the Quaker City Motor Club had only intended to have four divisions, they accepted this entry even though it would fall into a small car division. This must have been due to the small number of entries. In order for the E. M. F. to take part, another small car would have to be entered to provide it with some competition, and that ultimately would not happen.

On Wednesday, the spectators witnessed the worst accident, or at least the worst looking accident, in four years of the park race. Harvey Ringler raced up the West River Drive in his bright yellow Mercer on his second lap of the day, and it was a fast one. He approached the curve that leads onto Neill Drive, but did not appear to slow down. The car broke through an iron fence and bounded down a fifteen foot embankment as it left the road. Parts flew off the car as it rolled down the hill, and finally hit a stone wall that lined the Schuylkill River towpath. The somersaults threw Ringler and his mechanician, Thomas Bowen, from the car before it reached the bottom. Police and motor club officials quickly arrived on the scene and put both men in an ambulance bound for St. Timothy's Hospital. Ringler suffered a sprained wrist, bruised ribs, and various cuts and bruises on his face. Bowen was more seriously injured. He suffered bruises and a broken leg, from which the bone protruded. He would have to spend some time in the hospital.

"I am more worried about Bowen my mechanician, than I am about myself," Ringler said."[32] There were conflicting reports as to what caused the accident. The *Philadelphia Evening Bulletin* reported that Ringler said that the steering gear had broken as he approached the turn.[33] The *Philadelphia Evening Times*, on the other hand, reported that Ringler admitted taking the turn too fast.[34] Either way, both driver and mechanician would fully recover. They were lucky to come away with such relatively minor injuries.

The car did not come out quite as well. It was almost unrecognizable, just a pile of twisted metal lying at the bottom of the hill. Spectators gazed at it in amazement, shocked that what lay before them used to be a speeding racecar. Very little evidence remained to show that it had actually been an automobile. The luckiest person in this accident was Stella Werntz who lived at 52nd and Irving Streets. Ringler had promised to take her on a ride around the course, but she arrived late because her alarm clock did not go off. After hearing what had transpired, Stella said that she did not "feel any ill will towards the clock."[35]

Hughie Hughes took to the track first on Wednesday in his Mercer. He did not turn a lap in less than nine minutes. The only drivers to make any real attempts were Erwin Bergdoll and Ralph Mulford. Bergdoll again had the best lap of the day of 7:42. Mulford trailed close behind with a lap of 7:47, and Zengle had the third best time of 8:03. It sure seemed like the three men who controlled the previous year's race were set to do the same thing again in 1911. Wednesday was a dreary morning, with an ever present chance of rain overhead, but despite that, over 5,000 fans arrived in the park to see the practice spins.

On Wednesday night, the Quaker City Motor Club convened a meeting at the Hotel Walton to draw numbers. Lee Oldfield chose #1. The club's belief in superstition seemed to change from year to year, but in 1911, they decided to skip #13. Harvey Ringler attended the meeting and announced that he would not be able to

Erwin Bergdoll, and mechanician Frank Johnson, speed down the Concourse in their No. 8 Benz. Bergdoll has just passed the scoring stand and is heading toward the first turn. In the background, one of the scorers is perched high on a ladder, writing a time on the scoreboard. (1911). Courtesy of Jerry Helck.

drive because of his sprained wrist. A replacement car was on the way though, and the Mercer Company chose a new driver to pilot the machine. That driver would be Ralph DePalma. DePalma was an Italian who came to the United States at the age of ten. He began racing in 1908, and won seventy-four of the one hundred and eleven races he had entered since then. DePalma had a reputation that rivaled that of Barney Oldfield. The Quaker City Motor Club could not have asked for a more famous driver to take part in their race, because there simply wasn't one. DePalma was better known as a track racer than a road racer, and many referred to him as "the greatest track driver in the country."[36]

On Thursday, Lee Oldfield made his first appearance in the park, and his presence caused quite a stir. Oldfield participated in an oval track race at Syracuse, New York in September, during which he ran his car off the track and crashed into a crowd of people. Nine people were killed by the accident, and fourteen others suffered injuries. Certainly, an accident involving spectators was one of the worst possibilities at an auto race. Syracuse authorities, and the AAA, investigated the accident and found that Oldfield was not at fault. Some fans did not agree with that conclusion. They considered Oldfield reckless, and many of his detractors went to the Thursday morning practice session to let him know that they were not happy that he was participating. As soon as Oldfield appeared on the course, a crowd surrounded his car. "Are you Oldfield?" one of them asked. "Yes. That is my name," responded the driver.[37] His admission led to questions and a berating from the crowd, who let it be known that he was not welcome. As soon as he could get away, he began his practice laps, but the criticism affected him, and he could only manage to make a few slow laps. Frank Hodson, the entrant of the car, rode along with Oldfield that morning, and he took exception to the treatment of his young driver. "If there had been any doubts in my mind about Oldfield's skill as a driver, I would not have gone out to the course to ride with him in an attempt to beat the record this morning. Of course, after what happened, we made no attempt to speed."[38] Hodson said that he intended to go to the Quaker City Motor Club and explain why he chose Oldfield, but he really did not have to do that. The club had no problem with him, and had accepted his entry. Officially, the AAA and the Quaker City Motor Club considered Oldfield to be a safe driver. The accident only damaged Oldfield's reputation.

Thursday also brought a change of drivers. Louis Disbrow would take over the reigns of the National car that was originally to be driven by Harry Koopman, who was injured in a race that Saturday. Disbrow was a veteran who had been racing for six years. The local newspapers made much of his rivalry with Ralph DePalma. A match race that was supposed to take place at Point Breeze between the two drivers had been rained out recently, so now Philadelphia fans would get to see the two of them battle on a different type of course.

Grover Bergdoll made a few practice laps on Thursday morning, having decided to re-enter the race. The Louis J. Bergdoll Motor Company must have come to the conclusion that the car was good enough to compete after all. About 15,000 spectators watched Thursday's practice, and the drivers did not disappoint them. Erwin Bergdoll continued to turn fast laps, making two consecutive laps of 7:41, tying the record set by Zengle during the 1909 race. It seemed as though nobody else could touch Bergdoll. Zengle's fastest time of the day was 8:02, Mulford's was 8:23, and John F. Betz climbed amongst the leaders with an 8:06. DePalma slowly felt his way around the course, and only managed a 9:14.

Bergdoll's fast lap times were not the only excitement of the day. William Wallace furnished some of his own, though he would have much rather not. Wallace sped up the West River Drive at upwards of 60 mph and approached the "dip of death," that narrow downhill turn under the railroad bridge and onto Neill Drive that made every driver hold his breath. Although he made this turn many times before, this time he misjudged it. He turned in too tightly and struck the bridge with his left front tire. The impact spun the car around and sent it into the outside wall of the abutment. Luckily for Wallace, the car did not turn over, and both he and his mechanician, Alfred Hammel, remained in their seats unharmed. The car suffered a broken front axle, which could be repaired before Saturday. It was the type of accident that everyone expected whenever a car went through that turn at speed, but without the horrific results that everyone expected to go along with it. The police showed how serious they were about people being on the track when they arrested several spectators for trespassing during Thursday's practice. Among the people arrested were members of some prominent Philadelphia families, thus

Spencer Wishart's Mercedes looks speedy as it tears down Belmont Avenue. The Mercedes was second only to Bergdoll's Benz after a week of practice. (1911). Courtesy of Jerry Helck.

proving that the police would not discriminate when arresting those who broke the rules.

Police again estimated Friday's crowds at over 15,000 and they were in for a real treat. On his second time around, Erwin Bergdoll shattered Len Zengle's record of 7:41 with an amazing lap of 7:33, and that was not the only fast lap that he made. His next three laps totaled 7:55, 7:56, and 7:45. The only other driver able to consistently turn laps that fast was Spencer Wishart, who made a lap of 7:42 on his first time around, and followed it up with a 7:50 and a 7:39. He would have broken Zengle's record had Bergdoll not already set a new mark. Ralph Mulford and Len Zengle tried to keep up with the pace. Zengle turned a lap of 7:57, and Mulford had a 7:56, but they could not make fast laps as consistently as Bergdoll and Wishart. Mulford and Zengle were veterans, who probably did not feel that they needed to go that fast during practice. They could save it for the race rather than risk everything during practice. Since Zengle made his record lap during the 1909 race, he still held the official track record. The AAA considered Bergdoll and Wishart's laps unofficial practice times.

While Parker made a practice lap in his Ohio, the connecting rod in his engine broke, tearing up the crank case as it continued to spin around. His car would have to be repaired before Saturday if he was to take part. Hughie Hughes had a close call on one of his practice laps. He flew down the Concourse in his Mercer when a dog ran out onto the track, directly into his path. Hughes swerved his car to the

Table 10. 1911—Fastest time of Each Driver in Practice

Car	Driver	Time
Fiat	Oldfield	No Laps Recorded
National	Zengle	7:57
Lozier	Mulford	7:47
Cole	Basle	9:40
Mercer	DePalma	8:43
National	Herr	7:56
Case	Jagersberger	7:58
Benz	E. Bergdoll	7:33
Lozier	Grant	8:08
Stutz	Anderson	8:13
Mercer	Hughes	7:59
Ohio	Parker	9:03
Mercer	Ringler	No Laps Recorded
Bergdoll	G. Bergdoll	No Laps Recorded
Fiat	Betz	8:05
National	Koopman	8:17
Mercedes	Wishart	7:39
Mercedes	Wallace	9:03
Ohio	Matthews	9:08
E.M.F.	Tower	No Laps Recorded

right and narrowly avoided the dog. The crowds in the grandstand held their breath collectively as they watched.

One noticeable absence from practice was Grover Bergdoll, who entered, then withdrew, then entered again. His absence from practice seemed to indicate that he would not take part, although he had not withdrawn the car. Frank Hodson did make it known that he intended to withdraw the Fiat that was to be driven by Lee Oldfield. Oldfield, who felt the wrath of the fans on Thursday, decided not to drive in the race. His reason was that he could not concentrate on driving the car, knowing that the crowds surrounding the track blamed him for the deaths at Syracuse. William Wallace returned to the track on Friday. His car had been repaired, but he soon encountered engine trouble and had to cut his final practice session short.

On Friday night, the drivers met at the Hotel Walton to receive their final instructions. Quaker City Motor Club officials reviewed the rules with the drivers. Another problem that they took care of on Friday was the choice of the race starter. The Quaker City Motor Club's starter, G. Hilton Gantert, was designated as the starter of the race, as he had been for two of the previous years. The question of whether or not he was the best person for the job had come up during his first appointment in 1909, but Gantert always proved himself to be more than capable. This year the AAA decided that they did not want Gantert to be the starter; they wanted Fred Wagner, the Vanderbilt Cup veteran starter, who they had tried to replace Gantert with in 1909. Wagner ended up serving as assistant referee that year. The argument between the AAA and the Quaker City Motor Club had been going on for weeks behind closed doors, but now, the day before the race, the matter was still not resolved, and the issue came to a head.

To settle the matter S. M. Butler, the chairman of the AAA, said that Wagner would be the starter, or the AAA sanction would be revoked.[39] This would effectively end the race because any driver who took part in an unsanctioned race would be banned from AAA contests, as often happened, especially when the AAA and ACA were not getting along. Neither side would budge, until finally, Wagner settled things by removing himself from the conflict. He said that he would not act as starter even if the Quaker City Motor Club relented. This left Gantert as the most qualified person available on such short notice. The AAA appointed an assistant starter to help Gantert as they did in 1909, but it really was not necessary.

This episode should have never occurred. Gantert proved himself before, and could hardly be called an amateur after holding the position for the previous two years. This was another example of the battle for control over the race between the national club and the local club. The Quaker City Motor Club planned the race for four years, and obviously felt ownership over it, but with racing on Long Island a thing of the past, the Fairmount Park Race was much more important to the AAA than it had ever been before. The *Philadelphia North American* reported that the AAA felt that "the importance of the event made it imperative that a starter of national reputation should officiate."[40] The Quaker City Motor Club held their ground and did not allow the AAA to have their way, thus helping their effort to keep control of the race. This was the best result for everyone, since the Quaker City Motor Club demonstrated that they could stage a much safer race than the AAA could.

G. Hilton Gantert found himself in the center of a power struggle between the AAA and the Quaker City Motor Club. The AAA wanted their starter, Fred Wagner, to start all of the major races, but the Quaker City Motor Club had confidence in Gantert and did not feel that they needed to cede any control over the event to the AAA. (1911). Photograph by Nathan Lazarnick, courtesy of the Detroit Public Library, National Automotive History Collection.

With the week of practice completed, there was little doubt that Erwin Bergdoll had the fastest car. The question was whether he had learned his lesson from the previous year, when he pushed his car too hard and cost himself the race. He certainly did not hold back during the practice sessions, and it seemed as though it was his intent to push the car to its limit every time he got behind the wheel. He and the car just needed to do it on one more day, for 200 miles.

9

The Fourth Annual Fairmount Park Race

A heavy rain fell on the City of Philadelphia from Friday night into Saturday morning. Undeterred by the rain and cold weather, the fans began their trek to the park as early as 8:00 A.M., for the 12:00 P.M. race. The police and park guards took their places to keep things in order, but the chance of a contest taking place was slim. Quaker City Motor Club officials met at the Hotel Walton to decide whether or not to cancel the race, while Referee Dunlap went to the park to inspect the course. He concluded that the race should be postponed. "It looks bad-very bad," he said, "and I think it would be too risky to hold the race today."[1] But the motor club really wanted to get the race in, as did many of the drivers who had to get out of town to participate in other events. The Contest Committee decided to appoint six drivers to go out and test the course to see if they thought it was safe. The committee chose Ralph DePalma, Len Zengle, Ralph Mulford, Harry Grant, Hughie Hughes, and Charles Basle. During their inspection, they found muddy roads that the cars dug deep ruts into. The brick section of the track on Parkside Avenue was so slick that their cars slid, even at slow speeds. The drivers reported back to Referee Dunlap that they felt the track was too dangerous, so he reported back to the Quaker City Motor Club that the race would have to be postponed. They made the decision around 10:45 A.M. By this time there were over 20,000 people in the park. Although disappointed, the crowd understood that the postponement was just as much for their safety, as it was for the drivers. The only people who really had a problem with it were the sandwich vendors, who after making so many sandwiches would now have to take it as a loss. One of the Quaker City Motor Club officials mentioned that the race could be held the following Saturday, but the police would not hear of it. One lieutenant said, "Nothin' doin' next Saturday. We hold the police carnival on next Saturday and nothin' is goin' to interfere with that."[2] Saturday would not be a good day for anyone, since several of the cars and drivers were entered in the Santa Monica Race which was scheduled for that day. They generally did not race on Sundays back then, in observance of the Sabbath, so the motor club rescheduled the race for Monday. This would be a slight problem since people had to go to work, or to school, but the motor club really had no other choice if they wanted to keep the cars and drivers from withdrawing.

The club planned their traditional dinner party for Saturday night at the Hotel Walton. Drivers, entrants, and other guests had already been invited. Since this had already been planned, the club held the event on Saturday night despite the fact that they cancelled the race; the only difference was that they could not use the occasion to celebrate the winner's victory.

Improved weather arrived on Sunday. The combination of sunshine and a strong wind quickly dried the wet course. Motor club officials inspected the surface on Sunday afternoon and found it to be in great shape. The sun also shone brightly on Monday morning, although it was a little cold early on as a steamroller traversed the course to give the roadway a final packing before the big event. A couple of groups camped in the park during the night, staking claim to some of the prime viewing locations, but for the most part, the crowds did not begin to gather in earnest until around nine o'clock. Trolleys, automobiles, and people on foot streamed into the park, as in previous years, although the numbers were not quite as high. Police estimated the crowd to number 300,000, the lowest it had ever been, and half that of the previous year. This was mainly due to the postponement of the race. That so many people went to the race on a Monday is amazing in itself. Philadelphia businesses and schools must have had long absentee lists that day. The standing room spaces filled early, but the grandstand seats and parking spaces did not begin to look full until eleven o'clock, since those holding tickets had reserved spaces and did not have to worry about arriving early. Once again, many of those in the grandstands and parking spaces had prominent roles in industry and commercial endeavors. Store owners James D. Lit and Morris Clothier reserved parking spaces. Local industrialists such as Henry Disston and Arthur Dorrance had returned, and Senator James P. McNichol attended as always.

Twelve wire stations surrounded the course, each with two members of the electrical bureau inside. They had megaphones to inform the crowd from their raised platforms, which towered 10 feet above the track. They could also communicate with any of the other stations and the medical teams. A hospital tent was constructed near the Smith Memorial, in addition to the ambulances and patrol wagons stationed around the course.

When the teams arrived at the track, the crowds besieged them in the hope of getting an up close view of the drivers, but the police cleared the way and the teams were able to set up their pits, which were not located in front of the grandstand in 1911, but a little further up the Concourse. As the fans picnicked and awaited the race, the drivers arrived in the pits and prepared themselves as well. Len Zengle and

9. The Fourth Annual Fairmount Park Race

The famous racer Ralph DePalma and mechanician Louis Suhrmann await the start of the 1911 Fairmount Park Race in their Mercer car. Behind the car is the scoring stand, where timers from the Quaker City Motor Club are seated. (1911). Photograph by Nathan Lazarnick, courtesy George Eastman House.

Ralph Mulford had a conversation as they awaited the start. "Have you passed that big Benz?" Zengle asked; questioning whether Mulford had reached a speed that bettered Bergdoll. "No, I haven't passed him, but I have seen him go by," responded Mulford.[3] Clearly, both knew that Bergdoll was the one to beat, but they certainly did not consider him unbeatable. Bergdoll was fast in 1910 as well, but Zengle came away the winner. He believed that he could do the same in 1911. "Well, George Robertson won the park race twice in succession, and Harry Grant was a two-time winner of the Vanderbilt Cup race. I expect to start in first place in this year's Park race, and it won't be my fault or that of the National if I fail to finish in the same position," he said.[4] In other words, if he lost, it was going to be because someone else was faster, not because he did not give it his best effort.

Among other notable people who chatted with the drivers before the race were Harvey Ringler, who seemed to be just fine only a few days after his accident, and George Robertson who had attended every Fairmount Park Race, either as a competitor or as a spectator. Ringler was sorry that he could not participate. "If I had a pair of goggles, I would start in the race as a mechanician," he said.[5] At 11:30 A.M., the drivers began to make their way to the starting line, each passing by Starter Gantert, who gave them some final instructions, and a wish of good luck. As the min-

The cars are lined up in rows of two for the start of the Fourth Annual Fairmount Park Race. Many drivers and mechanicians can be seen in this photograph. Mechanician Louis Suhrmann is seated in the No. 5 Mercer. Donald Herr and his mechanician are in the No. 6 car, and Erwin Bergdoll and Frank Johnson, in car No. 8, can be seen talking to a member of the Lozier team. (1911). Photograph by Nathan Lazarnick, courtesy of the Detroit Public Library, National Automotive History Collection.

utes ticked by, and the start of the race approached, a noticeable absence in the grandstand could not be ignored. Mayor Reyburn did not take his seat in the grandstand as he had in previous years. The controversy of the 1910 race continued to bother him, and he decided not to attend.

With Lee Oldfield and Grover Bergdoll's cars withdrawn, only sixteen cars lined up at the start in rows of two. Lee Oldfield's Fiat was the #1 car, but he had withdrawn. This meant that Len Zengle's #2 National would be the first car to start. As long as he was able to start, he would be the only driver to take part in all of the Fairmount Park events thus far. The cars would start at twenty second intervals. At twelve o'clock noon, Starter Gantert gave Zengle the signal, and his blue National car jumped from the line and sped off into the distance. The race was on. Zengle's mechanician, Frank Faber, waved "so long" to Mulford as they left, but twenty seconds later, Mulford pursued Zengle in his Lozier, as usual decked out in the ghostly white garb that was standard for the Lozier team. Charles Basle started next in his green Cole car, and then came the Mercer of Ralph DePalma. Donald Herr followed DePalma in the #6 National. Jagersberger's Case car approached the line next,

Table 11. 1911 Starting Lineup

No.	Car	Driver	Piston Displacement	Mechanician	Tires
2	National	Zengle	589	Frank Faber	Michelin
3	Lozier	Mulford	544	William Chandler	Michelin
4	Cole	Basle	286	James Hyers	Michelin
5	Mercer	DePalma	300.6	Louis Suhrmann	Michelin
6	National	Herr	477	Frank Martin	Michelin
7	Case	Jagersberger	300.7	Fred Pfeister	Michelin
8	Benz	E. Bergdoll	712	Frank Johnson	Michelin
9	Lozier	Grant	544	George Ainslee	Michelin
10	Stutz	Anderson	389.9	Mr. Andrews	Michelin
11	Mercer	Hughes	300.6	Edward Pullen	Michelin
12	Ohio	Parker	299	William G. Rollston	Michelin
15	Fiat	Betz	615	George Tompkins	Michelin
16	National	Disbrow	477	Richard Ulbrecht	Michelin
17	Mercedes	Wishart	583	Robert Willoughby	Michelin
18	Mercedes	Wallace	583	Alfred Hammel	Michelin
19	Ohio	Matthews	299	Frank J. Huber	Michelin

and for those who had not seen it in practice, it must have looked quite strange. One newspaper man described the torpedo shaped car as "the freak car."[6] At this point, Bergdoll approached the starter. In a cloud of smoke and dust, Bergdoll dashed away from the line. He intended to lead from the beginning to the end, saying before the race that the way to win was, "to take the lead and hold it."[7] Harry Grant's #9 Lozier started twenty seconds later, followed by Gil Anderson in the Stutz. The thick clouds of smoke, which filled the space between the grandstand and the scoreboard, camouflaged the cars as they started.

Hughie Hughes made the start in his #11 Mercer, and close behind him George Parker followed in the #12 Ohio. Since no car bore the #13, and Grover Bergdoll's withdrawn car was designated as #14, the #15 car started next. John F. Betz's Fiat had that number, and he received a large round of applause when he approached the starter. He commented just before the start, "My 90-horsepower Fiat is in great shape. Hope I'll have better luck than last year."[8] With that he darted away and disappeared around the first curve. The last of the National cars started next, car #16 with Louis Disbrow at the wheel. Then came the two Mercedes of Spencer Wishart and William Wallace, and finally, Matthews' #19 Ohio. It took five minutes to get the sixteen cars under way. Starter Gantert did another excellent job and proved once again that he had the qualifications for the position, despite what the AAA officials thought.

The crowd in the grandstand only had to wait two minutes and fifty-one seconds for the first car to come back around, yet it must have seemed like an eternity as they glanced at their watches and then at the road, and then back again, in great anticipation to see who would be the first one to complete a lap. Len Zengle's National appeared in the distance and hurtled down the Concourse and across the line. Ralph Mulford trailed only a few seconds behind Zengle, and then came Ralph DePalma who had already passed the third starter, Charles Basle. The car that fol-

John F. Betz passes the Belmont Waterworks at the intersection of the West River Drive and Montgomery Avenue. The city used cinders from the waterworks to surface the drive. The photograph for this postcard was taken from atop the Columbia Bridge. (1911). Collection of the author.

lowed DePalma must have been quite a surprise, although based on practice; maybe it did not surprise everyone. Erwin Bergdoll crossed the line next. He reeled off a record breaking lap of 7:34, and this time it was official. He held first place at the conclusion of the first lap, followed by Len Zengle. John F. Betz and Spencer Wishart lagged only one second behind, tied for third place. Bergdoll had physically passed three cars on his first lap in order to be the fourth car to cross the line. Ralph Mulford found himself in fourth place after the first lap. Besides leading the race, Bergdoll also led the 6C Division. Len Zengle led the 5C Division, and the #6 National of Donald Herr led the 4C Division by thirty-one seconds over Gil Anderson. Ralph DePalma led Division 3C by only one second over his teammate Hughie Hughes in the Mercer. The first incident of the day occurred on the first lap, as Jagersberger slid on the bricks of Parkside Avenue. He kept the car under control, but a tool kit flew from his car and headed toward the crowd at the side of the road. Luckily it did not hit anyone, as members of the crowd jumped to get out of the way.

On the second lap, Bergdoll increased his lead even further by once again breaking the track record, which he had just set. This time he made a lap in 7:28, six seconds faster than his first time around. Zengle remained in second, but trailed thirty-eight seconds behind the leader, despite turning some very fast laps himself. As he made the turn off of City Avenue onto Belmont Avenue on his second lap, the car skidded and his right rear wheel slammed into a tree. Zengle did not stop, and finished the lap with a quick time of 7:49. Spencer Wishart tied Zengle for second place. They led the fourth place car of John F. Betz by seven seconds. A little further back Ralph DePalma began to fall behind, ceding way to the much more powerful cars of Wallace and Disbrow, but also to his teammate Hughie Hughes, who held off those two drivers despite the difference in power. Seeing that Bergdoll had no intention of slowing down, the crowd really got behind the local driver, urging him to once again break the track record.

George Robertson volunteered to work in the pits as a member of John F. Betz's Fiat team. Around this time, a reporter talked to Robertson in the pits. "I would like to be on the track again," the former driver said.[9] Just as he spoke those words, Betz's car rolled in for service and Robertson cut the conversation short. Betz's bad luck at Fairmount Park continued. The car had a mechanical problem. Robertson and the other Fiat mechanics looked at it, and found that they could do nothing to get the car back into the race. The car had a broken connecting rod. Betz could not believe it. Once again he dropped out of the race through no fault of his own. Len Zengle pulled into the pits on the next lap. He lost about 5 minutes making a tire change; a long time considering the fast laps that Bergdoll continued to make in his Benz. Bergdoll made his third lap in 7:39, slower than his first two, but faster than any lap made by any of the other drivers. Wishart assumed second place in the Mercedes, one minute and eleven seconds behind the Benz. With the withdrawal of Betz, and Zengle's misfortune, Mulford moved into third place. Proving that power was not everything, Disbrow moved past Wallace for sixth even though his car was a division below Wallace's. At the completion of the third lap, Zengle placed twelfth overall, and last in his division.

The next lap produced no changes. Bergdoll's Benz tore up the track, and although Wishart hung on, he lost about fifteen seconds per lap to Bergdoll. With the positions holding steady, lap five did not see any change other than Len Zengle moving ahead of Gil Anderson for eleventh. Since Betz already dropped out of the race, Bergdoll automatically won the 6C Division. In Division 5C, Wishart led Mulford by eleven seconds, with Harry Grant in third. Louis Disbrow had the first place spot in the 4C Division, and had a lead of about one minute over Donald Herr's National. In the 3C Division, the Mercer of Hughie Hughes held the first spot, but only twenty-three seconds separated him from Ralph DePalma. Jagersberger took up a distant third place in the Case.

Bergdoll led the race, but because of the interval, Mulford actually led the field on the track, with Bergdoll closing in from behind. Zengle provided the only real action on lap six, climbing up another position into tenth place, and sending Jagersberger back to eleventh. The rest of the order remained the same. Then on lap seven, Bergdoll made another spectacular lap of 7:28, tying his own record from lap two. In the process, he gained track position by passing Mulford, who could not do anything to stop him. By the end of the lap, Bergdoll put twenty seconds between himself and Mulford on the track and continued to pull away. This was just track position. In terms of time, only Zengle moved up through the order, this time getting ahead of Donald Herr, his teammate, to take ninth spot. He valiantly tried to get back up amongst the leaders, though it must have seemed almost impossible at

John F. Betz made two fast laps, and was running in fourth, when a connecting rod broke on lap three. Making the switch from a Simplex to a Fiat didn't stop the bad luck that haunted Betz in his attempts to win the Fairmount Park Race. (1911). Courtesy of Jerry Helck.

the rate that Mulford and Bergdoll circulated around the track. The #4 car, the Cole of Charles Basle, retired due to engine trouble on this lap. Basle and his mechanician, James Hyers, could not fix the problem so they parked the car at the side of the road.

The signalmen waved yellow flags on this lap to warn the drivers of danger on the course. This was because Basle had pulled the Cole off to the side of the road. Some drivers, Louis Disbrow among them, complained that there was no danger, perhaps not seeing the Cole car. They claimed that they lost time by slowing down, when there was no real danger, but this was not true. A glimpse at the drivers lap times from laps seven to nine, shows no noticeable drop in time due to the yellow flags. In fact, Disbrow's times actually improved during these laps. Just because the drivers did not see the car pulled off to the side, did not mean that it was not there, or that the signalmen waved the yellow flags unnecessarily.

Everything remained static on lap eight, although Mulford began to catch up to the second place Wishart. On the following lap, he caught him, and the two drivers

Two-time Vanderbilt Cup winner Harry Grant tries to hold off Spencer Wishart, who is quickly gaining on him. Drivers were not allowed to turn around, so Lozier mechanician, George Ainslee, is looking back to keep tabs on the Mercedes. (1911). Photograph by Nathan Lazarnick, courtesy of the Detroit Public Library, National Automotive History Collection.

tied for second place at the completion of the ninth lap. George Parker stopped his Ohio on Sweet Briar Hill around this time to change a tire. He stayed put for about twelve minutes and now lagged several laps behind the leader, in last place. Jagersberger made a pit stop to change tires on this lap without losing a position.

Also on lap nine, Louis Disbrow's National finally moved past Hughes' Mercer for fifth place. Hughes had occupied that position for six laps, even though he was in the 3C Division, with a less powerful car. On the next lap, Mulford and Wishart decided their battle, with the Lozier coming out on top in second place. Mulford moved ahead due to an uncharacteristically slow lap by Wishart. Meanwhile, Wallace seemed to be having some problems in his Mercedes. A lap of 9:44 dropped him back to tenth place, from seventh.

At the conclusion of lap ten, Mulford led the 5C Division by forty-nine seconds over Wishart, with Harry Grant another 1:30 behind them. Disbrow's National had the 4C Division well in hand with almost two minutes between him and his teammate Don Herr. In the 3C Division, Hughie Hughes still had first place, but Ralph DePalma trailed him by only thirteen seconds. Jagersberger lagged a full five minutes behind them, so it seemed as though it would be a struggle between the Mercers for the 3C Division victory.

Referred to by some as the "freak car," because of its odd shape, the Case actually represented the most forward-looking design of any car in the Fairmount Park Races. Jagersberger was not able to match his fast practice times during the race, and ultimately crashed out on lap sixteen. (1911). Courtesy of Jerry Helck.

Things held fairly steady on lap twelve, but Zengle continued his push up to the front by moving ahead of both DePalma and Hughes to take over sixth position. William Wallace fell back three positions to thirteenth spot when he brought his car into the pits for a stop to change tires. During the stop, he flooded the engine and could not get the car underway. This caused the stop to be much longer than usual, about eight minutes in length. Zengle continued to be the only man making any progress through the field as the speed of his car showed that he did not deserve to be so far back. By lap fourteen, he had moved up another two places to take over fourth place. Harry Grant helped him along in this endeavor, by stopping at his pit to pick up oil and water. Grant dropped back to seventh place with this stop. Zengle climbed ahead of Hughie Hughes' Mercer, which did not have the power to compete with the big National.

Grant lost more time and fell back an additional spot on the following lap when he had to stop his car near the Strawberry Mansion Bridge to repair a tire after just having stopped at his pit. This moved DePalma into seventh, behind Hughes, who had sixth place. Ralph Mulford also had an eventful fifteenth lap, or at least his mechanician William Chandler did. On Sweet Briar Hill, the daring mechanician climbed onto the back of the car to fix a broken fuel valve. With that problem solved, the Lozier continued up the West River Drive towards Neill Drive and the "dip of death." As they took the turn under the railroad bridge, it was obvious to the spectators that Mulford approached it too fast. The car skidded to the outside, toward the wall of the bridge. Chandler jumped out of the car and rolled on the ground, believing that the car would hit the wall. Mulford hit the brakes and stopped the car in the nick of time, and enveloped in a cloud of dust, he averted catastrophe. Yellow flags waved as Mulford ran back to check on his mechanician, who jumped back to his feet and headed for the car. They climbed back in and continued on, but this incident allowed Bergdoll, the leader, to climb right up behind them as they traversed the Neill Drive. By the time they settled down on City Avenue, Bergdoll moved ahead of Mulford on the track, in addition to overall time. Despite the near accident, Mulford did not lose his second place position.

Herr and Anderson fought for second place in the 4C Division. They raced close to each other as they came down City Avenue. Herr made the turn onto Belmont Avenue with the Stutz in close pursuit. Both drivers made the turn too fast, each determined not to slow down and give the other an advantage. Herr's National went wide on the turn, running into the gutter and glancing off of a tree and a fireplug as it ran up onto the sidewalk. Meanwhile, as is so often seen in the sport of automobile racing, Anderson concentrated on the car in front of him. When Herr went wide, Anderson made the same mistake and also flew up onto the sidewalk, hitting the same tree that Herr did. Both cars slowed immediately, and got back onto the track where they resumed their contest, barely losing a few seconds in the ordeal.

At this point in the race, Mulford led the 5C Division by fourteen seconds over Wishart. In Division 4C, Disbrow held first place with a comfortable lead of about six minutes over his fellow National driver Herr. In Division 3C, Hughie Hughes led, with Ralph DePalma just within striking distance.

On lap sixteen, Ralph DePalma fell from seventh to tenth when he made a pit stop. Jagersberger's Case also dropped out of the race on this lap. It was just another case of a driver trying to take a slow turn a little too fast. The car lost its grip as Jagersberger tried to make the hairpin turn at the bottom of Sweet Briar Hill, and slammed into a telegraph pole on the inside of the track. The accident threw Fred Pfeister, the mechanician, out of the car and onto the course. Jagersberger held on and stopped the car after it glanced off the pole. Police had to hold back the crowds that tried to run to the mechanician's aid. A number of cars approached just behind Jagersberger, and their drivers had to hit their brakes and slowly make their way through the hairpin. Pfeister jumped up and got back in the car, as Jagersberger started cranking the machine in an attempt to get it going again. The car started and they continued on. Before they could finish the lap, they had to pull off and park the car for the day. The accident had damaged the engine and it would go no further.

DePalma had a 22:34 lap time for his sixteenth lap. He had been experiencing problems with his steering rod throughout the race that made it difficult for him to control the car. On the next lap, with the problem solved, he resumed the chase, but followed sixteen minutes behind his teammate Hughes, whom he had to catch for the 3C Division win.

Matthews' No. 19 Ohio roars past Pencoyd Farm, the City Avenue home of iron magnate George B. Roberts. Roberts must have invited friends and family to watch the race from the grounds of his estate. On the opposite side of the road, a scoreboard has been erected so that his guests can more easily follow the race. In the distance Matthews' teammate, George Parker, follows in the No. 12 Ohio. (1911). Photograph by Nathan Lazarnick, courtesy of the Detroit Public Library, National Automotive History Collection.

On lap seventeen, things heated up a bit. The leader, Bergdoll, came into the pits to change tires. Mulford also stopped on this lap, allowing Spencer Wishart to assume the lead in his Mercedes. Bergdoll came out in second place with Mulford third and Len Zengle fourth, about two minutes behind Mulford. While the leaders made lap sixteen, the last place car of George Parker made his eleventh lap, and he got into some trouble at Sweet Briar. While descending the hill, one of his tires came loose and fell off of the car. Parker moved at a fast clip, but he hit the brakes and brought the car to a stop near the telegraph pole that Jagersberger had hit a few laps earlier. Parker and his mechanician, William Rollston, leaped from the car, put on a new tire, and continued on.

Now the real battle began. Only 3:17 separated the top four positions. It was anyone's race to win. Bergdoll began his pursuit of Spencer Wishart, cutting the time between himself and the leader from thirty seconds to nineteen seconds on the next lap. Zengle, after having worked so hard to get back up amongst the leaders, experienced more tire trouble and had to make another stop for repairs. While he did not lose a position, the two minute interval between he and Mulford expanded to four minutes.

On lap nineteen, Bergdoll cut Wishart's lead to two seconds, and then on lap

9. The Fourth Annual Fairmount Park Race

Erwin Bergdoll's Benz is followed by the National of Louis Disbrow as they negotiate the "S" turn on Neill Drive. The park's "natural grandstands" are very evident in this photograph, as the spectators overlook the fray from grass covered hills. In the background, the steeple of St. Bridget's Church towers over the East Falls section of the city. (1911). From the Collections of Henry Ford Museum & Greenfield Village, Neg. No. 1774.FP.11.1.

twenty, he re-took the lead and quickly put thirteen seconds between himself and the Mercedes. Zengle's problems continued, as he experienced some *déjà vu* from lap two. He made the turn from City Avenue onto Belmont Avenue and skidded just as he did on lap two, only this time he slammed his right rear tire into a tree. He continued on, but lost some time on the lap, putting the victory even further out of reach. His accident pushed him back to sixth. On the following lap, Gil Anderson ran into a ditch while making the very same turn. He and his mechanician had to push the car out and get it back on track, causing him to lose about two minutes. He also had problems with this turn back on lap fifteen.

On lap twenty-two, Wishart lost his second place position when his Mercedes blew a tire near the Catholic Fountain. Wishart and his mechanician, Robert Willoughby, jumped out of the car and changed the tire, and then Wishart hopped back in the car and drove off without his mechanician. When he got onto the Concourse and realized that Willoughby was not on board, he stopped at the pits and picked up a member of his pit crew. Wishart fell to third, allowing Mulford to take

Starter Gantert waves the checkered flag as Erwin Bergdoll crosses the finish line to take the win in the 1911 Fairmount Park Race. Although it would not be known that Bergdoll was the winner until the other cars crossed the line, the crowd had a good idea of who the winner was. (1911). Photograph by Nathan Lazarnick, courtesy of the Detroit Public Library, National Automotive History Collection.

second, but Mulford's luck would be no better than Wishart and Zengle's. Mulford went through the Sweet Briar Curve when one of his rear tires burst. He did not stop immediately, but continued up the West River Drive before he eventually stopped to change it. This allowed Wishart to take second place, with Mulford falling back to third again.

While his main rivals had all sorts of trouble, Bergdoll attempted to put as much distance as possible between himself and his competitors. He had a 2:40 lead on the second place car of Spencer Wishart. As Bergdoll passed the grandstands at the end of lap twenty-four, Starter Gantert waved a green flag to signal the beginning of his final lap. Bergdoll waved in acknowledgement, and never letting up, he took his car around at a blistering 7:38, and took the checkered flag at the end of lap twenty-five. Bergdoll pulled his Benz off the track in the designated area near the Smith Memorial, where Philadelphians immediately converged upon him to congratulate their new local hero. Bergdoll knew that his time put him safely in first place, but he waited for the other contenders to cross the line. In thirty-one seconds, Ralph Mulford finished his twenty-fifth lap. Bergdoll's time was 3:18:41. Mulford's time was slower by 3:11, but what position he finished in would not be known until Spencer Wishart

Table 12. 1911—Winner in Each Division

Division	No.	Car	Driver	Time
6C	8	Benz	E. Bergdoll	3:18:41
5C	3	Lozier	Mulford	3:21:52
4C	16	National	Disbrow	3:28:22
3C	11	Mercer	Hughes	3:29:45

crossed the line a few minutes later. The crowds waited for Wishart, and when one hundred and forty seconds passed, an explosive cheer went up for Bergdoll. Wishart came across the line in second place with a time of 3:20:11, beating Mulford by 1:41, and taking second place. The race continued for about another twenty minutes. Disbrow brought his National over the line at 3:28:22, taking the victory in the 4C Division by almost twelve minutes over Anderson and Herr. Hughes took the 3C Division in his Mercer, and he was the only driver in that class to finish the twenty-five laps. Matthews, who had completed twenty-two laps, and Parker, who completed twenty laps, were still running at the time that the race was stopped. Ralph DePalma dropped out during his twenty-third lap, when his steering knuckle, which had been troubling him throughout the race, finally put an end to his day.

Bergdoll, basking in the victory and the cheers of Philadelphians, did not take all of the credit for the win, saying after the race that much of it was due to his mechanician Frank Johnson.[10] There were several reasons for Bergdoll's victory over a few of America's most experienced veteran drivers. The well prepared car had something to do with it. Bergdoll pushed his machine harder than anyone, and experienced no mechanical problems. When he had to change tires, he and Johnson did it very quickly, and it cost them little time. Bergdoll also had the most powerful car in the field, which certainly helped, but what really won it for him was his own desire to win. From the moment practice began, Bergdoll did not let up. He went as fast as he could, and in 1911, he had a car that could take it. While Bergdoll did not take part in every Fairmount Park Race, he had been around since the beginning, and he possessed a determination to win his local race, which not only took place in his hometown, but just about in his own neighborhood. Tires definitely factored into the race, as many of the cars encountered tire trouble. All of the machines carried Michelin tires, so it really came down to luck, with some cars having plenty of tire problems, while others held up fairly well.

Not only did Bergdoll set a new track record, but he also set a new race record, besting the time that had been set by Zengle in 1910. Bergdoll was not the only one to lower the record. The top six drivers each had times lower than Zengle's winning time of the previous year.

When the race was completed, the fans left the park without incident, the large police presence once again helped to make everything go smoothly and safely. Although the race had been run and the crowds started on their way home, the Quaker City Motor Club did not consider the results to be official. Bergdoll took home the $2,500 for finishing in first place overall, plus $1,000 for first place in the 6C Division. The prize money did not matter much to him, as he was already a mil-

Erwin Bergdoll (arrow) is surrounded by the crowd after his victory in the Fourth Annual Fairmount Park Race. Judging by the way Bergdoll and a few others are raised above the crowd, it is likely that he is still in his car. Photograph by Nathan Lazarnick, Courtesy of the Detroit Public Library, National Automotive History Collection.

lionaire, and had spent much more than that trying to win the race over the last few years. Winning was all that mattered. Herr won $1,000 for the 4C Division win, and Hughes won $1,000 for winning in the 3C Division. In addition, all of the winners, except for Herr, won additional monetary prizes from the Bosch Magneto Company for winning while using their products. The 5C Division remained undecided.

Ralph Mulford and the Lozier team filed a protest against the results, claiming that Wishart violated the rules when he drove his car from George's Hill to the pits without his mechanician. On Monday night, after the Lozier team discussed the situation in their rooms at the Bellevue-Stratford, they proceeded down the street to the Hotel Walton where the Quaker City Motor Club convened a meeting of the Contest Committee to hear the protest. Lozier claimed that Wishart violated two rules during the race which gave him an advantage. Rule 109 of the AAA rules stated that two men must ride in the car, and rule 110 said that a substitution of the driver or mechanician had to be approved by the referee. Wishart broke both of these rules by riding without a mechanician and by substituting a new mechanician without permission. As a result, the Quaker City Motor Club disqualified Wishart, and sustained Lozier's protest. Fred C. Dunlap, the referee, released this statement concerning the disqualification:

> Without justification or excuse Mr. Wishart continued around the course without a mechanician. While he finished second in the race, he did not live up to the rules of

the American Automobile Association. Rule No. 106 [*sic*] states that a contesting car must carry two men, a driver and mechanician. Wishart did not do this throughout the race and therefore the Lozier's protest is sustained and said car, No. 17, is disqualified.[11]

The decision infuriated Wishart. "I didn't know that my mechanician Willoughby, was not in the car until I was well under way along the Concourse," he said.[12] "The action of the Quaker City Motor Club in disqualifying me is an outrage."[13] He said that the club should have disqualified Mulford since his mechanician had fallen off, and that Bergdoll kept looking back, which the drivers were not allowed to do, in an attempt to deflect the attention from his own rule breaking. Wishart really had no defense for his actions. He never denied that he drove without his mechanician, or that he substituted a new one. He basically admitted that he did not realize that his mechanician was not sitting next to him, but just did not want to take responsibility for it.

On Tuesday afternoon, Wishart and a representative from the Boulevard Garage, the local Mercedes dealer, got in Wishart's racecar and drove to New York to file an appeal with the AAA. The result of Wishart's appeal would not be known until 17 November 1911, over a month later, when the AAA Contest Board had a meeting in New York. One of those on the board was P. D. Folwell, a member of the Quaker City Motor Club. The AAA upheld the decision of the Quaker City Motor Club, by agreeing that Wishart's actions violated the rules. The board officially awarded Mulford the victory in the 5C Division, and second place overall.

Although the 1911 Fairmount Park Race ended with some controversy, it once again proved that Philadelphia could stage a road race better than anywhere else. The race was totally devoid of injury. The racing may not have appeared quite as exciting as in previous years. It was pretty much a walk for Bergdoll, but Wishart and Mulford were not that far behind at the end. With the Fairmount Park course being so hard on tires and machines, anything could happen, and while Bergdoll had it easy for most of the race, it tightened up at the end.

Fairmount Park had asserted itself as the best place for road racing. In his syndicated newspaper column, Barney Oldfield, who ran into some problems when trying to enter the race in 1909, did not hold it against the Quaker City Motor Club, and claimed that Fairmount Park was the best racing venue. He liked it so much, and thought that the Quaker City Motor Club did such a good job, that he wanted Philadelphia to stage the Vanderbilt Cup. "The Vanderbilt race should either be abandoned altogether or be assigned to Philadelphia to be run in conjunction with the Fairmount Park race, over the Fairmount course as the Vanderbilt Cup race," he said.[14] "It should be a survival of the fittest. Philadelphia has shown that it can run a big road race in an almost perfect manner. New York has shown clearly that it cannot do the same."[15] While other East Coast races folded up, and the focus of American auto racing began to move westward, Philadelphia put on the best race possible. Oldfield predicted, "that the Philadelphia race will continue to be run long after other road events are abandoned because of lack of police protection."[16] Oldfield did not realize that the Fairmount Park Race was in danger of being banned, regardless of its popularity and safety record.

10

Opposition

Resolved: That in the opinion of the Fairmount Park Commissioners it is inadvisable to continue the automobile races in the Park in future years, and that, to avoid disappointment and misunderstanding, this opinion be transmitted to the persons chiefly concerned and be made public.[1]

Just two days after the 1911 Fairmount Park Race, Dr. J. William White, a member of the Fairmount Park Commission, offered the above resolution for adoption. The commission took no action that day, as Edward Stotesbury moved to delay the decision until the resolution could be further considered, but the line had been drawn in the sand. After four years of successful racing, a member of the Fairmount Park Commission suddenly attempted to ban the race. Given what we now know of the Fairmount Park Motor Races, the idea that someone would try to ban it almost sounds unbelievable. Why would anyone want the City of Philadelphia to lose a world class sporting event; one that Barney Oldfield suggested as the stage for the next Vanderbilt Cup Race? Philadelphia had beaten New York. It had taken a form of the sport popularized on Long Island and made it even better and safer. Yet, the Fairmount Park Race was still not secure in its status as an annual event.

The Quaker City Motor Club feared that something like this would happen from the very beginning. As has been discussed earlier, the Quaker City Motor Club knew that some members of the Fairmount Park Commission would simply not find an automobile race in the park to be acceptable. So, they tried to appease those opponents by taking on all of the responsibility, and later by turning the race into a charitable event. It seemed as if those plans had worked. Philadelphia society filled the grandstands for the past three events, and the Quaker City Motor Club had encountered no problems in getting the necessary approval from the commission

Dr. J. William White led the campaign to ban the Fairmount Park Motor Races, claiming that it was not safe for drivers or spectators. (c. 1911). From Agnes Repplier's *Dr. J. William White M.D.: A Biography* (Boston: Houghton Mifflin Company, 1919).

for the previous two. But suddenly, a member of the commission attacked the race, supposedly in the interest of safety. One must ask, who was J. William White, and why was he opposed to the Fairmount Park Races? Was this the patrician-influenced opposition that the Quaker City Motor Club had expected all along? A closer look at the events following the 1911 race, and a more detailed examination of the make-up of the Fairmount Park Commission provides some insight to these questions.

Dr. J. William White was born in Philadelphia in 1850. He was the son of a doctor, and eventually aspired to follow in his father's footsteps. He attended the Medical College of the University of Pennsylvania and became a surgeon. Well-respected for his surgical abilities, Dr. White's peers considered him to be one of the best in his field. He had been resident physician at Eastern State Penitentiary early in his career, and the surgeon for the First City Troop, a bastion of old Philadelphia society. He rose to be the Chief of Surgery at the Philadelphia Hospital, and also served as a professor at the University of Pennsylvania, holding many prominent positions there, such as the John Rhea Barton Professor of Surgery, and the Chair of Clinical Surgery. Probably most important to this study, was his appointment in 1884 as Director of Physical Education. It is fair to say that Dr. White was a health fanatic, and to be healthy, he believed, a person had to be active. He encouraged all forms of physical exercise, and he believed that the best way to exercise was to participate in sports. Dr. White's vacations consisted of climbing mountains and swimming for miles through the oceans. He filled his scrapbooks with newspaper clippings describing University of Pennsylvania sports teams. His particular favorite seemed to be the football team. He followed the team everywhere, also acting as its surgeon, which was necessary in those days, because football was not a particularly safe sport. Dr. White brought the Army-Navy football game to Philadelphia in 1899, through his position as a member of the Board of Visitors at the Annapolis Naval Academy. Like the Fairmount Park Races, the Army-Navy Game was a charitable event, with the proceeds of ticket sales going to the Army-Navy Relief Fund. While Dr. White encouraged sports of all kinds for their health benefits, he mainly concerned himself with college sports such as football, swimming, running, and wrestling, especially the University teams in particular.

Dr. White's professional positions, his affiliation with the University of Pennsylvania, and his connection to the First City Troop, are all signs of his status in Philadelphia society. John Lukacs described him as, "a patrician physician, athlete, and *literatus*, a quintessential Kiplingite in his appearance, attitudes and preferences."[2] In other words, in Dr. White, one could see all of the defining attributes of the patricians described earlier. Patricians were fond of France and England, and Dr. White was no exception. He frequently vacationed in Europe, and had many prominent friends abroad. In fact, he did not become a member of the Quaker City Motor Club, but he did join the Automobile Club of London. Dr. White resided at 1810 S. Rittenhouse Square, the favorite place to live of many a Philadelphia patrician. According to E. Digby Baltzell, in his book, *Philadelphia Gentlemen: The Making of a National Upper Class*, patricians considered Rittenhouse Square to be "*the* address."[3]

When Dr. White proposed his resolution, his fellow commissioners immediately suspected his motives. "I move that we refer the matter to The Committee on Police and Superintendence," said James Pollock. "No, no," replied Dr. White, "I think this matter should be taken up by the whole board, and I suggest that it be laid over to a future meeting, when it can be discussed."[4] Moving the issue to the Committee on Superintendence & Police obviously concerned Dr. White. That group might have killed the resolution before he had a chance to convince other members of the commission to support him. The make-up of the smaller committee probably would not have helped him, since it was that group which suggested that the race be allowed in the first place. They also had oversight of the actual planning of the race for the previous four years. There had been no changes in the make-up of the Fairmount Park Commission since the death of Samuel Gustine Thompson, and the appointment of Dr. White as his replacement in 1909.

At the meeting, Fred Dunlap, who held a commission seat due to his position as Chief of the Water Bureau, questioned Dr. White's motives. Dunlap was a member of the Quaker City Motor Club, and had served as referee for the 1911 race. He thought that the idea of banning the race due to safety was absurd, since the races had proven to be safe for four years. "Foot ball is more dangerous, as statistics of accidents and fatalities of that game will show. If we withdraw the motor races in Fairmount Park will the University of Pennsylvania stop foot ball games on Franklin Field?" he asked. "You know you injure more men at foot ball than we do in the motor races." "Oh, that is another matter entirely," the doctor replied.[5] Dunlap made a good point. If Dr. White truly wanted to ban the races because of safety reasons, wouldn't he have had to feel the same about football, or any other sport for that matter? James Pollock, who wanted to send the question to the smaller committee, said that he would need to hear a convincing argument before he would support the resolution. "It ought to be considered well before it is approved. When the race was first proposed four years ago, I did not look favorably upon the suggestion because I feared for the safety of the spectators and the drivers," he said. "The contests have proved, though, that my fear was not justified, and now I am in favor of having the races held in the Park."[6]

Archibald T. James, the Secretary of the Quaker City Motor Club, believed that another reason, besides safety, caused J. William White to take action. Several days before the 1911 race, the Athletic Association of the University of Pennsylvania made a request of the Quaker City Motor Club. They wanted the announcer at Fairmount Park to make announcements during the race concerning the progress of the football game between the university and Ursinus, which took place the same day. If that was not possible, they at least wanted some sort of announcement informing those at the race that a game was underway. Mr. James told the Athletic Association that the motor club could not make the announcements because they would then get requests from every theater and sporting venue in the area asking them to make similar announcements. Declining all of those requests would be difficult if they extended the favor to the University of Pennsylvania. "It is possible that Dr. White, in his enthusiasm for the interests of the University team and general athletics, took my refusal as a personal slight," said Mr. James.[7] Whether it was because of this incident, or because of the absurdity of the safety argument, some people thought that Dr. White must have other motives.

Certainly, the timing of Dr. White's opposition could not have been better for his cause. The recent accident involving Lee Oldfield, that killed nine spectators at Syracuse, gave the doctor a good reason to present the safety argument. There is also another factor to be considered. Mayor Reyburn had been a big supporter of the race, such a big supporter, that the event probably would not have ever happened without his assistance. Even though the Mayor was no longer fond of the Quaker City Motor Club, and did not attend the race in 1911, he did not stand in the way, and still believed that holding the race was good for the city, regardless of who organized it. When Dr. White presented his resolution, the mayor was on his way out. It was an election year, and Mayor Reyburn did not run for re-election. At the time, Dr. White did not know who the next mayor would be, but he had a better chance of getting his resolution passed since Reyburn would not be around anymore. He certainly had a better chance than he would have had previously.

It is needless to say that the Fairmount Park Race was very popular, and there were some who did not intend to let the Fairmount Park Commission ban the race. They let their voices be heard by writing to the city's newspapers. One unidentified writer, know only as "Disgusted" called for Dr. White's removal from the commission. He saw the doctor's attempt to ban the race as another example of Philadelphia being led down the path of the patricians. "New York and other cities refer to us as [sic] contemptuously as 'slow.' Shall we always deserve this epithet?" he asked.[8] The papers themselves also showed their support for the race. "It is not fair to the tens of thousands of citizens interested in the yearly automobile races in Fairmount Park to insist, without good reason, that the park commissioners shall put the ban on this event," argued the editor of the *Philadelphia Evening Times*.[9] According to *Motor Age*, there was not "a motorist or enthusiast in the city but who has not expressed his or her indignation."[10]

Meanwhile, Dr. White prepared to make another attempt at the December commission meeting. At that meeting, he once again moved for the consideration of his resolution, but this time he had prepared some arguments to go along with it. He did not limit himself to the safety issue, but instead brought several reasons why the race should not be held, in the hope that the commissioners would vote in his favor for one reason or another. The safety argument topped his list, and answering the critics who had said that football was a more dangerous sport, he said, "The essential difference between such games, for example, as football, of which I have always been an advocate, or baseball, which I heartily approve of and greatly enjoy, and the automobile races of the present day lies in the unavoidable and excessive risk of life, not only of the participants, but of the spectators, that is inseparable from the latter events."[11] With this argument, he had a point, but it still did not hold much weight. Spectators have always taken a risk when attending an automobile race, especially in those days, but it is a risk that they take voluntarily. If a person can choose to take a risk in driving a race car, or playing in a football game, why can't a spectator choose to take a risk by watching an automobile race?

The doctor would have the commission believe that the lack of accidents had been because of luck, and that something could go wrong at any time, but that just was not the case. There was luck involved in some of the accidents that took place in the park, but the lack of serious injury, especially to spectators, had more to do with the planning of the race. The Quaker City Motor Club and the Philadelphia Police Department had proven time and again that they were more than capable of keeping people out of danger. They did not allow spectators to stand in dangerous places, which is why nobody was ever hit by a car at the races, with the exception of a policeman during the 1910 race. The policeman put himself in a dangerous spot, but the spectators were not in danger. This is why there were never any serious injuries, even though cars had left the track just as many times at Fairmount Park as they had at other race courses around the country. It was not that there were fewer accidents at Fairmount Park; it was just that nobody was ever positioned in the path of them.

The doctor moved on to say that not only was the race dangerous, but that if anything bad happened, the Fairmount Park Commission would have it on its conscience. He admitted that he had attended the race in the past, but that he now realized his part in putting the crowds at risk. "I imagine that a similar change of feeling would take place in many—perhaps the majority—of the spectators if they were obliged to assume the responsibility," he said.[12] This argument had been used before, in 1909, when certain commissioners, such as Samuel Gustine Thompson, feared that they would be held liable if someone were killed. This was another argument that seemed weak considering the fact that the commissioners had accepted that responsibility for four years. Besides, the Quaker City Motor Club had always deposited money with the commission to cover such unfortunate incidents if necessary. It was also likely that the AAA and the Quaker City Motor Club would take responsibility for any serious injuries or deaths that occurred, since they organized the race. All that the commissioners had to do was allow the event to take place in the park.

Dr. White also made the argument that automobile races no longer served any useful purpose. He claimed that people only went to watch them because they wanted to see the accidents. He used one of the most popular racing driver's words to advance his argument. Barney Oldfield had written an article in *Popular Mechanics* in which he claimed that the reason for the existence of automobile racing was "the blood-hunger of the spectator."[13] Dr. White quoted Oldfield on this matter, and also on the idea that automobile racing did not help the development of the motor car any longer. "The science of speed has reached a point where any manufacturer can produce a car which will satisfy any sane buyer," wrote Oldfield. "There is no demand and little need for a further development along speed lines."[14] Whether Oldfield believed this himself is questionable. He made his living as a racing driver, so if he did not believe in the sport, why did he participate in it? Oldfield was never a fan of the AAA, and based on his articles where he said that the Vanderbilt Cup should be run in Philadelphia, it seemed that he was unhappy with safety precautions at other race tracks, and the AAA's lack of action to make racing safer. When Oldfield made these comments, he was probably venting, and trying to damage the AAA in some way, or spur them to make changes that would improve safety. Dr. White's use of the famous driver's words about his own sport certainly must have helped his argument, but he left out the fact that in other articles, Oldfield had heaped praise on the Fairmount Park Race because it was so safe, and so unlike other venues. Dr. White also left something else out. Whether the crowds enjoyed automobile races for one reason or another, or whether they served a purpose in the further development of the motor car was not the issue. The important issue was the fact that the race benefited the city. It advertised the city, and brought in visitors from out of town. It also helped businesses, such as hotels and restaurants, and boosted the city's automobile trade.

Perhaps the most unbelievable point that White made during his speech was that the people of Philadelphia did not favor it. He said that of the people he had polled, "not more than two per cent" said that they would not support his resolution.[15] But what is interesting is exactly who he polled. He said that among those that he had asked were the members of a literary club, the board of a financial institution, and a large committee of medical men. These were all patrician, or mostly patrician, organizations. Doctors, bankers, and members of literary clubs, were not the same as the average man on the street. The literary club may well have been a group that consisted only of himself, Agnes Repplier, and author Horace Howard Furness. In other words, Dr. White only asked people who were just like him. He was such a renowned patrician figure at the time, who amongst the patricians would disagree with him, or would admit to him that they actually enjoyed the race and wanted it to continue? Dr. White cited George Wharton Pepper as being in agreement with him. Pepper, a prominent lawyer, and a member of a well known Philadelphia family, was a famous patrician figure on par with Dr. White. He also happened to be the solicitor of the Fairmount Park Commission. Dr. White also spoke with

George P. Rich, another lawyer, who claimed that the commissioners did not have the right to close the park for the purposes of the race. Dr. White admitted that Pepper disagreed with Rich on this argument, Pepper saying that the commission did have the power to permit the race, but Dr. White put the argument forward anyway. Even though Pepper believed that the commission had the power to allow the race, he was not in favor of it. "If I were a Commissioner I should vote against it, for the reasons which you have so clearly set forth," he wrote to White.[16]

White suggested that since most Philadelphians were not interested in the race, many of those who attended the race were from out of town. He said, "While there are collateral benefits to certain merchants and businessmen from the influx to the City of outsiders, they are to some extent counterbalanced by the interference, experienced by others, with the orderly processes of trade or manufacture."[17] Patricians did not like visitors coming to the city. They just wanted to be left alone, and preferred not to receive the attention, or the visitors, that the race brought to town. As has already been shown, this was one of the characteristics of the patricians that gave Philadelphia its reputation for being a backwards and boring city.

Off to the Race!
Service on the "High Speed" for Motorists at Wanamaker's

The Fairmount Park Races brought thousands of people into the city. Local business benefited greatly from this, and attempted to bring the race fans into their stores. This detail from an advertisement for the John Wanamaker Department Store is just one of many examples that show how important an event of this magnitude could be to a city and its businesses. From the *Philadelphia Record*, 8 October 1910.

In Dr. White's arguments, we see that there were more reasons behind his efforts to ban the race, rather than simply the safety issue. His choice of supporters, his portrait of the race as a problem that caused trouble by attracting *outsiders* who cause *interference*, and his view that automobile races are not necessary to automobile development, are signs that his patrician background motivated, or at least helped, his crusade. Unlike the average working man or businessman, Dr. White could not see the race as sport. If it did not contribute to the development of the motor car, he would argue, then why do it? His arguments also show his feelings toward the people who watched automobile races. He portrayed them as bloodthirsty spectators, who put themselves at risk and did not know any better.

Despite the doctor's well-prepared arguments, the commission still did not act on his resolution. Thomas DeWitt Cuyler moved that it be sent to the Committee on Superintendence & Police for recommendation. The rest of the commissioners agreed, because it was a decision that they did not want to make. True, four years previously, they did not want to approve the race at all, but now they did not want to ban it. It was going so well, and made money for charity, so why change things? Now they had Dr. J. William White, who they respected, and did not want to cross, asking them to support his efforts to ban the race. If they did so, it would be a very unpopular decision with the public, so they kept putting it off, hoping that the whole question would just go away. The Quaker City Motor Club, and all of those who supported the race, also hoped that it would go away, and in fact, many believed that it would. *Motor Age* said, "It is hard to conceive how favorable action on the resolution can be taken, in view of the fact that the race has become or was thought to have been a fixture."[18]

Motor club officials and other interested parties quickly tried to deflect Dr. White's arguments. Edward H. Fitch, manager of the Diamond Rubber Company, again compared the race to football, knowing that if the numbers were compared, it was an argument that Dr. White could not win. "I think the record of four annual motor races without accidents would look well alongside the statistics of the casualties on Franklin Field for the same number of years in football history," he said.[19] Paul Huyette, of the Quaker City Motor Club, found fault with Dr. White's survey, implying that he did not ask a representative group of people, and that it was impossible that all of the spectators came from out of town. "If this half million is only two percent of the population of Philadelphia and vicinity, then we can boast a population of nearly 25 millions, which is nearly seventeen times more than we are credited with on the census books," he pointed out.[20] G. Douglas Bartlett, vice-president of the Quaker City Motor Club, took notice of Dr. White's portrayal of the race as something that people only went to see for the accidents. He said, "This excitement may be noted at any sport in which there is a keen struggle for the honors, and fatalities do not necessarily result. We have shown that fast motor races can be conducted without accident and if we must stop everything in which a chance of danger exists, then contractors should be forced to quit work on all buildings and bridges, and all progress should come to an end."[21]

The commission moved the resolution to the Committee on Superintendence & Police, and that committee stalled on making their decision for months. The issue did not come up again until 10 April 1912, when the Quaker City Motor Club made their annual request for permission to hold the race, which they planned to hold on 5 October. Since the approval of the race depended on the report of the committee concerning Dr. White's resolution, Mr. Pollock moved that the motor club's request also be referred to the smaller committee. The commission agreed, and once again set the issue aside. The Committee on Superintendence & Police did not meet until 8 May 1912, almost a full month later. The only three members to attend the meeting were James Pollock, Eli Kirk Price Jr., and Sydney W. Keith. These three commissioners did not want to make the decision on their own, so they referred the issue back to the full commission without recommendation "in view of the small number of members present at the meeting."[22] They instructed the commission to vote on Dr. White's resolution first, and suggested that if it did not pass, the Quaker City Motor Club's request should be granted. In effect, they recommended the approval of the race, but they did not want to make the decision on Dr. White's resolution. Nobody wanted to be the one to disagree with him, because of what he represented. The full Fairmount Park Commission met later that same day. Only ten members attended. They were Edward T. Stotesbury, Mayor Blankenburg, Thomas DeWitt Cuyler, Fred Dunlap, James Elverson, Sydney W. Keith, James Pollock, Eli K. Price, George Webster, and Dr. White. The secretary read Dr. White's resolution, and Mr. Cuyler moved for its adoption. Fred Dunlap voiced his opinion, making the argument that the race had been safe for four years, and the fact that it was extremely popular. The new mayor, on the other hand, did not want the races to continue under his watch. "I feel it would be a mistake to allow these races to continue. They do not accomplish any good at all and serve no useful purpose. It has been said that they have been enjoyed by a great many people. That is true; but I know a great many people who would enjoy attending a hanging…I am very strongly opposed to having the races continued," he said.[23] The commissioners voted, and the resolution passed. The Fairmount Park Motor Race had come to an end.

Of the ten members present, only Fred Dunlap voted against the resolution. This raises the question, if the Committee on Superintendence & Police seemed to imply that the race should continue, why would the three members of that body, who attended the full meeting, vote for the resolution? Reports suggested that the commissioners decided to vote for the resolution when they discovered that the mayor was not in favor of the race. Without the mayor's support, the police would not be authorized to serve as guards, but that reason alone really does not explain their action. Without the mayor's support, there were other alternatives. The commissioners could have voted down Dr. White's resolution, and then discussed the matter of course protection with the Quaker City Motor Club. Without the mayor's support, the club could have used the profits of the race to rent the park, and to hire guards for the course, rather than giving all of the proceeds to charity. They also could have asked the governor for military protection. This might not be the ideal situation, but it could have been discussed. With the adoption of the White Resolution, all hope was lost. The answer to the question may lie in the fact that most of the commissioners were patricians who did not want to cross Dr. White, who they saw as one of their own. A closer look at the professions and residences of the

Fairmount Park Commission members, both those who were present, and those whose absence contributed to the passage of the resolution, shows just how similar many of these commissioners were in terms of social status.

Most of the commissioners who held seats through appointment, were neighbors, who lived in the exclusive area around Rittenhouse Square. Besides living in the most patrician neighborhood, these commissioners worked in occupations that could be classified as acceptable patrician professions. First, let's take a look at those who attended the meeting. Eli Kirk Price Jr. was a lawyer who lived at 1834 Spruce Street. Thomas DeWitt Cuyler was also a lawyer, and vice president of the Commercial Trust Company. He lived just two doors away from Mr. Price at 1830 Spruce Street. Cuyler said during the meeting that the races were not sport, but "advertisements for the cars entered."[24] He seems to have held a very patrician view of auto racing. If the game was not played on a college campus, he did not consider it to be a sport. He also must have found fault with advertising a product by unconventional means.

Sydney W. Keith was a manager at Edward B. Smith & Company, a firm of bankers. He lived at 226 S. 21st Street, only two blocks from Rittenhouse Square.

James K. Pollock was one of the exceptions when it came to the appointed members, which may explain why he was initially in favor of the race. He was born in Ireland, and now owned a large carpet manufacturing company in the Kensington section of the city. By virtue of his trade, Pollock was not a patrician. He also lived in the Chestnut Hill section of the city, where many wealthy industrialists like him also resided.[25] Although Chestnut Hill was a wealthy neighborhood, it was not a patrician bastion like Rittenhouse Square or the Main Line.

James Elverson Jr. was the son of the vice president of the *Philadelphia Inquirer*, and was himself the general manager. He lived at 2028 Walnut Street, just a block away from Rittenhouse Square. Very close by, was the home of Edward T. Stotesbury, a banker with Drexel & Company. He lived at 1925 Walnut Street. In writing of Stotesbury, James T. Maher said, "even though he was, undeniably, a Philadelphian, he was, just as undeniably, not a *Philadelphian*."[26] While he was not a patrician, and was regarded by them to be "new money," he desperately wanted to be accepted into their patrician social circle. This aspiration explains why he favored the race at the meeting of the Committee on Superintendence & Police, but ultimately voted to ban it when faced with Dr. White's resolution. In order to make himself fit in with the patricians, Stotesbury could not, or would not, oppose them.

Three of those in attendance held ex-officio seats. George Webster was the Chief Engineer & Surveyor, who lived at 4900 Penn Street in the Frankford section of the city. He can not be classified as a patrician by either his occupation, or his place of residence. Mayor Blankenburg lived at 214 W. Logan Square, just around the corner from Senator Jim McNichol. He was a merchant and manufacturer by occupation. Although Blankenburg was originally a Republican, he did not approve of the machine politics of McNichol, Penrose, and Reyburn. He had won the mayoral election as a member of the Keystone Party, a political party intent on reform. Blankenburg's motives for being against the continuation of the race had nothing to do with his social standing. He was not a patrician, and so had no social-connection as a reason to support Dr. White's arguments. It is more likely that Blankenburg truly did not want to be responsible if an accident occurred, or that he saw the race as a relic of the Reyburn Administration. While Reyburn operated within the machine's web, Blankenburg did not. During his administration, he would eliminate much of the extra spending that had occurred when municipal contracts had been let to members of the machine. The race may have been one of the first victims of this reform. The close ties between machine members and the race, which helped it to come about in the first place, may have helped to make it go away. The new mayor may have viewed it as another method by which the previous political machine wasted the city's money. Blankenburg, as a reformer, could not justify spending money on something such as the race, when he had promised to cut excess spending and invest in basic city services.

Fred Dunlap was the last of the commission members who attended the meeting. As we know, Dunlap was the Chief Engineer of the Waterworks, a member of the Quaker City Motor Club, and referee for the 1911 race. He lived in North Philadelphia at 6621 N 12th Street, well outside of the accepted areas favored by the patricians.

Among those who did not attend the meeting was John G. Johnson, a lawyer who lived at 506 S. Broad Street. Peter A. B. Widener also did not attend. He was a former butcher who had become very wealthy, first as a supplier of food to Union troops during the Civil War, and then as a streetcar magnate. At the time, Widener lived in a sizable mansion in Elkins Park, Pennsylvania, but had previously lived on North Broad Street. Like Pollack, he did not fit the typical profile of a Fairmount Park Commissioner.

A. Louden Snowden was President of the Electric Company of America. He lived at 1812 Spruce Street, just down the street from Mr. Price and Mr. Cuyler, and just around the corner from Rittenhouse Square. The others were ex-officio members such as Commissioner of City Property, A. S. Eisenhower, who lived in North Philadelphia at 1725 N 17th Street. President of Common Council, George McCurdy, and President of Select Council, Harry Ransley, also did not attend. Ransley was a mercantile appraiser who lived in South Philadelphia at 1120 S 10th Street, and McCurdy was a lawyer who lived at 124 N 17th Street.

Many of the members of the commission were patricians, who worked in similar occupations, and lived very close to each other in the Rittenhouse Square area. They attended the same churches, went to the same parties, and joined the same clubs. So it is certainly within reason that they would all support Dr. White, regardless of how they personally felt. Defying a prominent member of their own social class, in support of an event that was organized and enjoyed by "new money" and middle class citizens was out of the question. The proximity of the residences of the Fairmount Park Commission members, especially those who were appointed to the commission, is striking. Just as striking, is that fact that local supporters of the race, such as Quaker City Motor Club members and race participants, lived in areas that were anything but acceptable to the patricians. None of the race supporters resided near Rittenhouse Square. They generally lived outside of the downtown area, in North, West, and South Philadelphia. When the race was voted on, seven of the commissioners present at the meeting held their seats by appointment, and they were the ones who were most likely to agree with Dr. White. With the mayor also against the race, it had no chance. Perhaps if more of the ex-officio commission members had attended, the vote would have turned out differently. In the past, Mayor Reyburn had threatened to get involved in Fairmount Park Commission business if the commissioners did not vote in favor of the race. He also urged ex-officio commission members to attend the meetings to ensure that there would be enough votes in favor of the event. Those same ex-officio commissioners now had to answer to a new mayor, who was not in favor of the race. With Mayor Reyburn and the political machine no longer around to organize the ex-officio commissioners against the appointed commissioners, the race did not have a chance.

The Quaker City Motor Club did not attempt to find a new location for the race. They knew that the venue was one of the major elements of its success. Fairmount Park was the best place to hold the race, and no other location would provide the same benefits. Instead, the motor club preferred not to push the matter. They waited a full year before making another proposal. The attempt to revive the race for 1913 provides further evidence that the decision to ban the race had more to do with support for Dr. J. William White, and less to do with the mayor's approval. In April of 1913, a committee from the Quaker City Motor Club visited the mayor to discuss his opposition to the race, and the possibility of finding a way to hold the event in the future that would be agreeable to him. The meeting went very well. The mayor told the club members that he opposed the race, but would not stand in the way. "I told them that if they asked Councils to request the Park Commission to permit, and if the Commission granted the request; I would not oppose the race," he said. He continued on to say that he still did not think it was a good idea. "I made it quite plain that I stood, as I did last year, against the race. I have not changed my opinion, and I told the committee so. However, if the Park Commission wants to grant permission, it is up to them. But I do not want the responsibility of it."[27]

The club made their annual request to the Fairmount Park Commission, which dealt with the matter in June 1913. By then, the Common and Select Councils had passed resolutions requesting that the commission allow the race in the park. Those in attendance at the meeting were Edward T. Stotesbury, who was now the president of the commission following the death of A. Loudon Snowden in September, Mayor Blankenburg, James Elverson Jr., Sydney W. Keith, James Pollock, Eli K. Price Jr., J. William White, President of Common Council George McCurdy, Commissioner of City Property William H. Ball, and Chief Engineer and Surveyor George Webster. Carleton E. Davis, who replaced Fred Dunlap as Chief Engineer of the Waterworks, was also in attendance. The Chairman of the Committee on Superintendence & Police, Mr. Price, read the application of the motor club, and offered a resolution for adoption. He included the conditions that would have to be met in order for the race to occur, just in case it actually passed. In the resolution, Mr. Price stated that the park guards, the police, and the mayor would have to agree to cooperate in staging the race. He also said that profits would go to charity, and that the charities involved would be the Police Pension Fund and the Park Guard Pension Fund. When the resolution was put on the table, various members voiced their opinions on the matter.

Dr. White made his usual arguments, reminding the commission that they had already banned racing in the park, and their reasons for doing so. This time he made it a bit more personal. If there was any doubt about how Dr. White looked down upon the races and those involved, there could not be any longer after he said, "While it may be a minority, still it is a large minority of drivers in these races who are mentally and morally irresponsible. It is demoralizing to see such type of man exalted as a hero."[28] So, according to Dr. White's arguments, a racing driver could not be a hero, but a football player could. Death on a race course was irresponsible, while death on Franklin Field was accidental and just part of the game. Dr. White was a patrician who did not see automobile racing as a sport. He looked down upon the working class men and women who watched the races and participated in them, believing that their judgment was flawed. He felt that he knew what was best for them.

The mayor informed the commission that the director of the police did not feel that he could spare the number of men necessary to patrol the course. He did not say that the police would not be available; he just said that he was not sure whether the police would be available. This should not have mattered when voting on the resolution, because Mr. Price worded the resolution in a way which stated that it would not take place without police protection. This was also a strange argument for the mayor to make, since the police department had guarded the course for four years, with no reports of widespread crime due to so many police being at the park.

The strongest advocate for the race was George McCurdy, President of Common Council. McCurdy had held that position throughout the Reyburn Administration, and knew that the race was good for the city. He called it "a clean healthful sport," and went on to talk about its safety record, the number of spectators who enjoyed it, and the benefits to the city.[29] Finally, the commissioners voted and chose not to support the resolution by a vote of eight to two. Mayor Blankenburg did not vote, as he had promised not to interfere. The only two votes for the resolution were George McCurdy and James Elverson Jr., who it seems, decided to vote favorably now that the mayor did not object. Everyone else agreed with Dr. White that the race must remain banned. McCurdy was furious at the decision, sarcastically referring to the other commissioners as, "a bunch of good sports."[30]

The Quaker City Motor Club was out of luck for another year. Meanwhile, another group looked to try something different. Since 1911, the major road races in the East had disappeared, and the focus of the auto racing community moved to the West. Both the Vanderbilt Cup Race and the Grand Prize were held in Milwaukee in 1912 and then in Santa Monica in 1914. Oval track racing was also on the rise with the Indianapolis 500 being the biggest event of the year. In August 1913, the first rumblings began to be heard about the possibility of an Indianapolis style speedway in the vicinity of Philadelphia. The Quaker City Motor Club did not make the plans. A group of prominent Philadelphians and suburbanites who called themselves The Philadelphia Motor Speedway Association were behind the effort.

Although The Philadelphia Motor Speedway Association was not affiliated with the Quaker City Motor Club, there were some men involved in it who had been involved with the motor club, or with the park races. Frank Hardart, who had served on the Board of Governors of the Quaker City Motor Club, was involved, as was Harvey Ringler, who crashed in practice for the 1911 race. G. Henry Stetson, who had contributed prize money for the Fairmount Park Race, was also a member of the new association, along with John F. Betz. Many of the other individuals involved were operators of Philadelphia hotels, such as Mahlon W. Newton, President of the Philadelphia Hotel Association. He believed that like the Fairmount Park Race, such a facility would draw people to the city and increase business. They planned to build a speedway in Bucks County, just north of Philadelphia. It would be easier to find open land in Bucks County, and in addition, it would benefit from not having to deal with the Philadelphia city government.

The Philadelphia Motor Speedway Association was a membership organization. According to Charles L. Betts Jr., in an article about the speedway, membership would mean free access to the speedway, as well as the golf course and tennis courts that were to be built along with it.[31] Basically they were going to build a country club that would include a speedway. By February 1914, the association had obtained the land in Warminster Township, Bucks County. Old York Road, County Line Road, Street Road, and the Pennsylvania Railroad tracks bounded the property. The proximity to the railroad, as well as these three major roads in Bucks County, would make it easy to travel to the speedway from Philadelphia, which was exactly what the hotel men wanted.

Meanwhile, the Quaker City Motor Club prepared for yet another attempt at resurrecting the park race. They again had much support when approaching the Fairmount Park Commission. John P. Connelly, a member of the Common Council, had introduced a resolution advising the Fairmount Park Commission to allow the race in the park. The resolution laid out the reasons why the Common Council believed that allowing the race would be a good thing. He pointed to the benefits to charity, the large number of citizens who enjoyed it, the boost in tourism, and the advertisement value for the city.[32] He urged Mayor Blankenburg and the Fairmount Park Commission to support it. The resolution passed unanimously in the Common Council, and then was sent to the Select Council, where it also passed without a single negative vote. The Market Street Merchants Association also made a request to the Fairmount Park Commission, asking that they allow the race because of the economic benefits to their businesses. The motor club had high hopes that with this level of support, the commission would have to allow the race.

The Fairmount Park Commission met on the afternoon of 12 March 1914 to consider the matter. Edward Stotesbury presided. Also present were Mayor Blankenburg, Thomas DeWitt Cuyler, James Elverson Jr., Sydney W. Keith, Eli Kirk Price Jr., George McCurdy, Commissioner of City Property William Ball, Chief Engineer Webster, and Theodore Justice, who took the seat opened with the death of A. Loudon Snowden. Dr. J. William White was on a round-the-world trip at the time. The request from the Quaker City Motor Club was read, and Mr. Cuyler, Dr. White's friend, who had supported him in his effort to ban the race from the beginning, moved that the commission refuse it. Mr. Justice moved that the issue be put in the hands of the Committee on Superintendence & Police, but Cuyler explained to the commission that the issue had been decided two years earlier, and that there was no sense in debating it any longer. The commission voted down Justice's motion, and so Cuyler moved that his resolution to refuse permission be adopted. A vote was taken, and it passed, but then the requests from the City Councils and The Market Street Merchants Association were read before the commission. In an effort to be fair, Mr. Cuyler withdrew his previous resolution and suggested that the commission re-evaluate the issue now that they had these additional requests. He offered the following resolution:

> Resolved: That the Commissioners, after due consideration of the application of the Quaker City Motor Club, the Resolution of Request of Select and Common Councils and the communication from the Market Street Merchants' Association, deem it inadvisable to grant the request.[33]

The commissioners voted again, and the resolution was adopted. The race was again voted down, this time, twice in a single day. The press reported that there was not a single dissenting vote. The minutes of the commission do not mention the vote tally, but it is hard to believe that George McCurdy, who argued for the race a year earlier, and James Elverson who moved that permission be granted in 1913, would vote against it. The only explanation is that the mayor may have once again implied that he would not cooperate. With this vote, the Fairmount Park Race was effectively ended for good. There would be no other attempts to revive it. Philadelphia's hope for a major automobile race now hinged on the Philadelphia Motor Speedway Association.

Having acquired the necessary land, the Philadelphia Motor Speedway Association moved forward with its plans to construct a speedway in Bucks County. They hired the Philadelphia architectural firm of Heacock & Hokanson to design the complex. In May, they sent one of the partners, J. Linden Heacock, to Indianapolis to witness the fourth running of the Indianapolis 500. Heacock's mission was to see what made Indianapolis such a great track, and determine what Philadelphia could do to make their track even better. Like the Quaker City Motor Club, and their view of the Vanderbilt Cup, The Philadelphia Motor Speedway Association felt the same way about Indianapolis. It was something to emulate, but it was also something to be improved upon. Indianapolis had already had its share of fatal accidents, and the Philadelphia Motor Speedway was intended to be much safer.

Heacock returned with many useful observations. He loved the Indianapolis track, and felt that it was the greatest in the world, but he also thought that he could eliminate many of its problems. One thing that Heacock noticed was that the track had grown in popularity so quickly that the infrastructure was not prepared for it. His plans would include more necessities such as restrooms and concessions. The biggest problem he found in Indianapolis was getting there. He found the congestion on the roads that led to the track to be not only inconvenient, but dangerous as well. At the Philadelphia Motor Speedway, getting in and out would be made easy, not only by the three major roads that surrounded the property, but also by built-in trolley stations that dropped spectators off right at the grandstands, and a built-in train station with eighteen tracks. Two additional train tracks afforded a view of the racetrack, so that travelers would not be required to leave their seats on the train in order to view the race. This idea was probably inspired by Fairmount Park, where trains parked on the nearby Pennsylvania Railroad tracks. He also included parking for 30,000 cars in the center of the track with sixteen tunnels leading under the racing surface for easy access.

Another problem that Heacock found with Indianapolis was the view of the race. "The chief desire of each spectator is to see as much of the race as possible, yet at Indianapolis practically no attempt was made to follow the course of the cars after they passed the immediate vicinity of the spectator, both because the track was too large to take in from one point, and because of the many obstructions on the stands and within the track enclosure."[34] Heacock's plans called for a 2 mile speedway, as opposed to the 2.5 mile track at Indianapolis, thus making it easier to follow the cars all the way around. There would also be no tall structures in the infield to block a person from seeing the entire track. The only exception would be the judges' stand. Heacock felt that despite the shorter track, speeds would be higher. He predicted an average speed of over 90 mph, and top speeds over 110 mph.[35] The increased speed would be due to high banked turns.

To call the Philadelphia Motor Speedway simply a racetrack is a bit of an understatement. Heacock's plans called for much more. "It is, in fact, a question as to whether this great undertaking had not been better named a National Playground, instead of going down through history as the Philadelphia Speedway," he said.[36] In addition to the two mile track, there was to be a one-mile horse track and stables, a horse show ring, hangars and an aviation field, tennis courts, a golf course, a baseball diamond, and swimming pools. There would also be a 60,000 seat stadium for football and track events, which, rather than being built up, would be dug into the ground. The main feature for club members would be the spectacular clubhouse which would include billiard rooms, a conservatory, bowling alleys, a gymnasium, a library and dining rooms. Members of the Philadelphia Motor Speedway Association would have free access to these facilities year-round. They would even be allowed to drive on the speedway when it was not in use.

Early plans were for a brick track, much like Indianapolis, but those plans quickly changed to wood when other board tracks proved that it was faster and safer for automobile racing. Construction began early in 1915. Workers cleared the land and the banked turns began to rise up on the former Bucks County farmland. Heacock, and members of the Philadelphia Motor Speedway Association, visited with the AAA in New York to discuss the future of the facility, and its place among the country's great racing venues. From this meeting came "the Big Seven," a group of seven speedways which would include Philadelphia, Indianapolis, Des Moines, Chicago, Sheepshead, Sioux City and Minneapolis. These seven tracks would have the exclusive right to conduct races in their respective areas, and as the AAA's premier events, would be the basis of a "grand circuit of automobile racing."[37] Construction continued throughout 1915 and into 1916. The Philadelphia Chamber of Commerce lent its endorsement, further securing the success of the project. By late 1916, 2,700,000 feet of lumber had been used in the construction. Everything seemed

10. Opposition

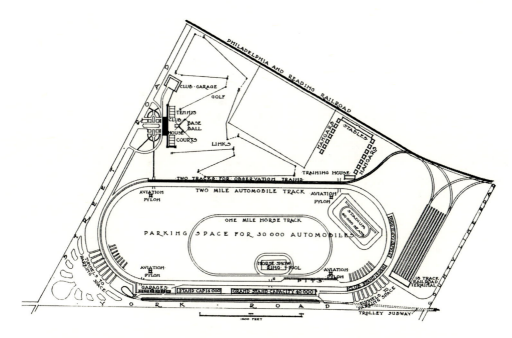

A plan of the proposed Philadelphia Motor Speedway, by Heacock & Hokanson, Architects. The speedway plan included innovative ideas, such as a football stadium that was to be dug into the ground, and tracks for observation trains. This plan shows the facilities that would have been available for a wide variety of sporting events, as well as the easy access to and from the track provided by the major roads, railroad, and trolley lines. From the *Journal of the Philadelphia Chamber of Commerce* (November 1915).

to be going well. Drivers expected it to be one of the fastest and safest courses in the country. The famous driver Dario Resta, who won the 1915 and 1916 Vanderbilt Cup Races commented, "Wood tracks, such as are to be laid at the Philadelphia speedway make the racing surface preferred by most drivers." "A brick track like Indianapolis," he said, "sets up a vibration that racks the nerves of drivers and destroys the car."[38] The Philadelphia Chamber of Commerce hoped that the new facility and its stadium would help the area to once again secure the Army-Navy Game, which had taken place at the Polo Grounds in New York for three of the previous four years. Heacock even thought that the facility might be a good place to hold the Olympics.[39]

In November of 1916, the track was reported as "favorably progressing."[40] The banking had been completed, and workers were laying the boards for the racing surface. The association expected it to be finished in 1917, but the work took longer than expected, and then stopped altogether. Charles L. Betts Jr. surmised that it could have been the fact that so many tracks were being built at the time that caused the project to come to an end, but this probably was not the case. The AAA had already committed to the Philadelphia Motor Speedway, guaranteeing it a date on the racing circuit, and giving it the right to control racing in the area. It is more likely that World War I caused the speedway's demise. When the United States

The Philadelphia Motor Speedway Association had grand plans for their speedway project, as evidenced by this rendering of the proposed clubhouse by the architectural firm of Heacock & Hokanson. The clubhouse was to contain many amenities for members of the association, such as a library, bowling alleys, and dining rooms. From *The Yearbook of the Twenty-Second Annual Architectural Exhibition* (Philadelphia: The T-Square Club and the Philadelphia Chapter of the American Institute of Architects, 1916).

declared war in 1917, men and materials suddenly became in short supply, causing construction to stall. A newspaper article from 1924 supports this observation, noting, "the war stepped in to stop operations and later the project was abandoned."[41] Subscribers, who had pledged money, began to default because they were not sure if it would ever get finished. The Philadelphia Motor Speedway Association sued some of its members in February of 1918 to obtain the money they had pledged. In March, the judge decided that the subscribers had to pay, but the war was still on, and work did not resume. In 1921, The Philadelphia Motor Speedway Association went to court to dissolve itself, and the judge appointed the association's president, William L. Ferguson, liquidating trustee. A plan was created in which the land would be divided into lots and sold, thus allowing the association to pay its debts and give its members a return on their investment. In June of 1924, the lots were auctioned. Demolition crews removed the completed sections of the speedway, and Philadelphia's hope of returning itself to a place of prominence amongst the country's premier racing venues was again brought to a halt.

Conclusion

This book has attempted to achieve several goals. A first goal was to demonstrate that the Fairmount Park Motor Race is just as important as its contemporaries such as the Vanderbilt Cup and the Grand Prize when it comes to the history of motor racing, if not more so. Although the Fairmount Park Race ultimately did not achieve the same long-term recognition as those two races, for a time, it was the finest example of road racing in the United States of America.

There are a number of reasons why the Fairmount Park Race was so successful. The course itself was spectacular. There is no question that the Fairmount Park course was the most scenic road course of the time. The cars traveled on a winding journey through the well-manicured park that took them past historic mansions and monuments, spraying fountains, remnants of the Centennial Exhibition such as Memorial Hall, and the wonderful view along the Schuylkill River. The natural grandstands such as hills, bridges and rooftops provided excellent accommodations for those who did not have grandstand seats, or who preferred to watch from a different part of the course.

The layout of the course was pioneering in its nature. The Quaker City Motor Club made a good decision in making the course shorter than most other road courses, and then it happened to be made two miles shorter by a decision of the park commissioners. The motor club realized that the shorter track enabled the spectators to see the cars come by more often. It also produced much more side-by-side action to thrill the crowds. The club also knew that a shorter course was easier to handle from a safety perspective. There was not as much area to protect, and spectators were not as spread out, making them easier to watch over. The path of the course was also a benefit. The mix of straight sections and twisting turns allowed for a spectacular contest, and challenged the drivers, unlike other tracks that relied on speed alone to provide the excitement.

Although proposed as a means of gaining support for the continuation of the event, the donation of the proceeds to charity was also a key to the success of the Fairmount Park Races. The charitable organizations benefited greatly from 1909-1911, and new fans of the sport were undoubtedly created when they attended their first race simply to support a good cause. The racing surface was always well prepared, making for great racing, and safe racing as well. The drivers were always happy with the condition of the roads, and frequently said so. Medical and police personnel were exemplary in performing their assigned tasks every year. To put it simply, the planning of the Fairmount Park Motor Races was second to none. The cooperation between the Quaker City Motor Club and the municipal government made for a perfect event, and with only a few exceptions, the spectators were well behaved and cooperative. These factors made the job considerably easier for everyone involved.

The Fairmount Park Motor Races succeeded not only because of their good planning, but also because of the dramatic action that took place on the track. The drivers always put on a good show. George Robertson captured the hearts of thousands of Philadelphians by taking the win in the inaugural event, and then came back the following year to repeat his victory. Len Zengle, the Philadelphia native, in a locally-built car, won the 1910 race to the crowd's delight in the closest finish in road racing history up to that point, beating Ralph Mulford by only six seconds in a dramatic finish that was made more exciting as both suffered tire punctures on their final lap. Then, in 1911, the hometown amateur, Erwin Bergdoll, set a furious pace and beat a field of veterans in a race that an amateur was not expected to win.

In addition to these glorious moments, many tortuous scenes were also witnessed. Ralph Mulford was a very successful driver and had a brilliant racing career. He came very close to victory at Fairmount Park, but never managed to finish first overall. Many others felt that they had the race in hand, only to suffer a mechanical problem, a tire puncture, or an accident. Unforgiving turns such as the Sweet Briar Curve, and the "dip of death" under the railroad bridge at Neill Drive, provided constant excitement and frayed nerves.

Despite the difficulty of the course, and a few dangerous turns, there was not a single death. No injury was so serious that its victim would not make a full recovery. Perhaps this is why the Fairmount Park Motor Races have been all but forgotten. Maybe Barney Oldfield was right when he said that he did not become popular until he went through a fence and killed a spectator.[1] In a time when racing drivers died in accidents with great regularity at other circuits, Fairmount Park was an oddity. A number of drivers who faced the starter in Fairmount Park died in racing accidents at other venues. The 20 year old, Tobin De Hymel, died just a few weeks after racing in the 1910 park race, in a crash at San Antonio, Texas. Louis Strang died during the 1911 Wisconsin Reliability Run. Spencer Wishart died at age 24 in the 1914 Elgin National Trophy Race, and Bob Burman was killed in an accident in Corona, California, in 1916. This is by no means a complete list, but it demonstrates the dangerous nature of the sport and the comparative safety of Fairmount Park.

This book has also attempted to place the event into the social and political atmosphere that existed in Philadelphia at the time. No event, not even a sporting event, is limited to the action that takes place in front of the spectators. The character of any sporting event is determined by a number of factors. The location, the planners, the participants, the spectators, and the venue, all contributed to make the Fairmount Park Race the success that it was. Some of those factors ultimately led to its demise. The Fairmount Park Motor Races were great sporting events, but they were also great examples of class attitudes and influence. The industrial nature of the city, and its industrial leaders, supported the idea of the race. A political machine, which was partial to industry and shared the same feeling about the event, helped to make it a reality. At the same time, the patrician influence in the Fairmount Park Commission caused the race to remain in constant jeopardy. Eventually, that influence brought the Fairmount Park Race to an end, despite its success and its perfect safety record. Dr. J. William White made it clear with his demeaning comment about the drivers that he looked down upon the race, no matter what he would have others believe. But even if we were to take Dr. White at his word; if he truly wanted to end the race in the interest of safety, he was able to do so because of the influence he carried due to his position in society and due to the similar positions of his fellow commission members.

The Fairmount Park race came to an end because a single person did not want racing to take place in the park, and that person had the social clout to guarantee that it would not continue. The impact of Dr. White on auto racing history may extend beyond Philadelphia. As racing in the park came to an end, the focus of automobile racing moved west. The Fairmount Park Race was the only major road race scheduled to take place in the East in 1912, and when that did not happen, it spelled the end of the big East Coast races. The Vanderbilt Cup and the Grand Prize moved from Savannah to Milwaukee, and then on to Santa Monica. Safety problems continued to plague West Coast and Midwestern road races, and dirt and board oval tracks grew in popularity. Unlike other cities, where safety was truly a problem, public demand and safety concerns did not end the Fairmount Park Race. We can only imagine how American automobile racing would have developed differently, had the Fairmount Park Race continued as the country's premier road racing venue.

The next best thing to the Fairmount Park Race, the Philadelphia Motor Speedway, also might have achieved similar success, if not for the interference of World War I. The speedway was a direct result of the success of the Fairmount Park Races, and its goal was to be better than Indianapolis. Philadelphia's business leaders would not settle for anything less. They had staged the best road race in the country, and they intended to have the best oval track as well.

Philadelphia's closest brush with big time automobile racing after Fairmount Park was the one-mile oval at Langhorne, Pennsylvania, about 15 miles outside of the city. In use from 1926 through the 1960s, Langhorne more closely echoed the racing that took place at Point Breeze, rather than that which took place in the park. Langhorne never approached the same level of success or the same level of importance to Philadelphians, as the Fairmount Park race had with its hundreds of thousands of spectators. None of the aspects of racing in the city, that benefited the park race, were present at Langhorne. For those who witnessed races in Fairmount Park that were on the same level as the Vanderbilt Cup and the Grand Prize, a track like

Langhorne must have been a small consolation, but Dr. White had his way. Philadelphia was no longer a major venue for American automobile racing, and the "droll city" that his biographer, Agnes Repplier, wrote about was made a little droller. The Fairmount Park Race faded into history, and in the words of Miss Repplier, "the press dropped the matter, the public forgot it, and the world moved unconcernedly on."[2]

Appendix

In the early days of automobile racing, result tables, like the ones that appear in this appendix, were published in most automotive periodicals as well as in newspapers local to the event. These tables were often presented as the "official" times, and usually included both lap times and a cumulative total. The publications almost always agreed on the cumulative totals, but the published lap times often varied, and sometimes the lap times did not add up to the given cumulative total. Circumstances at the 1909 Fairmount Park Race worsened the errors. Because of a mechanical problem with the automatic timer for the first few laps of that race, the lap times initially written on the scoreboard were three to four minutes too slow. The Quaker City Motor Club recognized the error and fixed the scoreboard by erasing the incorrect times and writing in the correct times, which had been recorded manually. When the scorers erased the incorrect times, the chalkboard became smeared with white chalk dust and the new times were difficult to read. As a result, some publications printed the old, incorrect times, and others printed a mix of incorrect times and corrected ones. No published table was completely correct.

To correct errors in the published results, I began by using the tables that appeared in *Motor Age* as a starting point. I recalculated the lap times to identify inconsistencies with the cumulative totals. When I discovered errors, I compared the table with existing photographs of the scoreboards, tables in other periodicals such as *The Automobile* and *Horseless Age*, and those in local newspapers, in order to find the correct lap times that would add up to the official cumulative totals. The resulting tables are a compilation of many sources, and I believe them to be the most accurate representation of what actually occurred. They are certainly more reliable than any individual table published at the time of the races.

Appendix

1908 Table of Results

CAR & DRIVER	1	2	3	4	5	6	7	8	9	10	11
#10 Locomobile, d Robertson	0:09:52	0:19:36 0:09:44	0:29:07 0:09:31	0:38:07 0:09:00	0:48:04 0:09:57	0:57:31 0:09:27	1:06:55 0:09:24	1:16:26 0:09:31	1:25:48 0:09:22	1:35:16 0:09:28	1:44:33 0:09:17
#14 Acme d Patchke	0:10:19	0:20:26 0:10:07	0:30:32 0:10:06	0:40:43 0:10:11	0:51:56 0:11:13	1:01:32 0:09:36	1:11:32 0:10:00	1:21:31 0:09:59	1:32:26 0:10:55	1:41:37 0:09:11	1:51:39 0:10:02
#17 Lozier d Mulford	0:14:41	0:24:04 0:09:23	0:33:29 0:09:25	0:42:48 0:09:19	0:52:44 0:09:56	1:01:37 0:08:53	1:11:05 0:09:28	1:20:03 0:08:58	1:31:04 0:11:01	1:39:36 0:08:32	1:49:13 0:09:37
#3 Peerless d Mauche	0:09:57	0:24:24 0:14:27	0:34:23 0:09:59	0:44:31 0:10:08	0:56:51 0:12:20	1:05:14 0:08:23	1:15:04 0:09:50	1:26:11 0:11:07	1:36:37 0:10:26	1:47:14 0:10:37	1:57:41 0:10:27
#9 Locomobile d Florida	0:09:59	0:19:37 0:09:38	0:29:11 0:09:34	0:38:45 0:09:34	0:48:20 0:09:35	0:57:51 0:09:31	1:07:25 0:09:34	1:17:04 0:09:39	1:26:37 0:09:33	1:36:14 0:09:37	1:45:57 0:09:43
#2 Apperson d Davis	0:10:28	0:19:39 0:09:11	0:29:11 0:09:32	0:38:41 0:09:30	0:48:15 0:09:34	0:59:36 0:11:21	1:11:05 0:11:29	1:20:34 0:09:29	1:29:56 0:09:22	1:39:30 0:09:34	1:48:52 0:09:22
#11 American Locomotive d L. Bergdoll	0:10:03	0:20:54 0:10:51	0:29:41 0:08:47	0:39:40 0:09:59	0:49:37 0:09:57	0:59:41 0:10:04	1:09:47 0:10:06	1:19:54 0:10:07	1:30:02 0:10:08	1:40:03 0:10:01	1:49:50 0:09:47
#12 Palmer & Singer d Wallace	0:09:27	0:18:42 0:09:15	0:27:58 0:09:16	0:37:16 0:09:18	0:46:43 0:09:27	0:55:15 0:08:32	1:05:39 0:10:24	1:21:42 0:16:03	1:30:07 0:08:25	1:39:35 0:09:28	1:48:58 0:09:23
#6 Studebaker d Yerger	0:12:40	0:22:45 0:10:05	0:33:09 0:10:24	0:43:32 0:10:23	0:54:23 0:10:51	1:04:27 0:10:04	1:14:50 0:10:23	1:25:29 0:10:39	1:35:38 0:10:09	1:46:03 0:10:25	1:56:12 0:10:09
#16 Pennsylvania d Zengle	0:10:08	0:20:10 0:10:02	0:30:07 0:09:57	0:40:47 0:10:40	0:51:56 0:11:09	1:02:46 0:10:50	1:12:54 0:10:08	1:28:56 0:16:02	1:40:09 0:11:13	1:59:18 0:19:09	2:10:25 0:11:07
#7 Chadwick d Harkins	0:11:33	0:23:23 0:11:50	0:33:16 0:09:53	0:43:18 0:10:02	0:53:53 0:10:35	1:11:40 0:17:47	1:29:28 0:17:48	1:39:50 0:10:22	1:49:55 0:10:05	2:00:06 0:10:11	2:29:02 0:28:56
#5 Thomas d Salzman	0:08:57	0:17:37 0:08:40	0:26:32 0:08:55	0:38:47 0:12:15	0:47:32 0:08:45	0:56:22 0:08:50	Out (Crankshaft)				
#8 Stoddard-Dayton d Ireland	0:10:29	0:20:45 0:10:16	0:31:00 0:10:15	0:41:21 0:10:21	0:53:21 0:12:00	1:43:14 0:49:53	Out (Pump Gear)				
#4 Pullman d La Roche	0:10:44	0:24:34 0:13:50	0:34:23 0:09:49	0:47:20 0:12:57	Out (Tire)						
#1 Maxwell d Bitner	0:11:31	0:22:42 0:11:11	0:33:46 0:11:04	Out (Crankshaft)							
#15 Lozier d Michener	0:09:47	Out (Car Overturned)									

1908 Table of Results *cont.*

12	13	14	15	16	17	18	19	20	21	22	23	24	25	Total
1:54:12	2:03:43	2:13:09	2:22:28	2:32:11	2:46:31	2:55:53	3:05:14	3:14:41	3:24:06	3:33:30	3:43:15	3:52:52	4:02:30	4:02:30
0:09:39	0:09:31	0:09:26	0:09:19	0:09:43	0:14:20	0:09:22	0:09:21	0:09:27	0:09:25	0:09:24	0:09:45	0:09:37	0:09:38	
2:01:36	2:11:38	2:21:37	2:31:31	2:41:27	2:51:26	3:02:38	3:12:49	3:23:15	3:33:33	3:43:49	3:54:09	4:04:26	4:14:54	4:14:54
0:09:57	0:10:02	0:09:59	0:09:54	0:09:56	0:09:59	0:11:12	0:10:11	0:10:26	0:10:18	0:10:16	0:10:20	0:10:17	0:10:28	
1:58:51	2:08:32	2:18:08	2:31:58	2:42:12	2:51:47	3:01:30	3:11:13	3:26:45	3:36:21	3:45:54	3:55:30	4:06:55	4:17:26	4:17:26
0:09:38	0:09:41	0:09:36	0:13:50	0:10:14	0:09:35	0:09:43	0:09:43	0:15:32	0:09:36	0:09:33	0:09:36	0:11:25	0:10:31	
2:08:02	2:18:17	2:26:46	2:38:41	2:49:08	3:01:22	3:11:20	3:21:25	3:31:29	3:41:29	3:51:29	4:01:28	4:11:35	4:21:26	4:21:26
0:10:21	0:10:15	0:08:29	0:11:55	0:10:27	0:12:14	0:09:58	0:10:05	0:10:04	0:10:00	0:10:00	0:09:59	0:10:07	0:09:51	
1:55:31	2:05:13	2:14:59	2:24:46	2:34:36	2:46:21	2:56:53	3:05:44	3:15:22	3:27:39	3:37:37	4:03:30	4:14:56	Running	
0:09:34	0:09:42	0:09:46	0:09:47	0:09:50	0:11:45	0:10:32	0:08:51	0:09:38	0:12:17	0:09:58	0:25:53	0:11:26		
1:58:23	2:07:50	2:17:20	2:26:46	2:39:11	2:48:46	2:58:17	3:07:50	3:17:36	3:27:59	Out (Engine)				
0:09:31	0:09:27	0:09:30	0:09:26	0:12:25	0:09:35	0:09:31	0:09:33	0:09:46	0:10:23					
1:59:54	2:09:53	2:19:59	2:29:57	2:40:00	2:49:55	2:59:58	3:10:01	3:20:00	Out (Cylinder)					
0:10:04	0:09:59	0:10:06	0:09:58	0:10:03	0:09:55	0:10:03	0:10:03	0:09:59						
1:58:23	2:07:48	2:26:32	2:36:10	2:45:33	2:54:31	3:04:15	3:13:41	3:27:59	Out (Steering Gear)					
0:09:25	0:09:25	0:18:44	0:09:38	0:09:23	0:08:58	0:09:44	0:09:26	0:14:18						
2:06:19	2:16:29	2:59:23	3:09:30	3:19:49	3:30:02	3:45:14	3:55:43	Running						
0:10:07	0:10:10	0:42:54	0:10:07	0:10:19	0:10:13	0:15:12	0:10:29							
Out (Engine)														
2:38:58	Out (Tire)													
0:09:56														

APPENDIX

1909 Table of Results

CAR & DRIVER	1	2	3	4	5	6	7	8	9	10	11
#4 Simplex d Robertson	0:09:18	0:17:40 0:08:22	0:25:24 0:07:44	0:33:55 0:08:31	0:42:25 0:08:30	0:50:57 0:08:32	0:59:31 0:08:34	1:08:09 0:08:38	1:16:55 0:08:46	1:25:31 0:08:36	1:35:17 0:09:46
#5 Chalmers-Detroit d Dingley	0:10:12	0:18:00 0:07:48	0:26:57 0:08:57	0:36:28 0:09:31	0:44:47 0:08:19	0:53:46 0:08:59	1:02:50 0:09:04	1:11:50 0:09:00	1:21:01 0:09:11	1:29:56 0:08:55	1:38:54 0:08:58
#8 Apperson d Harding	0:13:18	0:23:06 0:09:48	0:32:55 0:09:49	0:41:27 0:08:32	0:50:38 0:09:11	0:59:45 0:09:07	1:08:51 0:09:06	1:18:02 0:09:11	1:27:35 0:09:33	1:36:33 0:08:58	1:45:30 0:08:57
#18 Chadwick d Parkin	0:09:13	0:18:12 0:08:59	0:29:11 0:10:59	0:40:01 0:10:50	0:49:04 0:09:03	0:58:05 0:09:01	1:07:10 0:09:05	1:16:17 0:09:07	1:25:14 0:08:57	1:34:11 0:08:57	1:43:05 0:08:54
#17 Isotta d Strang	0:09:30	0:18:38 0:09:08	0:27:40 0:09:02	0:37:00 0:09:20	0:46:29 0:09:29	0:55:39 0:09:10	1:05:10 0:09:31	1:14:25 0:09:15	1:23:45 0:09:20	1:32:59 0:09:14	1:42:16 0:09:17
#10 Palmer & Singer d Wallace	0:09:13	0:18:18 0:09:05	0:28:28 0:10:10	0:41:30 0:13:02	0:51:05 0:09:35	1:00:20 0:09:15	1:09:41 0:09:21	1:19:18 0:09:37	1:28:49 0:09:31	1:38:24 0:09:35	1:48:15 0:09:51
#3 Benz d Howard	0:10:36	0:23:32 0:12:56	0:51:06 0:27:34	1:00:54 0:09:48	1:10:46 0:09:52	1:20:28 0:09:42	1:29:47 0:09:19	1:39:41 0:09:54	1:49:37 0:09:56	2:00:06 0:10:29	2:08:33 0:08:27
#1 Simplex d Betz	0:09:36	0:18:41 0:09:05	0:27:50 0:09:09	0:36:53 0:09:03	0:46:30 0:09:37	0:55:06 0:08:36	1:04:12 0:09:06	1:13:14 0:09:02	1:22:22 0:09:08	1:32:32 0:10:10	1:40:26 0:07:54
#2 American d Drach	0:08:59	0:17:40 0:08:41	0:26:10 0:08:30	0:35:25 0:09:15	0:48:37 0:13:12	0:57:51 0:09:14	1:06:57 0:09:06	1:16:06 0:09:09	1:25:11 0:09:05	1:34:18 0:09:07	1:43:25 0:09:07
#9 Buick d Burman	0:20:20	0:28:27 0:08:07	0:36:42 0:08:15	0:45:05 0:08:23	0:53:26 0:08:21	1:02:02 0:08:36	1:10:27 0;08;25	1:54:40 0·44·13	2:03:21 0:08:41	2:11:43 0:08:22	2:26:15 0.14.32
#16 Chadwick d Zengle	0:08:49	0:17:33 0:08:44	0:26:17 0:08:44	0:35:56 0:09:39	0:43:37 0:07:41	0:51:45 0:08:08	1:00:55 0:09:10	1:09:40 0:08:45	1:18:27 0:08:47	1:27:00 0:08:33	1:35:31 0:08:31
#23 Selden d Young	0:45:48	0:59:15 0:13:27	1:10:52 0:11:37	1:20:25 0:09:33	1:40:22 0:19:57	1:50:48 0:10:26	2:01:12 0:10:24	2:13:24 0:12:12	2:23:58 0:10:34	2:34:16 0:10:18	2:44:41 0:10:25
#15 Thomas d L. Bergdoll	0:09:24	0:18:28 0:09:04	0:27:45 0:09:17	0:37:16 0:09:31	0:46:59 0:09:43	0:56:27 0:09:28	1:07:13 0:10:46	1:22:15 0:15:02	1:32:39 0:10:24	1:43:04 0:10:25	2:26:52 0:43:48
#13 Buick d Chevrolet	0:08:40	0:17:02 0:08:22	0:25:21 0:08:19	1:07:56 0:42:35	1:16:59 0:09:03	1:26:12 0:09:13	1:35:19 0:09:07	1:44:19 0:09:00	1:53:30 0:09:11	2:02:35 0:09:05	2:11:40 0:09:05
#7 Acme d Leinau	0:14:53	0:27:44 0:12:51	0:53:56 0:26:12	1:10:06 0:16:10	1:20:47 0:10:41	1:29:56 0:09:09	1:58:12 0:28:16	3:05:15 1:07:03	Out (Engine)		
#12 American d Hayes	0:09:03	0:19:42 0:10:39	0:29:15 0:09:33	0:38:39 0:09:24	0:49:38 0:10:59	0:59:17 0:09:39	1:09:11 0:09:54	Out (Crash)			
#19 Chalmers-Detroit d Lorimer	0:09:40	0:18:31 0:08:51	0:27:36 0:09:05	0:45:38 0:18:02	Out (Broken Frame)						
#6 Thomas d Haupt	0:14:59	0:36:20 0:21:21	0:47:19 0:10:59	Out (Engine)							
#20 Welch d E. Bergdoll	0:10:44	0:19:43 0:08:59	Out (Engine)								
#14 Columbia d Coffey	0:12:47	0:31:02 0:18:15	Out (Collision)								
#22 Lozier d Seymour	Did Not Start (Water Pump)										
#11 Alco d Grant	Did Not Start (Steering)										

Appendix 195

1909 Table of Results *cont.*

12	13	14	15	16	17	18	19	20	21	22	23	24	25	Total
1:43:52	1:52:23	2:01:00	2:11:45	2:20:30	2:29:08	2:37:52	2:46:32	2:55:04	3:03:41	3:12:19	3:21:07	3:29:55	3:38:58	3:38:58
0:08:35	0:08:31	0:08:37	0:10:45	0:08:45	0:08:38	0:08:44	0:08:40	0:08:32	0:08:37	0:08:38	0:08:48	0:08:48	0:09:03	
1:47:57	1:56:53	2:05:54	2:14:52	2:23:49	2:32:48	2:41:49	2:50:41	2:59:46	3:08:34	3:17:30	3:26:23	3:35:24	3:44:20	3:44:20
0:09:03	0:08:56	0:09:01	0:08:58	0:08:57	0:08:59	0:09:01	0:08:52	0:09:05	0:08:48	0:08:56	0:08:53	0:09:01	0:08:56	
1:54:33	2:03:29	2:13:10	2:21:17	2:30:03	2:38:53	2:47:54	2:58:34	3:07:38	3:16:38	3:26:34	3:34:26	3:43:13	3:52:17	3:52:17
0:09:03	0:08:56	0:09:41	0:08:07	0:08:46	0:08:50	0:09:01	0:10:40	0:09:04	0:09:00	0:09:56	0:07:52	0:08:47	0:09:04	
1:51:56	2:00:47	2:09:45	2:18:53	2:33:08	2:42:00	2:50:50	3:00:06	3:10:39	3:19:38	3:28:33	3:37:33	3:46:30	3:55:31	3:55:31
0:08:51	0:08:51	0:08:58	0:09:08	0:14:15	0:08:52	0:08:50	0:09:16	0:10:33	0:08:59	0:08:55	0:09:00	0:08:57	0:09:01	
1:51:37	2:00:45	2:10:09	2:19:27	2:28:38	2:37:53	2:47:01	3:00:48	3:10:04	3:19:33	3:28:57	3:38:09	3:47:30	3:56:54	3:56:54
0:09:21	0:09:08	0:09:24	0:09:18	0:09:11	0:09:15	0:09:08	0:13:47	0:09:16	0:09:29	0:09:24	0:09:12	0:09:21	0:09:24	
1:57:28	2:07:23	2:24:20	2:33:39	2:42:32	2:51:32	3:02:37	3:11:31	3:20:20	3:29:09	3:37:59	3:46:41	3:57:15	Running	
0:09:13	0:09:55	0:16:57	0:09:19	0:08:53	0:09:00	0:11:05	0:08:54	0:08:49	0:08:49	0:08:50	0:08:42	0:10:34		
2:21:04	2:30:31	2:40:31	2:50:30	3:00:24	3:10:22	3:20:20	3:30:19	3:40:25	3:50:31	Running				
0:12:31	0:09:27	0:10:00	0:09:59	0:09:54	0:09:58	0:09:58	0:09:59	0:10:06	0:10:06					
1:49:50	1:58:51	2:07:51	2:16:51	2:36:01	2:44:51	2:53:40	3:02:30	3:11:30	Out (Broken Pump)					
0:09:24	0:09:01	0:09:00	0:09:00	0:19:10	0:08:50	0:08:49	0:08:50	0:09:00						
1:55:10	2:04:22	2:21:54	3:09:49	3:19:19	3:28:46	3:38:10	3:47:30	3:57:01	Out (Auxiliary Gas Tank)					
0:11:45	0:09:12	0:17:32	0:47:55	0:09:30	0:09:27	0:09:24	0:09:20	0:09:31						
2:34:54	2:43:24	2:55:44	3:04:36	3:13:32	3:25:49	Out (Radiator)								
0:08:39	0:08:30	0:12:20	0:08:52	0:08:56	0:12:17									
1:45:10	1:54:41	2:38:00	2:51:56	3:02:07	Running									
0:09:39	0:09:31	0:43:19	0:13:56	0:10:11										
2:55:03	3:05:49	3:21:50	3:31:11	3:40:28	3:51:42	Running								
0:10:22	0:10:46	0:16:01	0:09:21	0:09:17	0:11:14									
2:43:21	Out (Water Circulation)													
0:16:29														
Out (Inlet Valve)														

APPENDIX

1910 Table of Results

CAR & DRIVER	1	2	3	4	5	6	7	8	9	10	11
Division 6C: Piston Displacement of 601 to 750 Cubic Inches											
#12 Chadwick		0:17:07	0:25:45	0:34:07	0:42:20	0:50:46	0:58:59	1:07:15	1:17:00	1:25:17	1:33:29
d Zengle	0:08:43	0:08:24	0:08:38	0:08:22	0:08:13	0:08:26	0:08:13	0:08:16	0:09:45	0:08:17	0:08:12
#5 Benz		0:17:07	0:25:23	0:33:39	0:41:39	0:49:41	0:57:48	1:06:03	1:14:12	1:22:25	1:30:35
d E. Bergdoll	0:08:50	0:08:17	0:08:16	0:08:16	0:08:00	0:08:02	0:08:07	0:08:15	0:08:09	0:08:13	0:08:10
#25 Chadwick		0:16:48	0:25:07	0:33:18	0:41:30	Out (Crash)					
d Mitchell	0:08:10	0:08:38	0:08:19	0:08:11	0:08:12						
#13 Simplex		0:19:26	0:28:11	Out (Cracked Cylinder)							
d Mullen	0:09:49	0:09:37	0:08:45								
#22 Simplex		0:17:33	Out (Crash)								
d Beardsley	0:08:45	0:08:48									
#19 Simplex d Betz	Out (Crankshaft)										

CAR & DRIVER	1	2	3	4	5	6	7	8	9	10	11
Division 5C: Piston Displacement of 451 to 600 Cubic Inches											
#4 Lozier		0:16:53	0:25:17	0:33:40	0:41:58	0:50:22	0:58:39	1:06:54	1:15:07	1:23:20	1:31:33
d Mulford	0:08:32	0:08:21	0:08:24	0:08:23	0:08:18	0:08:24	0:08:17	0:08:15	0:08:13	0:08:13	0:08:13
#29 Stoddard-Dayton		0:17:07	0:25:32	0:34:17	0:42:39	0:51:14	0:59:36	1:08:04	1:16:26	1:24:47	1:33:10
d De Hymel	0:08:25	0:08:42	0:08:25	0:08:45	0:08:22	0:08:35	0:08:22	0:08:28	0:08:22	0:08:21	0:08:23
#20 Mercedes		0:17:58	0:26:43	0:35:35	0:44:25	0:53:36	1:02:22	1:11:09	1:19:50	1:28:34	1:37:37
d Jagersberger	0:08:54	0:09:04	0:08:45	0:08:52	0:08:50	0:09:11	0:08:46	0:08:47	0:08:41	0:08:44	0:09:03
#9 Apperson		0:19:14	0:28:31	0:37:54	0:47:11	0:56:30	1:05:39	1:14:07	1:24:05	1:34:30	1:43:50
d Davis	0:09:44	0:09:30	0:09:17	0:09:23	0:09:17	0:09:19	0:09:09	0:08:28	0:09:58	0:10:25	0:09:20
#1 Apperson		0:18:47	Out (Stripped Gear)								
d Hanshue	0:09:31	0:09:16									
#7 Stoddard-Dayton		0:23:47	Out (Engine)								
d Harding	0:08:47	0:15:00									

CAR & DRIVER	1	2	3	4	5	6	7	8	9	10	11
Division 4C: Piston Displacement of 301 to 450 Cubic Inches											
#3 National		0:17:46	0:26:26	0:35:07	0:43:54	0:52:47	1:01:33	1:10:16	1:19:10	1:28:23	1:37:19
d Aitken	0:09:01	0:08:45	0:08:40	0:08:41	0:08:47	0:08:53	0:08:46	0:08:43	0:08:54	0:09:13	0:08:56
#14 Jackson		0:17:58	0:26:58	0:36:22	0:45:31	0:55:04	1:04:10	1:13:30	1:22:36	1:31:51	1:40:58
d Cobe	0:09:06	0:08:52	0:09:00	0:09:24	0:09:09	0:09:33	0:09:06	0:09:20	0:09:06	0:09:15	0:09:07
#23 Wescott		0:18:37	0:27:27	0:36:50	0:46:01	0:55:07	1:04:09	1:13:12	1:22:14	1:31:12	1:40:07
d Knight	0:09:11	0:09:26	0:08:50	0:09:23	0:09:11	0:09:06	0:09:02	0:09:03	0:09:02	0:08:58	0:08:55
#11 Marmon		0:21:20	0:29:55	0:40:02	0:48:22	0:57:15	1:06:04	1:14:50	1:23:32	1:32:11	1:41:53
d Harroun	0:12:05	0:09:15	0:08:35	0:10:07	0:08:20	0:08:53	0:08:49	0:08:46	0:08:42	0:08:39	0:09:42
#17 Benz		0:28:25	0:37:22	0:46:00	0:54:40	1:03:14	1:11:51	1:20:28	1:29:12	1:37:48	1:46:23
d Haupt	0:20:02	0:08:23	0:08:57	0:08:38	0:08:40	0:08:34	0:08:37	0:08:37	0:08:44	0:08:36	0:08:35
#16 National		0:17:49	0:26:42	0:37:49	0:47:08	1:00:51	1:12:19	1:21:01	1:29:38	1:38:16	1:47:01
d Wilcox	0:08:54	0:08:55	0:08:53	0:11:07	0:09:19	0:13:43	0:11:28	0:08:42	0:08:37	0:08:38	0:08:45
#26 Benz		0:33:53	0:43:36	0:53:03	1:04:34	1:15:58	1:25:38	1:35:23	1:49:57	Out (Ignition)	
d Hearne	0:08:58	0:24:55	0:09:43	0:09:27	0:11:31	0:11:24	0:09:40	0:09:45	0:14:34		
#30 Benz d C. Bergdoll	Out (Lost Gas Cap)										

Appendix 197

1910 Table of Results *cont.*

12	13	14	15	16	17	18	19	20	21	22	23	24	25	Total

Division 6C: Piston Displacement of 601 to 750 Cubic Inches

1:41:42 1:49:55 1:58:10 2:06:18 2:14:26 2:22:23 2:30:37 2:38:46 2:46:50 2:54:57 3:03:09 3:11:22 3:19:31 3:29:07 3:29:07.88
0:08:13 0:08:13 0:08:15 0:08:08 0:08:08 0:07:57 0:08:14 0:08:09 0:08:04 0:08:07 0:08:12 0:08:13 0:08:09 0:09:36

1:38:40 1:47:01 1:55:17 2:03:32 Out (Oil Feed)
0:08:05 0:08:21 0:08:16 0:08:15

12	13	14	15	16	17	18	19	20	21	22	23	24	25	Total

Division 5C: Piston Displacement of 451 to 600 Cubic Inches

1:39:45 1:47:57 1:56:09 2:04:24 2:12:39 2:20:51 2:29:08 2:37:26 2:46:53 2:55:08 3:03:16 3:11:23 3:19:22 3:29:13 3:29:13.30
0:08:12 0:08:12 0:08:12 0:08:15 0:08:15 0:08:12 0:08:17 0:08:18 0:09:27 0:08:15 0:08:08 0:08:07 0:07:59 0:09:51

1:46:42 1:54:47 2:06:09 2:14:51 2:23:07 2:31:53 2:40:09 2:48:25 2:56:41 3:04:53 3:13:02 3:21:12 3:29:24 3:37:42 3:37:42.95
0:13:32 0:08:05 0:11:22 0:08:42 0:08:16 0:08:46 0:08:16 0:08:16 0:08:16 0:08:12 0:08:09 0:08:10 0:08:12 0:08:18

1:48:22 1:56:58 2:05:38 2:14:17 2:22:53 2:31:23 2:39:51 2:48:44 3:00:08 3:08:55 3:17:30 3:26:05 3:34:41 3:43:18 3:43:18.74
0:10:45 0:08:36 0:08:40 0:08:39 0:08:36 0:08:30 0:08:28 0:08:53 0:11:24 0:08:47 0:08:35 0:08:35 0:08:36 0:08:37

1:52:58 2:02:08 2:11:20 2:20:36 2:30:03 2:41:50 2:51:10 3:08:15 3:17:25 3:26:39 3:36:01 3:45:19 3:54:29 4:03:42 4:03:42.05
0:09:08 0:09:10 0:09:12 0:09:16 0:09:27 0:11:47 0:09:20 0:17:05 0:09:10 0:09:14 0:09:22 0:09:18 0:09:10 0:09:13

12	13	14	15	16	17	18	19	20	21	22	23	24	25	Total

Division 4C: Piston Displacement of 301 to 450 Cubic Inches

1:46:13 1:55:02 2:03:57 2:12:57 2:21:47 2:30:36 2:39:27 2:48:22 2:57:13 3:06:11 3:15:16 3:24:13 3:33:18 3:42:20 3:42:20.75
0:08:54 0:08:49 0:08:55 0:09:00 0:08:50 0:08:49 0:08:51 0:08:55 0:08:51 0:08:58 0:09:05 0:08:57 0:09:05 0:09:02

1:50:01 1:59:15 2:08:12 2:17:07 2:25:04 2:35:04 2:43:59 2:52:59 3:01:56 3:10:50 3:19:42 3:28:37 3:37:28 3:46:13 3:46:13.16
0:09:03 0:09:14 0:08:57 0:08:55 0:07:57 0:10:00 0:08:55 0:09:00 0:08:57 0:08:54 0:08:52 0:08:55 0:08:51 0:08:45

1:49:09 1:58:06 2:07:05 2:16:01 2:24:55 2:35:38 2:44:36 2:55:14 3:04:18 3:13:15 3:22:14 3:31:09 3:40:08 3:52:44 3:52:44.87
0:09:02 0:08:57 0:08:59 0:08:56 0:08:54 0:10:43 0:08:58 0:10:38 0:09:04 0:08:57 0:08:59 0:08:55 0:08:59 0:12:36

1:50:31 1:59:29 2:31:50 2:41:30 2:51:08 3:00:38 3:12:15 3:22:04 3:31:39 3:41:25 3:50:55 4:00:28 Running
0:08:38 0:08:58 0:32:21 0:09:40 0:09:38 0:09:30 0:11:37 0:09:49 0:09:35 0:09:46 0:09:30 0:09:33

1:55:06 2:03:51 2:12:33 2:21:21 2:30:23 2:39:02 2:47:38 2:56:09 Out (Shifting)
0:08:43 0:08:45 0:08:42 0:08:48 0:09:02 0:08:39 0:08:36 0:08:31

1:55:43 2:06:31 2:15:06 2:23:35 2:32:05 2:40:44 2:50:39 Out (Radiator)
0:08:42 0:10:48 0:08:35 0:08:29 0:08:30 0:08:39 0:09:55

And see next page

1910 Table of Results *cont.*

CAR & DRIVER	1	2	3	4	5	6	7	8	9	10	11
	Division 3C: Piston Displacement of 231 to 300 Cubic Inches
#10 Pullman		0:19:12	0:28:38	0:37:59	0:47:19	0:56:47	1:06:00	1:15:05	1:24:03	1:33:01	1:42:00
d Gellard	0:09:43	0:09:29	0:09:26	0:09:21	0:09:20	0:09:28	0:09:13	0:09:05	0:08:58	0:08:58	0:08:59
#15 Mercer		0:20:57	0:30:39	0:41:24	0:51:30	1:01:34	1:11:41	1:21:41	1:31:38	1:41:25	1:51:00
d Frey	0:10:12	0:10:45	0:09:42	0:10:45	0:10:06	0:10:04	0:10:07	0:10:00	0:09:57	0:09:47	0:09:35
#32 Otto		0:23:05	0:33:08	0:43:05	0:53:00	1:07:47	1:17:52	1:27:44	1:37:41	1:51:03	2:01:06
d Yerger	0:12:57	0:10:08	0:10:03	0:09:57	0:09:55	0:14:47	0:10:05	0:09:52	0:09:57	0:13:22	0:10:03
#28 Marmon		0:17:43	0:26:15	0:35:04	0:43:58	0:52:45	1:01:29	1:10:08	1:18:46	1:27:22	1:36:15
d Dawson	0:08:43	0:09:00	0:08:32	0:08:49	0:08:54	0:08:47	0:08:44	0:08:39	0:08:38	0:08:36	0:08:53
#31 Corbin		0:19:17	0:30:27	Out (Magneto)							
d Matson	0:09:25	0:09:52	0:11:10								
#8 Pullman	Out (Pump Shaft)										
d Hardesty	0:14:49										

CAR & DRIVER	1	2	3	4	5	6	7	8	9	10	11
	Division 2C-Piston Displacement of 161 to 230 Cubic Inches
#21 Abbott-Detroit		0:22:23	0:33:10	0:44:00	0:54:43	1:05:25	1:16:07	1:26:41	1:37:18	1:47:40	1:58:18
d Padula	0:11:28	0:10:55	0:10:47	0:10:50	0:10:43	0:10:42	0:10:42	0:10:34	0:10:37	0:10:22	0:10:38
#2 Abbott-Detroit		0:19:53	0:29:46	0:39:39	0:49:33	0:59:32	1:09:29	1:19:30	1:29:24	1:39:18	1:49:22
d Mortimer Roberts	0:10:43	0:09:10	0:09:53	0:09:53	0:09:54	0:09:59	0:09:57	0:10:01	0:09:54	0:09:54	0:10:04
#24 Ford		0:19:54	0:29:06	0:39:14	0:55:21	1:04:46	1:14:16	1:23:41	1:55:22	2:04:50	2:14:27
d Kulick	0:09:47	0:10:07	0:09:12	0:10:08	0:16:07	0:09:25	0:09:30	0:09:25	0:31:41	0:09:28	0:09:37
#18 Cole		0:20:07	0:29:24	0:40:01	0:50:03	1:00:02	1:10:05	1:20:03	1:29:52	1:39:54	1:49:43
d H. Endicott	0:09:52	0:10:15	0:09:17	0:10:37	0:10:02	0:09:59	0:10:03	0:09:58	0:09:49	0:10:02	0:09:49
#27 Cole		0:20:54	Out (Steering Gear)								
d B. Endicott	0:10:27	0:10:27									
#6 Abbott-Detroit		0:30:20	Out (Ignition)								
d Montague Roberts	0:11:42	0:18:38									

Appendix 199

1910 Table of Results *cont.*

12	13	14	15	16	17	18	19	20	21	22	23	24	25	Total

Division 3C: Piston Displacement of 231 to 300 Cubic Inches

12	13	14	15	16	17	18	19	20	21	22	23	24	25	Total
1:50:53	1:59:49	2:09:54	2:19:06	2:28:22	2:37:49	2:47:27	2:57:05	3:06:32	3:16:10	3:25:46	3:36:40	3:46:59	3:57:04	3:57:04
0:08:53	0:08:56	0:10:05	0:09:12	0:09:16	0:09:27	0:09:38	0:09:38	0:09:27	0:09:38	0:09:36	0:10:54	0:10:19	0:10:05	
2:00:34	2:10:07	2:19:39	2:29:08	2:41:43	2:51:18	3:00:51	3:10:20	3:19:56	3:29:36	3:39:11	3:48:49	3:58:22	Running	
0:09:34	0:09:33	0:09:32	0:09:29	0:12:35	0:09:35	0:09:33	0:09:29	0:09:36	0:09:40	0:09:35	0:09:38	0:09:33		
2:11:08	2:21:10	2:31:13	2:43:26	2:53:41	3:03:42	3:13:52	3:25:09	3:35:10	3:45:09	3:55:18	Running			
0:10:02	0:10:02	0:10:03	0:12:13	0:10:15	0:10:01	0:10:10	0:11:17	0:10:01	0:09:59	0:10:09				
1:44:59	Out (Broken Axle)													
0:08:44														

12	13	14	15	16	17	18	19	20	21	22	23	24	25	Total

Division 2C- Piston Displacement of 161 to 230 Cubic Inches

12	13	14	15	16	17	18	19	20	21	22	23	24	25	Total
2:08:49	2:19:17	2:29:53	2:40:25	2:52:31	3:03:05	3:13:25	3:24:03	3:34:27	3:44:50	3:57:27	Running			
0:10:31	0:10:28	0:10:36	0:10:32	0:12:06	0:10:34	0:10:20	0:10:38	0:10:24	0:10:23	0:12:37				
1:59:19	2:09:13	2:19:13	2:29:08	2:39:10	2:49:04	2:59:06	3:09:06	3:19:05	Out (Threw Wheel)					
0:09:57	0:09:54	0:10:00	0:09:55	0:10:02	0:09:54	0:10:02	0:10:00	0:09:59						
2:23:57	2:33:27	2:42:55	2:52:51	3:04:22	3:17:05	3:26:40	3:36:06	3:45:46	Disqualified					
0:09:30	0:09:30	0:09:28	0:09:56	0:11:31	0:12:43	0:09:35	0:09:26	0:09:40						
1:59:52	2:10:57	2:23:19	2:31:43	2:42:07	2:52:58	3:13:25	Out (Broken Spring Leaf)							
0:10:09	0:11:05	0:12:22	0:08:24	0:10:24	0:10:51	0:20:27								

Appendix

1911 Table of Results

CAR & DRIVER	1	2	3	4	5	6	7	8	9	10	11
Division 6C: Piston Displacement of 601 to 750 Cubic Inches- Non Stock												
#8 Benz d E. Bergdoll	0:07:34	0:15:02 0:07:28	0:22:41 0:07:39	0:30:28 0:07:47	0:38:19 0:07:51	0:46:02 0:07:43	0:53:30 0:07:28	1:01:06 0:07:36	1:08:48 0:07:42	1:16:47 0:07:59	1:24:33 0:07:46
#15 Fiat d Betz	0:07:52	0:15:41 0:07:49	Out (Connecting Rod)								
Division 5C: Piston Displacement of 451 to 600 Cubic Inches- Non Stock												
#17 Mercedes d Wishart	0:07:52	0:15:40 0:07:48	0:23:30 0:07:50	0:31:26 0:07:56	0:39:19 0:07:53	0:47:12 0:07:53	0:55:06 0:07:54	1:03:02 0:07:56	1:10:57 0:07:55	1:19:37 0:08:40	1:27:29 0:07:52
#3 Lozier d Mulford	0:07:55	0:15:47 0:07:52	0:23:40 0:07:53	0:31:34 0:07:54	0:39:30 0:07:56	0:47:32 0:08:02	0:55:23 0:07:51	1:03:13 0:07:50	1:10:57 0:07:44	1:18:48 0:07:51	1:26:36 0:07:48
#2 National d Zengle	0:07:51	0:15:40 0:07:49	0:27:43 0:12:03	0:35:38 0:07:55	0:43:34 0:07:56	0:51:27 0:07:53	0:59:15 0:07:48	1:07:03 0:07:48	1:14:55 0:07:52	1:22:59 0:08:04	1:30:55 0:07:56
#9 Lozier d Grant	0:08:17	0:16:25 0:08:08	0:24:34 0:08:09	0:32:41 0:08:07	0:40:51 0:08:10	0:48:58 0:08:07	0:57:02 0:08:04	1:05:04 0:08:02	1:13:08 0:08:04	1:21:13 0:08:05	1:29:43 0:08:30
#18 Mercedes d Wallace	0:08:27	0:16:41 0:08:14	0:24:59 0:08:18	0:33:19 0:08:20	0:41:31 0:08:12	0:49:44 0:08:13	0:57:57 0:08:13	1:06:07 0:08:10	1:14:20 0:08:13	1:24:04 0:09:44	1:32:29 0:08:25
Division 4C: Piston Displacement of 301 to 450 Cubic Inches-Non Stock												
#16 National d Disbrow	0:08:30	0:16:46 0:08:16	0:24:58 0:08:12	0:33:12 0:08:14	0:41:24 0:08:12	0:49:32 0:08:08	0:57:38 0:08:06	1:05:42 0:08:04	1:13:57 0:08:15	1:22:07 0:08:10	1:30:15 0:08:08
#10 Stutz d Anderson	0:09:09	0:17:55 0:08:46	0:26:36 0:08:41	0:35:24 0:08:48	0:44:18 0:08:54	0:53:22 0:09:04	1:02:18 0:08:56	1:11:07 0:08:49	1:20:21 0:09:14	1:29:20 0:08:59	1:38:02 0:08:42
#6 National d Herr	0:08:38	0:17:09 0:08:31	0:25:33 0:08:24	0:34:04 0:08:31	0:42:35 0:08:31	0:51:03 0:08:28	0:59:16 0:08:13	1:07:30 0:08:14	1:15:42 0:08:12	1:24:00 0:08:18	1:34:49 0:10:49
Division 3C: Piston Displacement of 231 to 300 Cubic Inches- Non Stock												
#11 Mercer d Hughes	0:08:21	0:16:27 0:08:06	0:24:51 0:08:24	0:33:06 0:08:15	0:41:15 0:08:09	0:49:23 0:08:08	0:57:36 0:08:13	1:05:51 0:08:15	1:14:05 0:08:14	1:22:24 0:08:19	1:30:39 0:08:15
#5 Mercer d DePalma	0:08:20	0:16:49 0:08:29	0:25:05 0:08:16	0:33:22 0:08:17	0:41:38 0:08:16	0:49:55 0:08:17	0:58:11 0:08:16	1:06:24 0:08:13	1:14:31 0:08:07	1:22:37 0:08:06	1:30:45 0:08:08
#19 Ohio d Matthews	0:09:58	0:19:54 0:09:56	0:29:49 0:09:55	0:39:39 0:09:50	0:49:23 0:09:44	0:59:04 0:09:41	1:08:47 0:09:43	1:19:00 0:10:13	1:28:57 0:09:57	1:38:44 0:09:47	1:48:24 0:09:40
#12 Ohio d Parker	0:09:29	0:18:46 0:09:17	0:27:47 0:09:01	0:36:49 0:09:02	0:45:44 0:08:55	0:54:35 0:08:51	1:16:43 0:22:08	1:25:36 0:08:53	1:34:34 0:08:58	1:43:34 0:09:00	1:54:57 0:11:23
#7 Case d Jagersberger	0:08:41	0:17:22 0:08:41	0:26:03 0:08:41	0:34:47 0:08:44	0:43:21 0:08:34	0:51:52 0:08:31	1:00:24 0:08:32	1:08:51 0:08:27	1:19:02 0:10:11	1:27:26 0:08:24	1:36:04 0:08:38
#4 Cole d Basle	0:09:24	0:18:58 0:09:34	0:28:22 0:09:24	0:37:42 0:09:20	0:47:39 0:09:57	0:57:45 0:10:06	Out (Carburetor)				

1911 Table of Results *cont.*

12	13	14	15	16	17	18	19	20	21	22	23	24	25	Total

Division 6C: Piston Displacement of 601 to 750 Cubic Inches- Non Stock

12	13	14	15	16	17	18	19	20	21	22	23	24	25	Total
1:32:31	1:40:08	1:49:13	1:56:43	2:04:25	2:14:48	2:22:20	2:29:53	2:37:28	2:45:06	2:52:37	3:02:07	3:11:03	3:18:41	3:18:41.35
0:07:58	0:07:37	0:09:05	0:07:30	0:07:42	0:10:23	0:07:32	0:07:33	0:07:35	0:07:38	0:07:31	0:09:30	0:08:56	0:07:38	

Division 5C: Piston Displacement of 451 to 600 Cubic Inches- Non Stock

12	13	14	15	16	17	18	19	20	21	22	23	24	25	Total
1:35:14	1:43:02	1:50:50	1:58:40	2:06:28	2:14:18	2:22:01	2:29:51	2:37:41	2:45:46	2:57:00	3:04:47	3:12:30	3:20:11	3:20:11.44
0:07:45	0:07:48	0:07:48	0:07:50	0:07:48	0:07:50	0:07:43	0:07:50	0:07:50	0:08:05	0:11:14	0:07:47	0:07:43	0:07:41	
1:34:19	1:42:00	1:49:50	1:58:34	2:06:26	2:15:19	2:23:03	2:30:47	2:38:31	2:46:15	2:55:50	3:06:37	3:14:18	3:21:52	3:21:52.78
0:07:43	0:07:41	0:07:50	0:08:44	0:07:52	0:08:53	0:07:44	0:07:44	0:07:44	0:07:44	0:09:35	0:10:47	0:07:41	0:07:34	
1:38:44	1:46:33	1:54:18	2:02:02	2:09:47	2:17:35	2:27:46	2:35:46	2:47:01	2:54:53	3:02:47	3:10:30	3:18:14	3:25:59	3:25:59.36
0:07:49	0:07:49	0:07:45	0:07:44	0:07:45	0:07:48	0:10:11	0:08:00	0:11:15	0:07:52	0:07:54	0:07:43	0:07:44	0:07:45	
1:37:18	1:45:24	1:55:32	2:05:55	2:13:59	2:22:05	2:30:20	2:38:20	2:46:28	2:55:42	3:03:54	3:12:08	3:20:16	3:28:50	3:28:50.37
0:07:35	0:08:06	0:10:08	0:10:23	0:08:04	0:08:06	0:08:15	0:08:00	0:08:08	0:09:14	0:08:12	0:08:14	0:08:08	0:08:34	
1:48:32	1:57:49	2:07:01	2:25:01	2:34:08	2:49:05	2:59:12	3:08:41	3:17:19	3:28:29	3:37:46	Running			
0:16:03	0:09:17	0:09:12	0:18:00	0:09:07	0:14:57	0:10:07	0:09:29	0:08:38	0:11:10	0:09:17				

Division 4C: Piston Displacement of 301 to 450 Cubic Inches-Non Stock

12	13	14	15	16	17	18	19	20	21	22	23	24	25	Total
1:38:16	1:46:24	1:54:30	2:02:35	2:11:12	2:21:00	2:29:18	2:38:57	2:47:09	2:55:22	3:03:37	3:11:52	3:19:59	3:28:22	3:28:22.32
0:08:01	0:08:08	0:08:06	0:08:05	0:08:37	0:09:48	0:08:18	0:09:39	0:08:12	0:08:13	0:08:15	0:08:15	0:08:07	0:08:23	
1:46:40	1:55:22	2:04:03	2:12:48	2:21:42	2:30:30	2:39:14	2:48:09	2:56:00	3:05:36	3:14:21	3:23:03	3:31:45	3:40:23	3:40:23.05
0:08:38	0:08:42	0:08:41	0:08:45	0:08:54	0:08:48	0:08:44	0:08:55	0:07:51	0:09:36	0:08:45	0:08:42	0:08:42	0:08:38	
1:43:29	1:51:46	2:00:01	2:08:14	2:16:30	2:24:48	2:33:10	2:41:30	2:49:47	2:58:01	3:06:23	3:15:12	3:31:57	3:40:33	3:40:33.87
0:08:40	0:08:17	0:08:15	0:08:13	0:08:16	0:08:18	0:08:22	0:08:20	0:08:17	0:08:14	0:08:22	0:08:49	0:16:45	0:08:36	

Division 3C: Piston Displacement of 231 to 300 Cubic Inches- Non Stock

12	13	14	15	16	17	18	19	20	21	22	23	24	25	Total
1:38:53	1:47:03	1:55:10	2:03:14	2:11:29	2:19:50	2:30:24	2:38:35	2:46:49	2:55:24	3:03:56	3:12:35	3:21:14	3:29:45	3:29:45.30
0:08:14	0:08:10	0:08:07	0:08:04	0:08:15	0:08:21	0:10:34	0:08:11	0:08:14	0:08:35	0:08:32	0:08:39	0:08:39	0:08:31	
1:38:54	1:47:17	1:55:40	2:05:42	2:28:16	2:36:43	2:45:06	2:53:28	3:02:05	3:11:36	3:21:38	Out (Steering)			
0:08:09	0:08:23	0:08:23	0:10:02	0:22:34	0:08:27	0:08:23	0:08:22	0:08:37	0:09:31	0:10:02				
1:58:13	2:07:50	2:17:35	2:27:22	2:37:03	2:46:44	2:56:22	3:06:09	3:15:49	3:25:36	3:35:21	Running			
0:09:49	0:09:37	0:09:45	0:09:47	0:09:41	0:09:41	0:09:38	0:09:47	0:09:40	0:09:47	0:09:45				
2:03:57	2:13:02	2:22:15	2:31:27	2:40:43	3:07:17	3:16:23	3:25:27	3:34:34	Running					
0:09:00	0:09:05	0:09:13	0:09:12	0:09:16	0:26:34	0:09:06	0:09:04	0:09:07						
1:44:30	1:53:02	2:01:40	2:13:34	Out (Crash)										
0:08:26	0:08:32	0:08:38	0:11:54											

Notes

1. An Unlikely Venue

1. Peter Helck, *The Checkered Flag* (New York: Castle Books, 1961), 4.
2. Frederick P. Henry, ed., *Founders' Week Memorial Volume* (Philadelphia: City of Philadelphia, 1909), 5–6.
3. "Law Prohibits Park Motor Race," *Philadelphia Evening Bulletin*, 15 August 1908.
4. Minutes, Fairmount Park Board of Commissioners, 14 August 1908, Philadelphia City Archives, p. 510.
5. "Plans Auto Speed Contest in Park," *Philadelphia Inquirer*, 15 August 1908.
6. Nathaniel Burt and Wallace E. Davies, "The Iron Age: 1876–1905," in *Philadelphia: A 300-Year History*, ed. Russell F. Weigley (New York: W. W. Norton & Company, 1982), 517.
7. Harrison Rhodes, "Who is a Philadelphian?" *Harper's Magazine* 133, no. 793 (June 1916): 9.
8. John Lukacs, *Philadelphia: Patricians & Philistines, 1900–1950* (New York: Farrar, Straus, Giroux, 1980), 6–7.
9. Nathaniel Burt, *The Perennial Philadelphians: The Anatomy of an American Aristocracy* (Boston: Little Brown & Co., 1963; Philadelphia: University of Pennsylvania Press, 1999), 529.
10. Isaac F. Marcosson, "The Millionaire Yield of Philadelphia," *Munsey's Magazine* 47 (July 1912): 505.
11. Burt, 18.
12. Lukacs, 30.
13. George Stewart Stokes, *Agnes Repplier: Lady of Letters* (Philadelphia: University of Pennsylvania Press, 1949), 2.
14. Agnes Repplier, *Philadelphia: The Place and the People* (New York: The Macmillan Company, 1898), 374.
15. "200-Mile Auto Race in the Park," *Philadelphia Public Ledger*, 15 August 1908.
16. "To Pick Park Auto Race Course Today," *Philadelphia Evening Times*, 20 August 1908.

17. "Mayor Views Auto Course in Park," *Philadelphia Record*, 21 August 1908.
18. "Mayor Approves Park Auto Route after Trip," *Philadelphia Inquirer*, 21 August 1908.
19. "Mayor Approves Park Auto Route after Trip," *Philadelphia Inquirer*, 21 August 1908.
20. "Quakerites Hope For Fairmount Race," *The Automobile* 19, no. 11 (10 September 1908): 362.
21. Clinton Rogers Woodruff, "Philadelphia's Republican Tammany," *Outlook* 69 (21 September 1901): 169–172.
22. Lloyd M. Abernethy, "Progressivism: 1905–1919," in *Philadelphia: A 300-Year History*, ed. Russell F. Weigley (New York: W. W. Norton & Company, 1982), 539.
23. Lukacs, 56.
24. "Favors Big Race," *Philadelphia Record*, 13 September 1908.
25. "Favors Big Race," *Philadelphia Record*, 13 September 1908.
26. "Quakertown's Projected Stock Car Race," *The Automobile* 19, no. 9 (27 August 1908): 309.
27. "Park Motor Races," *Philadelphia Evening Bulletin*, 1 September 1908.

2. *Making Plans*

1. "Founders Week Race Not Fully Settled," *Philadelphia Evening Times*, 1 September 1908.
2. "Final Plans for Park Motor Race," *Philadelphia Evening Bulletin*, 12 September 1908.
3. Minutes, Fairmount Park Board of Commissioners, 11 September 1908, Philadelphia City Archives, pp. 517–518.
4. "Why Fairmount Sanction Was Granted," *The Automobile* 19, no. 12 (17 September 1908): 394.
5. "Permission Given to Park Motor Race," *Philadelphia Evening Bulletin*, 11 September 1908.
6. Here and There Among Motorists, *Philadelphia Record*, 23 September 1908.
7. Here and There Among Motorists, *Philadelphia Record*, 23 September 1908.
8. "Final Plans for Park Motor Race," *Philadelphia Evening Bulletin*, 12 September 1908.
9. "Entry Blanks Out for Big Park Race," *Philadelphia Public Ledger*, 13 September 1908.
10. James J. Flink, *The Car Culture* (Cambridge: MIT Press, 1975), 31.
11. "Two More Great Cars Entered," *Philadelphia Record*, 27 September 1908.
12. Here and There Among Motorists, *Philadelphia Record*, 18 September 1908.
13. "Welch Car Entered," *Philadelphia Evening Bulletin*, 22 September 1908.
14. "Preparing for Park 200 Mile Auto Race," *Philadelphia Evening Times*, 5 September 1908.
15. Here and There Among Motorists, *Philadelphia Record*, 29 September 1908.
16. "Ready for the Big Park Race," *Philadelphia Record*, 4 October 1908.
17. "Motors Speed Mile a Minute in Park," *Philadelphia Evening Bulletin*, 5 October 1908.
18. "Racing Car Dashes Through Park Fog," *Philadelphia Evening Bulletin*, 6 October 1908.
19. "Racing Car Dashes Through Park Fog," *Philadelphia Evening Bulletin*, 6 October 1908.
20. "Racing Car Dashes Through Park Fog," *Philadelphia Evening Bulletin*, 6 October 1908.
21. Here and There Among Motorists, *Philadelphia Record*, 7 October 1908.
22. Robert Cutter and Bob Fendell, *The Encyclopedia of Auto Racing Greats* (Englewood Cliffs: Prentice Hall Inc., 1973), 429.
23. "Faster Speeding in Fairmount Park," *Philadelphia Evening Bulletin*, 7 October 1908.
24. "Faster Speeding in Fairmount Park," *Philadelphia Evening Bulletin*, 7 October 1908.

25. "Two Cars Damaged in Racing Practice," *Philadelphia Evening Bulletin*, 8 October 1908.
26. "Original Sixteen Passed for Race," *Philadelphia Evening Bulletin*, 9 October 1908.
27. "Twelve Entries in Fairmount Race," *Philadelphia Public Ledger*, 27 September 1908.

3. The Founders' Week Cup

1. "Fairmount Park Race Won by Locomobile," *Motor Age* 14, no. 16 (15 October 1908): 15.
2. "Locomobile 10 Runs First in 200-Mile Race," *Philadelphia Evening Times*, 10 October 1908.
3. "Park Auto Race Seen by Thousands," *Philadelphia Record*, 11 October 1908.
4. "Twelve Entries in Fairmount Race," *Philadelphia Public Ledger*, 27 September 1908.
5. "Multitude Sees Thrilling Auto Road Race in Park," *Philadelphia Public Ledger*, 11 October 1908.
6. "Locomobile Wins Park Motor Race in 4 Hours, 2 Minutes, 30 Seconds," *Philadelphia Evening Bulletin*, 10 October 1908.
7. "Multitude Sees Thrilling Auto Road Race in Park," *Philadelphia Public Ledger*, 11 October 1908.
8. "Locomobile Takes First in Auto Race," *Camden Post-Telegram*, 10 October 1908.
9. *The Automobile* 19, no. 16 (15 October 1908): 531.
10. "Fairmount Park Race Won by Locomobile," *Motor Age* 14, no. 16 (15 October 1908): 17.
11. "Ten Cars Crippled in Big Motor Race," *Philadelphia Evening Bulletin*, 10 October 1908.
12. "Multitude Sees Thrilling Auto Road Race in Park," *Philadelphia Public Ledger*, 11 October 1908.
13. "Crowd Hero-Mad Over Robertson," *Philadelphia Evening Bulletin*, 10 October 1908.
14. "Crowd Hero-Mad Over Robertson," *Philadelphia Evening Bulletin*, 10 October 1908.
15. "Crowd Hero-Mad Over Robertson," *Philadelphia Evening Bulletin*, 10 October 1908.
16. "Quakertown's 200-Mile Captured by a Locomobile—Robertson Driving," *The Automobile* 19, no. 16 (15 October 1908): 531.
17. Fairmount Park Race Won by Locomobile," *Motor Age* 14, no. 16 (15 October 1908): 14.
18. "What Winning Drivers Said," *Philadelphia Evening Bulletin*, 10 October 1908.
19. "What Winning Drivers Said," *Philadelphia Evening Bulletin*, 10 October 1908.
20. "Firestone Merit Proven," *Philadelphia Record*, 11 October 1908.
21. "Fairmount Park Race Won by Locomobile," *Motor Age* 14, no. 16 (15 October 1908): 15.
22. "Philadelphia Now Wants Annual Race," *The Automobile* 19, no. 17 (22 October 1908): 564.
23. "Philadelphia Now Wants Annual Race," *The Automobile* 19, no. 17 (22 October 1908): 564.
24. "New Tire Records," *Philadelphia Record*, 12 October 1908.
25. "Philadelphia Now Wants Annual Race," *The Automobile* 19, no. 17 (22 October 1908): 564.
26. "Where Race Was Run," *Philadelphia Evening Bulletin*, 10 October 1908.
27. United States Department of Transportation, Federal Highway Administration, *Highway Statistics, Summary to 1985* (District of Columbia: U. S. Government Printing Office, 1985), 35.
28. "40 Miles an Hour Over Park Roads," *Philadelphia Public Ledger*, 7 October 1908.

29. "Reyburn in Favor of Annual Contest," *Philadelphia Evening Times*, 12 October 1908.

30. Albert R. Bochroch, *American Automobile Racing: An Illustrated History* (New York: The Viking Press, 1974), 57.

4. A Charitable Event

1. "200-Mile Auto Race to be Run Next October by Quaker City Motor Club," *Philadelphia Evening Times*, 12 March 1909.

2. "Park Auto Race Sanction Given," *Philadelphia Inquirer*, 13 March 1909.

3. "Park Auto Race Sanction Given," *Philadelphia Inquirer*, 13 March 1909.

4. "Park Auto Race Sanction Given," *Philadelphia Inquirer*, 13 March 1909.

5. "Park Auto Race Sanction Given," *Philadelphia Inquirer*, 13 March 1909.

6. "Fairmount Park Race Committees," *Philadelphia Public Ledger*, 22 August 1909.

7. "Preparations for the Fairmount Park '200'," *The Automobile* 21, no. 5 (29 July 1909): 197.

8. "Course Will Be Made Very Fast," *Philadelphia Record*, 12 September 1909.

9. "Course Will Be Made Very Fast," *Philadelphia Record*, 12 September 1909.

10. "Autos to Speed in Fairmount Park," *Philadelphia Public Ledger*, 3 October 1909.

11. "Intense Interest in Big Auto Race," *Philadelphia Public Ledger*, 29 August 1909.

12. "Intense Interest in Big Auto Race," *Philadelphia Public Ledger*, 29 August 1909.

13. "Park Auto Race a Big Social Event," *Philadelphia Public Ledger*, 5 September 1909.

14. Missouri [pseud.], "The Park Auto Race," [Letter to the Editor] *Philadelphia Record*, 7 October 1909.

15. Missouri [pseud.], "The Park Auto Race," [Letter to the Editor] *Philadelphia Record*, 7 October 1909.

16. Missouri [pseud.], "The Park Auto Race," [Letter to the Editor] *Philadelphia Record*, 7 October 1909.

17. United States Department of Transportation, Federal Highway Administration, *Highway Statistics, Summary to 1985* (District of Columbia: U. S. Government Printing Office, 1985), 25.

18. Missouri [pseud.], "The Park Auto Race," [Letter to the Editor] *Philadelphia Record*, 7 October 1909.

19. "Fairmount Park Race," *Philadelphia Public Ledger*, 15 August 1909.

20. "Park Race Tickets Stir Up Criticism," *Philadelphia Evening Bulletin*, 7 October 1909.

21. "Award Race Prizes on Thursday Night," *Philadelphia Evening Bulletin*, 11 October 1909.

22. "Quakertown May Invite Foreigners to Compete," *The Automobile* 21, no. 2 (8 July 1909): 71.

23. "May Open Quaker Race to Foreigners," *The Automobile* 21, no. 4 (22 July 1909): 136.

24. "Foreign Cars Eligible in Fairmount Park Race," *The Automobile* 21, no. 6 (5 August 1909): 240.

25. Beverly Rae Kimes, *The Star and the Laurel, The Centennial History of Daimler, Mercedes and Benz* (Montvale, New Jersey: Mercedes Benz of North America, 1986), 134–136.

26. 1909 Benz Catalog, DaimlerChrysler Archives, Stuttgart, Germany.

27. "Barney Oldfield's Kick," *Philadelphia Record*, 7 October 1909.

28. "Barney Oldfield's Kick," *Philadelphia Record*, 7 October 1909.

29. "Strang to Drive in Park Auto Race," *Philadelphia Inquirer*, 5 October 1909.

30. "Hall Barred from Park Motor Race," *Philadelphia Evening Bulletin*, 5 October 1909.

31. "Hall Barred from Park Motor Race," *Philadelphia Evening Bulletin*, 5 October 1909.

32. "Hall Barred from Park Motor Race," *Philadelphia Evening Bulletin*, 5 October 1909.

33. "Hall Barred from Park Motor Race," *Philadelphia Evening Bulletin*, 5 October 1909.

34. "Drivers at Practice Go Fast Over Park Course," *Philadelphia North American*, 6 October 1909.
35. "Girl Dashes Round Park Motor Course," *Philadelphia Evening Bulletin*, 5 October 1909.
36. "Girl Dashes Round Park Motor Course," *Philadelphia Evening Bulletin*, 5 October 1909.
37. "Grand Stand Falls on Park Race Route," *Philadelphia Evening Bulletin*, 6 October 1909.
38. "Auto Driver Defies Death in Smashing Park Lap Record," *Philadelphia Evening Times*, 7 October 1909.
39. "Racing Motorist's Wife Not Alarmed," *Philadelphia Evening Bulletin*, 8 October 1909.
40. "Racing Motorist's Wife Not Alarmed," *Philadelphia Evening Bulletin*, 8 October 1909.
41. "Racing Motorist's Wife Not Alarmed," *Philadelphia Evening Bulletin*, 8 October 1909.
42. "Auto Driver Defies Death in Smashing Park Lap Record," *Philadelphia Evening Times*, 7 October 1909.
43. "Racing Motorist's Wife Not Alarmed," *Philadelphia Evening Bulletin*, 8 October 1909.

5. *The Second Annual Fairmount Park Race*

1. "Hotels Crowded with Auto Fans for Great Race," *Philadelphia Evening Times*, 9 October 1909.
2. "Bulletins of the Race," *Philadelphia Evening Bulletin*, 9 October 1909.
3. "Accidents Thrill Spectators, but no Serious Injury Mars the Record Breaking Event," *Philadelphia Inquirer*, 10 October 1909.
4. "200-Mile Nerve Racking Contest Told in Detail," *Philadelphia Evening Bulletin*, 9 October 1909.
5. "Bulletins of the Race," *Philadelphia Evening Bulletin*, 9 October 1909.
6. "Accidents Thrill Spectators, but No Serious Injury Mars the Record Breaking Event," *Philadelphia Inquirer*, 10 October 1909.
7. "More Than 500,000 in Vast Crowd See Race," *Philadelphia Press*, 10 October 1909.
8. "Robertson Is Again Victor," *Philadelphia Record*, 10 October 1909.
9. "Robertson Wins a Simplex Triumph Over Park Course," *Philadelphia North American*, 10 October 1909.
10. "Accidents Thrill Spectators, but No Serious Injury Mars the Record Breaking Event," *Philadelphia Inquirer*, 10 October 1909.
11. "Accidents Thrill Spectators, but No Serious Injury Mars the Record Breaking Event," *Philadelphia Inquirer*, 10 October 1909.
12. "Accidents Thrill Spectators, but No Serious Injury Mars the Record Breaking Event," *Philadelphia Inquirer*, 10 October 1909.
13. "Policeman Mad from Accidents," *Philadelphia Evening Times*, 9 October 1909.
14. Gossip of the Motor World, *Philadelphia Evening Times*, 13 October 1909.
15. "Accidents Thrill Spectators, but No Serious Injury Mars the Record Breaking Event," *Philadelphia Inquirer*, 10 October 1909.
16. "Robertson Is Again Victor," *Philadelphia Record*, 10 October 1909.
17. "No Protests in Auto Race," *Philadelphia Record*, 12 October 1909.
18. "Robertson Victor in Park Auto Race," *Philadelphia Public Ledger*, 10 October 1909.
19. "Robertson Wins Philadelphia Race," *Motor Age* 16, no. 16 (14 October 1909): 3.
20. "Simplex, Chalmers-Detroit, Apperson, Chadwick and Isotta Smash Fairmount Park Course Time," *Philadelphia Inquirer*, 10 October 1909.
21. "Smoker Ends Day of Great Auto Contest," *Philadelphia Press*, 10 October 1909.
22. "Smoker Ends Day of Great Auto Contest," *Philadelphia Press*, 10 October 1909.

23. "No Protest to Be Made Against Robertson's Car," *Philadelphia Evening Times*, 11 October 1909.
24. "Park Auto Race Prizes Delivered," *Philadelphia Record*, 15 October 1909.
25. "Daring Drivers Fear Their Own Friends," *Philadelphia Evening Times*, 15 October 1909.
26. "Fairmount Winners Receive Prizes," *The Automobile* 21, no. 17 (21 October 1909): 674.
27. "Robertson Fastest at Philadelphia," *The MotorWorld* 21, no. 3 (14 October 1909): 115.
28. "No Protests in Auto Race," *Philadelphia Record*, 12 October 1909.
29. "Fairmount Park Race a Financial Success," *Horseless Age* 24, no. 23 (8 December 1909): 653.
30. "Robertson Is Again Victor," *Philadelphia Record*, 10 October 1909.
31. "Robertson Fastest at Philadelphia," *The Motor World* 21, no. 3 (14 October 1909): 111–112.
32. "Award Race Prizes on Thursday Night," *Philadelphia Evening Bulletin*, 11 October 1909.
33. "Award Race Prizes on Thursday Night," *Philadelphia Evening Bulletin*, 11 October 1909.
34. "Robertson Is Again Victor," *Philadelphia Record*, 10 October 1909.
35. "Wants Park Race an Annual Event," *Philadelphia Record*, 18 October 1909.
36. "Wants Park Race an Annual Event," *Philadelphia Record*, 18 October 1909.

6. *Surpassing Vanderbilt*

1. "First Fairmount Entry," *Philadelphia Record*, 17 August 1910.
2. "Three Classics of Auto Racing," *Philadelphia Evening Times*, 10 August 1910.
3. "Harry Grant Entered in Fairmount Park Race," *Philadelphia Inquirer*, 21 August 1910.
4. "Motor Race Pilots and Who They Are," *Philadelphia Evening Bulletin*, 8 October 1910.
5. "Park Race Benefit, Says Mayor Reyburn," *Philadelphia Inquirer*, 18 September 1910.
6. Editorial, "Automobile Race in the Park a Public Event," *Philadelphia Evening Times*, 17 September 1910.
7. "Park Race Benefits, Says Mayor Reyburn," *Philadelphia Inquirer*, 18 September 1910.
8. "Motor Race Pilots and Who They Are," *Philadelphia Evening Bulletin*, 8 October 1910.
9. "Fairmount Park Auto Race Plans," *Philadelphia Evening Times*, 21 September 1910.
10. Helck, *The Checkered Flag*, 75.
11. Helck, *The Checkered Flag*, 75.
12. "Thousands Out at Park Race Trials," *Philadelphia Inquirer*, 4 October 1910.
13. "Thousands Out at Park Race Trials," *Philadelphia Inquirer*, 4 October 1910.
14. "Motor Race Pilots and Who They Are," *Philadelphia Evening Bulletin*, 8 October 1910.
15. "Robertson Will Retire," *Philadelphia Evening Bulletin*, 4 October 1910.
16. "Robertson Will Retire," *Philadelphia Evening Bulletin*, 4 October 1910.
17. "Public Protection in Big Auto Race," *Philadelphia Public Ledger*, 5 October 1910.
18. "New Police Rules for Motor Race," *Philadelphia Evening Bulletin*, 4 October 1910.
19. "Chadwick Throws Wheel but No One Is Injured," *Philadelphia Evening Bulletin*, 4 October 1910.
20. "Public Protection in Big Auto Race," *Philadelphia Public Ledger*, 5 October 1910.
21. "Car Smashed, 2 Hurt in Motor Race Spin," *Philadelphia Evening Bulletin*, 5 October 1910.

22. "Car Smashed, 2 Hurt in Motor Race Spin," *Philadelphia Evening Bulletin*, 5 October 1910.
23. "Car Smashed, 2 Hurt in Motor Race Spin," *Philadelphia Evening Bulletin*, 5 October 1910.
24. "Thirty-One Autos Entered for Race," *Philadelphia Inquirer*, 6 October 1910.
25. "Thirty-One Autos Entered for Race," *Philadelphia Inquirer*, 6 October 1910.
26. "Autos Take Final Practice Spins for Tomorrow's Race," *Philadelphia North American*, 7 October 1910.
27. "Park Auto Race Starts at Noon," *Philadelphia Inquirer*, 8 October 1910.

7. *The Third Annual Fairmount Park Race*

1. "Motor Cars Start in Race; Accident Puts Out Mr. Betz," *Philadelphia Evening Bulletin*, 8 October 1910.
2. Gordon Mackay, "Thousands Cheer as Mile-A-Minute Racers Flash Past," *Philadelphia Evening Times*, 8 October 1910.
3. "Big Crowd Views Dashing Motors," *Philadelphia Evening Bulletin*, 8 October 1910.
4. "Mayor Orders 6000 to Positions of Safety," *Philadelphia Evening Times*, 8 October 1910.
5. "Big Mercedes in Race Owned by Ed. Schroeder," *Philadelphia Evening Bulletin*, 8 October 1910.
6. "Half Million Persons on Hills and Slopes of Park," *Philadelphia North American*, 9 October 1910.
7. "Half Million View Thrilling Park Auto Race," *Philadelphia Inquirer*, 9 October 1910.
8. "Mrs. Harroun Ready with Surgeon's Kit for Her Husband's Auto Race," *Philadelphia Evening Times*, 5 October, 1910.
9. "J. Fred Betz 3rd Is Out of Race," *Philadelphia Evening Bulletin*, 8 October 1910.
10. "Zengle Victor in Auto Race," *Philadelphia Public Ledger*, 9 October 1910.
11. "Several Accidents to Machines Occur Along Neil Drive," *Philadelphia Inquirer*, 9 October 1910.
12. "Half Million View Thrilling Park Auto Race," *Philadelphia Inquirer*, 9 October 1910.
13. Gordon Mackay, "Thousands Cheer as Mile-A-Minute Racers Flash Past," *Philadelphia Evening Times*, 8 October 1910.
14. "Half Million View Thrilling Park Auto Race," *Philadelphia Inquirer*, 9 October 1910.
15. "Zengle Wins Mad Auto Race," *Philadelphia Record*, 9 October 1910.
16. M. Worth Colwell, "Quaker City Race Captured by Zengle in Chadwick," *Horseless Age* 26, no. 15 (12 October 1910): 512.
17. "Six Seconds Cost Ralph Mulford Race," *Philadelphia Inquirer*, 16 October 1910.
18. "Six Seconds Make Chadwick Victor in Exciting Park Race," *Philadelphia North American*, 9 October 1910.
19. "Park Course Good Test for the Auto," *Philadelphia Public Ledger*, 9 October 1910.
20. M. Worth Colwell, "Quaker City Race Captured by Zengle in Chadwick," *Horseless Age* 26, no. 15 (12 October 1910): 513.
21. "Park Course Good Test for the Auto," *Philadelphia Public Ledger*, 9 October 1910.
22. "Why the Lozier Lost," *Philadelphia Record*, 9 October 1910.
23. "Zengle Wins Mad Auto Race," *Philadelphia Record*, 9 October 1910.
24. "Charity Loses $1600 by Grab of Park Board," *Philadelphia Evening Times*, 10 October 1910.
25. "Charity Loses $1600 by Grab of Park Board," *Philadelphia Evening Times*, 10 October 1910.
26. "Fairmount Park Lap Record Stands," *Philadelphia Evening Times*, 12 October 1910.

27. "The Fairmount Cup," *Horseless Age* 26, no. 15 (12 October 1910): 513.
28. "Prizes for the Race," *Philadelphia Evening Bulletin*, 8 October 1910.
29. "More Honors for Len Zengle," *Philadelphia Record*, 15 October 1910.
30. "Winning Chadwick is Shown at Lits," *Philadelphia North American*, 16 October 1910.

8. *Controversy*

1. "Alco Car Wins Big Auto Race; 3 Men Killed," *Philadelphia Evening Times*, 1 October 1910.
2. "Will Hold Grand Prize Race Oct. 15," *Philadelphia North American*, 4 October 1910.
3. "Grand Prize Race Will Be Decided," *Philadelphia Evening Bulletin*, 4 October 1910.
4. "Benz Entries Rejected," *Philadelphia Public Ledger*, 5 October 1910.
5. "Indianapolis Wants Auto Race," *Philadelphia Public Ledger*, 7 October 1910.
6. "Savannah Seeks Grand Prize Race," *Philadelphia Evening Times*, 7 October 1910.
7. "Zengle Wins Mad Auto Race," *Philadelphia Record*, 9 October 1910.
8. "Zengle Wins Mad Auto Race," *Philadelphia Record*, 9 October 1910.
9. "Park Auto Race Starts at Noon," *Philadelphia Inquirer*, 8 October 1910.
10. "Half Million View Thrilling Park Auto Race," *Philadelphia Inquirer*, 9 October 1910.
11. "Grand Prize Race May Be Run Here," *Philadelphia Inquirer*, 10 October 1910.
12. "Grand Prize Here if Mayor Says So," *Philadelphia Evening Bulletin*, 10 October 1910.
13. "Grand Prize Here if Mayor Says So," *Philadelphia Evening Bulletin*, 10 October 1910.
14. "Noted Official Resigns," *Philadelphia Inquirer*, 18 November 1910.
15. "R. E. Ross Quits Q. C. Motor Club," *Philadelphia Evening Bulletin*, 17 November 1910.
16. "Ross Resigns from Quaker City M. C.," *Horseless Age* 26, no. 22 (30 November 1910): 753.
17. "Q. C. Motor Club Loses R. E. Ross," *Philadelphia Public Ledger*, 18 November 1910.
18. "Q. C. Motor Club Loses R. E. Ross," *Philadelphia Public Ledger*, 18 November 1910.
19. "Noted Official Resigns," *Philadelphia Inquirer*, 18 November 1910.
20. "Park Auto Races Give Charity $6623," *Philadelphia Inquirer*, 21 January 1911.
21. "Philadelphia's Mayor Denounces Management of 'Charity' Race," *Horseless Age* 27, no. 4 (25 January 1911): 204.
22. "Motor Club Denies Cash for Charity was Withheld," *Philadelphia Evening Bulletin*, 21 January 1911.
23. "Motor Club Made Profit in Park Race," *Philadelphia Public Ledger*, 21 January 1911.
24. "Motor Club Made Profit in Park Race," *Philadelphia Public Ledger*, 21 January 1911.
25. Quaker City Motor Club to Fairmount Park Commission, 27 April 1910, Automobiles Folder, History Subject Files, Fairmount Park Commission Archives, Philadelphia, Pennsylvania.
26. "Philadelphia's Mayor Denounces Management of 'Charity' Race," *Horseless Age* 27, no. 4 (25 January 1911): 204.
27. Minutes, Fairmount Park Board of Commissioners, 10 March 1911, Philadelphia City Archives, p. 113.
28. "Mayor Approves Park Auto Race," *Philadelphia Public Ledger*, 12 March 1911.
29. "Five Entries Already for Fairmount Park Race," *Philadelphia North American*, 17 September 1911.
30. "First Auto Classic Trials Postponed," *Philadelphia Public Ledger*, 3 October 1911.
31. "Bergdoll '40' Wrecked," *Philadelphia Record*, 4 October 1911.
32. "Mercer Car Wrecked and Crew Injured on Park Course," *Philadelphia Evening Bulletin*, 4 October 1911.
33. "Mercer Car Wrecked and Crew Injured on Park Course," *Philadelphia Evening Bulletin*, 4 October 1911.

34. "Ringler Hurt as Racing Car Dives Over Park Bank," *Philadelphia Evening Times*, 4 October 1911.
35. "Mercer Car Wrecked and Crew Injured on Park Course," *Philadelphia Evening Bulletin*, 4 October 1911.
36. "Cars in Tuning–Up Trials Furnish Thrills in Park," *Philadelphia North American*, 6 October 1911.
37. "Oldfield Rapped for Entering Race," *Philadelphia Evening Bulletin*, 5 October 1911.
38. "Oldfield Rapped for Entering Race," *Philadelphia Evening Bulletin*, 5 October 1911.
39. "Noted Drivers Will Shoot Fastest of Cars Over 200 Miles in the Park Race," *Philadelphia North American*, 7 October 1911.
40. "Noted Drivers Will Shoot Fastest of Cars Over 200 Miles in the Park Race," *Philadelphia North American*, 7 October 1911.

9. *The Fourth Annual Fairmount Park Race*

1. "Park Auto Race Postponed Until Tomorrow Noon," *Philadelphia Inquirer*, 8 October 1911.
2. "Park Auto Race Off Until Tomorrow," *Philadelphia Public Ledger*, 8 October 1911.
3. "Bergdoll in Benz, Fairmount Winner," *The Automobile* 25, no. 15 (12 October 1911): 608.
4. "Postponed Park Auto Race to be Run Off Today," *Philadelphia Inquirer*, 9 October 1911.
5. "Bulletins of the Race," *Philadelphia Evening Bulletin*, 9 October 1911.
6. "Bergdoll Wins Park Auto Race," *Philadelphia Public Ledger*, 10 October 1911.
7. "Bergdoll Wins Park Auto Race," *Philadelphia Public Ledger*, 10 October 1911.
8. "Bulletins of the Race," *Philadelphia Evening Bulletin*, 9 October 1911.
9. "E. Bergdoll Wins Park Auto Race; Sets New Record," *Philadelphia Inquirer*, 10 October 1911.
10. "E. Bergdoll Wins Park Auto Race; Sets New Record," *Philadelphia Inquirer*, 10 October 1911.
11. "Wishart Angry at Race Decision," *Philadelphia Evening Bulletin*, 10 October 1911.
12. "Wishart Will Appeal to A. A. A.," *Horseless Age* 28, no. 16 (18 October 1911): 592.
13. "Aftermath of Park Auto Race," *Philadelphia Record*, 11 October 1911.
14. Barney Oldfield, "Vanderbilt Race Should be Held in Fairmount Park," *Philadelphia Inquirer*, 17 December 1911.
15. Barney Oldfield, "Vanderbilt Race Should be Held in Fairmount Park," *Philadelphia Inquirer*, 17 December 1911.
16. Barney Oldfield, "Bergdoll at Head of the 'Amateurs'," *Philadelphia Inquirer*, 15 October 1911.

10. *Opposition*

1. Minutes, Fairmount Park Board of Commissioners, 11 October 1911, Philadelphia City Archives, p. 153.
2. John Lukacs, *Philadelphia: Patricians & Philistines, 1900–1950* (New York: Farrar, Straus, Giroux, 1980), 39.
3. E. Digby Baltzell, *Philadelphia Gentlemen: The Making of a National Upper Class* (Glencoe, Illinois: Free Press, 1958; New Brunswick, New Jersey: Transaction Publishers, 1995), 176.

4. "Seeks to Prohibit Park Auto Races," *Philadelphia Public Ledger*, 12 October 1911.
5. "Dr. White Against Park Auto Race," *Philadelphia Evening Bulletin*, 12 October 1911.
6. "Dr. White Against Park Auto Race," *Philadelphia Evening Bulletin*, 12 October 1911.
7. "Dr. White Against Park Auto Race," *Philadelphia Evening Bulletin*, 12 October 1911.
8. Disgusted [pseud.], "Motor Races in Fairmount Park," [Letter to the Editor] *Philadelphia Evening Bulletin*, 17 October 1911.
9. Editorial, "The Park Automobile Races," *Philadelphia Evening Times*, 13 October, 1911.
10. "Throws Bomb at Quaker City Road Race," *Motor Age* 20, no. 25 (21 December 1911): 14.
11. "Dr. White Condemns Auto Races in Fairmount Park," *Philadelphia North American*, 14 December 1911.
12. Dr. J. William White, Statement made to the Fairmount Park Commission, 13 December 1911, in "*In Re:* Automobile Races in Fairmount Park," Automobiles Folder, History Subject File, Fairmount Park Commission Archives, Philadelphia, Pennsylvania, p. 5.
13. Barney Oldfield, "Is the Game Worth the Candle?" *Popular Mechanics* 16, no. 3 (September 1911): 336.
14. Barney Oldfield, "Is the Game Worth the Candle?" *Popular Mechanics* 16, no. 3 (September 1911): 336.
15. Dr. J. William White, Statement made to the Fairmount Park Commission, 13 December 1911, in "*In Re:* Automobile Races in Fairmount Park," Automobiles Folder, History Subject File, Fairmount Park Commission Archives, Philadelphia, Pennsylvania, p. 7.
16. George Wharton Pepper to Dr. J. William White, 3 November 1911, in "*In Re:* Automobile Races in Fairmount Park," Automobiles Folder, History Subject File, Fairmount Park Commission Archives, Philadelphia, Pennsylvania, p. 15.
17. Dr. J. William White, Statement made to the Fairmount Park Commission, 13 December 1911, in "*In Re:* Automobile Races in Fairmount Park," Automobiles Folder, History Subject File, Fairmount Park Commission Archives, Philadelphia, Pennsylvania, p. 8.
18. "Throws Bomb at Quaker City Road Race," *Motor Age* 20, no. 25 (21 December 1911):14.
19. "Motorists Oppose White Resolution," *Philadelphia Inquirer*, 15 December 1911.
20. "Motorists Oppose White Resolution," *Philadelphia Inquirer*, 15 December 1911.
21. "Motorists Oppose White Resolution," *Philadelphia Inquirer*, 15 December 1911.
22. Minutes, Fairmount Park Committee on Superintendence & Police, 8 May 1912, Philadelphia City Archives, p. 79.
23. "Auto Race in Park Prohibited by Vote of the Commission," *Philadelphia North American*, 9 May 1912.
24. "Park Motor Races Barred," *Philadelphia Public Ledger*, 9 May 1912.
25. Baltzell, 207.
26. James T. Maher, *The Twilight of Splendor: Chronicles of the Age of American Palaces* (Boston: Little, Brown and Company, 1975), 26.
27. "Kill Plans for Park Race and Golf Course," *Philadelphia Record*, 12 June 1913.
28. "No 200-Mile Race in Park This Fall," *Philadelphia Public Ledger*, 12 June 1913.
29. "No 200-Mile Race in Park This Fall," *Philadelphia Public Ledger*, 12 June 1913.
30. "Kill Plans for Park Race and Golf Course," *Philadelphia Record*, 12 June 1913.
31. Charles L. Betts Jr. and J. Linden Heacock Jr. "The Philadelphia Motor Speedway," *Antique Automobile* 28, no. 3 (May–June 1964): 23.
32. City of Philadelphia, *Journal of the Common Council of the City of Philadelphia: 1914*, Vol. 1 (Philadelphia: William H. Sickels, Printer): 167–168.
33. Minutes, Fairmount Park Board of Commissioners, 12 March 1914, Philadelphia City Archives, p. 411.
34. Charles L. Betts Jr. and J. Linden Heacock Jr. "The Philadelphia Motor Speedway," *Antique Automobile* 28, no. 3 (May-June 1964): 26.

35. Charles L. Betts Jr. and J. Linden Heacock Jr. "The Philadelphia Motor Speedway," *Antique Automobile* 28, no. 3 (May-June 1964): 26.

36. Charles L. Betts Jr. and J. Linden Heacock Jr. "The Philadelphia Motor Speedway," *Antique Automobile* 28, no. 3 (May-June 1964): 26.

37. "Philadelphia's Proposed Speedway will be Fastest Track in the World," *Journal of the Philadelphia Chamber of Commerce* 4, no. 11 (November 1915): 40.

38. Mark W. Wilson, "Speedway Means Much to City," *Journal of the Philadelphia Chamber of Commerce* 5, no. 8 (August 1916): 35.

39. Charles L. Betts Jr. and J. Linden Heacock Jr. "The Philadelphia Motor Speedway," *Antique Automobile* 28, no. 3 (May-June 1964): 26.

40. "Inspect Speedway Site at Warminster," [Unidentified Newspaper Clipping], 20 November 1916, Clipping Morgue 1091, Bucks County Historical Society, Doylestown, Pennsylvania.

41. "To Sell Speedway Lots," [Unidentified Newspaper Clipping], 10 June 1924, Clipping Morgue 1091, Bucks County Historical Society, Doylestown, Pennsylvania.

Conclusion

1. Barney Oldfield, "Is the Game Worth the Candle?" *Popular Mechanics* 16, no. 3 (September 1911): 336.

2. Agnes Repplier, *J. William White M. D.: A Biography* (Boston: Houghton Mifflin Company, 1919), 200.

Bibliography

Books

Baltzell, E. Digby. *Philadelphia Gentlemen: The Making of a National Upper Class.* Glencoe, Illinois: The Free Press, 1958; New Brunswick, New Jersey: Transaction Publishers, 1995.

Bochroch, Albert R. *American Automobile Racing: An Illustrated History.* New York: The Viking Press, 1974.

Burt, Nathaniel. *The Perennial Philadelphians: The Anatomy of an American Aristocracy.* Boston: Little Brown & Co., 1963; Philadelphia: University of Pennsylvania Press, 1999.

City of Philadelphia. *Journal of the Common Council of the City of Philadelphia: 1914.* Philadelphia: William H. Sickels, Printer.

Collins, Herman Leroy, and Wilfred Jordan. *Philadelphia: A Story of Progress.* Philadelphia: Lewis Historical Publishing Company, 1941.

Cutter, Robert, and Bob Fendell. *The Encyclopedia of Auto Racing Greats.* Englewood Cliffs: Prentice Hall Inc., 1973.

Flink, James J. *America Adopts the Automobile, 1895–1910.* Cambridge: MIT Press, 1970.

_____. *The Automobile Age.* Cambridge: MIT Press, 1988.

_____. *The Car Culture.* Cambridge: MIT Press, 1975.

Georgano, Nick, ed. *The Beaulieu Encyclopedia of the Automobile.* Chicago: Fitzroy Dearborn Publishers, 2000.

Helck, Peter. *The Checkered Flag.* New York: Castle Books, 1961.

_____. *Great Auto Races.* New York: Harry N. Abrams, Inc., 1975.

Henry, Frederick P. ed. *Founders' Week Memorial Volume.* Philadelphia: City of Philadelphia, 1909.

Kimes, Beverly Rae. *The Star and the Laurel, The Centennial History of Daimler, Mercedes and Benz.* Montvale, New Jersey: Mercedes Benz of North America, 1986.

Klein, Esther M. *Fairmount Park: A History and a Guide.* Philadelphia: Fairmount Park Commission, 1974.

Lukacs, John. *Philadelphia: Patricians & Philistines, 1900–1950.* New York: Farrar, Straus, Giroux, 1980.

Maher, James T. *The Twilight of Splendor: Chronicles of the Age of American Palaces.* Boston: Little, Brown and Company, 1975.
Quattlebaum, Julian K., M. D. *The Great Savannah Races.* Columbia, South Carolina: R. L. Bryan Co., 1957; Athens, Georgia: The University of Georgia Press, 1983.
Repplier, Agnes. *J. William White, M. D.: A Biography.* Boston: Houghton Mifflin Company, 1919.
_____. *Philadelphia: The Place and the People.* New York: The Macmillan Company, 1898.
Scharf, J. Thomas, and Thompson Wescott. *History of Philadelphia, 1609–1884.* Philadelphia: L. H. Everts & Co., 1884.
Spofford, Ernest, ed. *Encyclopedia of Pennsylvania Biography.* New York: Lewis Historical Publishing Company, 1928.
Stokes, George Stewart. *Agnes Repplier: Lady of Letters.* Philadelphia: University of Pennsylvania Press, 1949.
United States Department of Transportation, Federal Highway Administration. *Highway Statistics, Summary to 1985.* District of Columbia: U. S. Government Printing Office, 1985.
Weigley, Russell F. ed. *Philadelphia: A 300-Year History.* New York: W. W. Norton & Company, 1982.
The Yearbook of the Twenty-Second Annual Architectural Exhibition. Philadelphia: The T-Square Club and the Philadelphia Chapter of the American Institute of Architects, 1916.

Periodicals/Newspapers

"Bergdoll in Benz Fairmount Winner," *Motor Age* 20, no. 15 (12 October 1911): 1–7.
"Bergdoll in Benz, Fairmount Winner," *The Automobile* 25, no. 15 (12 October 1911): 603–611, 643.
Betts, Charles L. Jr., and J. Linden Heacock Jr. "The Philadelphia Motor Speedway," *Antique Automobile* 28, no. 3 (May-June 1964): 21–26, 71.
Camden Post-Telegram, August 1908-November 1911.
Colwell, M. Worth. "Quaker City Race Captured by Zengle in Chadwick," *Horseless Age* 26, no. 15 (12 October 1910): 512–518.
Colwell, William. "The Fall Crop of Road Races," *Motor* 13, no. 1 (October 1909): 41–42.
"Commissioners Kill Fairmount Park Race," *The Automobile* 26, no. 19 (9 May 1912): 1070.
"Contest Board Overrules Wishart's Appeal–Boy Promoter Suspended," *Horseless Age* 28, no. 22 (29 November 1911): 825.
"Entries for Quaker City Race," *The Motor World* 21, no. 2 (7 October 1909): 68.
"Excellent Prospects for Fairmount Race," *The Automobile* 21, no. 12 (16 September 1909): 473.
"Fairmount Park Aftermath," *Motor Age* 18, no. 16 (20 October 1910): 10–11.
"Fairmount Park Aftermath," *Motor Age* 20, no. 16 (19 October 1911): 5.
"Fairmount Park Event Next Speed Contest," *Horseless Age* 26, no. 13 (5 October 1910): 483.
"Fairmount Park Field Big," *The Automobile* 23, no. 14 (6 October 1910): 600.
"The Fairmount Park Race," *The Automobile* 23, no. 12 (22 September 1910): 506–507.
"Fairmount Park Race a Bright Possibility," *Horseless Age* 31, no. 18 (30 April 1913): 754.
"Fairmount Park Race Comes Next," *The Automobile* 25, no. 12 (21 September 1911): 478.
"Fairmount Park Race Entry List Half Filled," *The Automobile* 21, no. 10 (2 September 1909): 411.
"Fairmount Park Race a Financial Success," *Horseless Age* 24, no 23 (8 December 1909): 653.
"The Fairmount Park Race, Philadelphia," *Motor* 13, no. 2 (November 1909): 60–61.
"Fairmount Park Race Successfully Run on Monday," *Horseless Age* 28, no. 15 (11 October 1911): 548–553.
"Fairmount Park Race Won by Locomobile," *Motor Age* 14, no. 16 (15 October 1908): 14–17.

"Fairmount Park Races," *Automobile Trade Journal* 16, no. 12 (1 June 1912): 88.
"Fairmount Park Road Racing," *Motor* 15, no. 1 (October 1910): 62–63.
"The Fairmount Park 200 Mile Stock Chassis Race," *Horseless Age* 24, no. 15 (13 October 1909): 411–413.
"Fairmount Park 200 Mile Stock Chassis Race," *The Automobile* 21, no. 15 (7 October 1909): 616.
"The Fairmount Park 200-Mile Stock Chassis Race," *Cycle and Automobile Trade Journal* 11, no. 5 (1 November 1911): 66–68.
"Fairmount Race Has Big Entry List," *Motor Age* 18, no. 14 (6 October 1910): 21.
"Fairmount 200-Mile Will Draw Big Crowd," *The Automobile* 25, no. 14 (5 October 1911): 570–571.
"Fairmount Winners Receive Prizes," *The Automobile* 21, no. 17 (21 October 1909): 674.
"Field Completed for Fairmount Park Race," *Motor Age* 16, no. 15 (7 October 1909): 8.
"Foreign Cars Barred," *Motor Age* 15, no. 21 (27 May 1909): 12.
"Foreign Cars Eligible in Fairmount Park Race," *The Automobile* 21, no. 6 (5 August 1909): 240.
"Grand Circuit Dates Are Announced, Racing High Spots Selected by Contest Board," *The Automobile* 24, no. 19 (11 May 1911): 1101.
"Hopes to Save Park Races, Quaker City Motor Club May Petition Commissioners for Rehearing," *Motor Age* 21, no. 20 (16 May 1912): 17.
"Little Hope for Revival of Fairmount Park Race," *The Automobile* 26, no. 20 (16 May 1912): 1114.
"Locomobile Wins Fairmount Park 200 Mile Race," *Horseless Age* 22, no. 16 (14 October 1908): 541.
"Long Island Automobile Club to Attend Fairmount Race," *The Automobile* 25, no. 14 (5 October 1911): 571.
Marcosson, Isaac F. "The Millionaire Yield of Philadelphia," *Munsey's Magazine* 47 (July 1912): 505.
"May Open Quaker Race to Foreigners," *The Automobile* 21, no. 4 (22 July 1909): 136.
"May Revive Fairmount Park Race," *Motor Age* 25, no. 9 (26 February 1914): 16.
"More Quaker Entries," *Motor Age* 14, no. 14 (1 October 1908): 11.
"Move to Hold Fairmount Park Race Defeated," *Horseless Age* 31, no. 25 (18 June 1913): 1097.
New York Times, August 1908–March 1965.
"1911 Rules Governing Contests," *The Automobile* 24, no. 9 (2 March 1911): 642–650.
"Nineteen in Fairmount Park Road Race," *Motor Age* 20, no. 14 (5 October 1911): 12.
"The 1912 Racing Situation," *Horseless Age* 29, no. 16 (7 April 1912): 683.
Oldfield, Barney. "Is the Game Worth the Candle?" *Popular Mechanics* 16, no. 3 (September 1911): 335–348.
"Park Race List Full," *Motor Age* 14, no. 15 (8 October 1908): 12.
"Permit Given For Fairmount Park Race," *Motor Age* 15, no. 11 (18 March 1909): 13.
"Permit Granted for Race," *Motor Age* 19, no. 11 (16 March 1911): 19.
"Petition for Renewal of Fairmount Park Race," *Automobile Trade Journal* 17, no. 3 (1 September 1912): 77.
Philadelphia Evening Bulletin, May 1901–March 1914.
Philadelphia Evening Times, August 1908–March 1914.
"Philadelphia Gets 'Speedway Bug'," *Horseless Age* 32, no. 6 (6 August 1913): 214.
Philadelphia Inquirer, August 1908–November 1917.
Philadelphia North American, August 1908–March 1914.
"Philadelphia Now Wants Annual Race," *The Automobile* 19, no. 17 (22 October 1908): 564.
"Philadelphia Park Road Race Certainty," *Motor Age* 14, no. 12 (17 September 1908): 4–5.
Philadelphia Press, October 1909.
Philadelphia Public Ledger, August 1908–March 1914.

Philadelphia Record, August 1908–March 1914.
"Philadelphia Speedway Project," *Horseless Age* 32, no. 14 (1 October 1913): 525.
"Philadelphia's Mayor Denounces Management of 'Charity' Race," *Horseless Age* 27, no. 4 (25 January 1911): 204.
"Philadelphia's Proposed Speedway Will Be Fastest Track in the World," *Journal of the Philadelphia Chamber of Commerce* 4, no. 11 (November 1915): 40–41.
"Philadelphia's 200-Mile Road Race," *Motor* 11, no. 2 (November 1908): 45–46.
"Preparations for the Fairmount Park '200'," *The Automobile* 21, no. 5 (29 July 1909): 197.
"Preparing for Fairmount Park Race," *The Automobile* 25, no. 13 (28 September 1911): 552.
"Protest Against Fairmount Race," *The Automobile* 25, no. 25 (21 December 1911): 1079.
"Quaker City to Have 200 Mile Race," *Cycle and Automobile Trade Journal* 13, no. 4 (1 October 1908): 44.
"Quakerites Hope for Fairmount Race," *The Automobile* 19, no. 11 (10 September 1908): 362.
"Quakers in Row with Mayor Over Fairmount Park Race," *The Automobile* 25, no. 3 (20 July 1911): 116.
"Quakers Satisfied with Race," *Motor Age* 14, no. 17 (22 October 1908): 9.
"Quakertown May Invite Foreigners to Compete," *The Automobile* 21, no. 2 (8 July 1909): 71.
"Quakertown's Projected Stock Car Race," *The Automobile* 19, no. 9 (27 August 1908): 309.
"Quakertown's Stock Chassis Race," *The Automobile* 19, no. 13 (24 September 1908): 448.
"Quakertown's 200-Mile Captured by a Locomobile—Robertson Driving," *The Automobile* 19, no. 16 (15 October 1908): 532–533.
"R. E. Ross Resigns from Q. C. M. C.," *The Automobile* 23, no. 21 (24 November 1910): 892.
"Refuse Sanction for Fairmount Park Race," *Horseless Age* 29, no. 20 (15 May 1912): 874.
Rhodes, Harrison. "Who Is a Philadelphian?" *Harper's Magazine* 133 no. 793 (June 1916): 1–13.
"Road Glory for Many at Philadelphia," *Motor Age* 18, no. 15 (13 October 1910): 1–9.
"A Road Race in Fairmount Park?" *The Automobile* 19, no. 8 (20 August 1908): 274.
"Robertson Again Wins Fairmount Race," *The Automobile* 21, no. 16 (14 October 1909): 627–633.
"Robertson Fastest at Philadelphia," *The Motor World* 21, no. 3 (14 October 1909): 111–116.
"Robertson Wins Philadelphia Race," *Motor Age* 16, no. 16 (14 October 1909): 1–7.
Rosenberger, E. H. "Fairmount Park Race Plans," *Motor* 29, no. 1 (October 1911): 34.
_____. "Fourth Running of the Fairmount," *Motor* 29 no. 2 (November 1911): 2–5.
"Ross Resigns from Quaker City M. C.," *Horseless Age* 26, no. 22 (30 November 1910): 753.
"Savannah to Get Grand Prize Race–Long Island Course Abandoned," *Horseless Age* 26, no. 15 (12 October 1910): 518.
"Six in Quaker Race So Far," *Motor Age* 20, no. 13 (28 September 1911): 9.
"Sixteen Entries for Fairmount Park Race," *The Automobile* 19, no. 14 (1 October 1908): 460.
"Speedways Organized," *Journal of the Philadelphia Chamber of Commerce* 5, no. 12 (December 1916): 29.
"Success of the Philadelphia 200 Mile Chassis Race Assured," *Cycle and Automobile Trade Journal* 14, no. 4 (1 October 1909): 60.
"3rd Fairmount Park Road Race," *The Automobile* 23, no. 15 (13 October 1910): 607–610.
"Thirteen Park Race Entries," *Motor Age* 16, no. 13 (25 September 1909): 11.
"Throws Bomb at Quaker City Road Race," *Motor Age* 20, no. 25 (21 December 1911): 14.
"Trade Association Considering Control of Racing in Philadelphia," *Horseless Age* 26, no. 21 (23 November 1910): 729.
"Why Fairmount Sanction was Granted," *The Automobile* 19, no. 12 (17 September 1908): 394.
Wilson, Mark W. "Speedway Means Much to City," *Journal of the Philadelphia Chamber of Commerce* 5, no. 8 (August 1916): 35–37.
"Winners in Quaker Race are Given Their Prizes," *Motor Age* 16, no. 17 (21 October 1909): 11.

"Wishart Fighting Fairmount Decision to a Finish," *Horseless Age* 28, no. 20 (15 November 1911): 749.

"Wishart Will Appeal to A. A. A.," *Horseless Age* 28, no. 16 (18 October 1911): 592.

Woodruff, Clinton Rogers. "Philadelphia's Republican Tammany," *Outlook* 69 (21 September 1901): 169–172.

"World's Progress Regulated by Speed," *The Automobile* 24, no. 12 (23 March 1911): 761–765.

Manuscript/Photograph Collections

Clark, Henry Austin. Photo Albums. Henry Austin Clark Collection. Henry Ford Museum & Greenfield Village Research Center, Dearborn, Michigan.

Clipping Morgue 1091. Bucks County Historical Society, Doylestown, Pennsylvania.

Fairmount Park Board of Commissioners. Minutes. Philadelphia City Archives, Philadelphia, Pennsylvania.

Fairmount Park Commission. Clipping Scrapbooks. Fairmount Park Commission Archives, Philadelphia, Pennsylvania.

Fairmount Park Commission. History Subject Files. Fairmount Park Commission Archives, Philadelphia, Pennsylvania.

Fairmount Park Committee on Superintendence & Police. Minutes. Philadelphia City Archives, Philadelphia, Pennsylvania.

Lazarnick, Nathan. Photographs. Nathan Lazarnick Collection. Detroit Public Library, Detroit, Michigan.

_____. Photographs. George Eastman House, Rochester, New York.

1909 Benz Catalog, DaimlerChrysler Archives, Stuttgart, Germany.

Quaker City Motor Club. Second Annual Fairmount Park Race Program, 1909. Antique Automobile Club of America Library & Research Center, Hershey, Pennsylvania.

_____. Third Annual Fairmount Park Race Program, 1910. Automobile Reference Collection. Free Library of Philadelphia, Philadelphia, Pennsylvania.

White, J. William. Papers, 1880–1925. J. William White Collection. University of Pennsylvania Archives, Philadelphia, Pennsylvania.

Index

Number in *italics* refer to pages with photographs.

Abbott-Detroit (automobile) 117–118, 122
Abbott-Detroit Company 107, 134
Abernethy, Lloyd M. 15
Acme (automobile): and 1908 park race 35, 41, 44, 47; and 1909 park race 64, 68, 79, 81–82, *82*, 86, 87
Acme Motor Car Company 26
Ainslee, George *159*
Aitken, John D.: and 1910 park race 107, 111, 117, 119–121, 123–125, *124*, 131; and 1910 Vanderbilt Cup 110
Ajax Tires 51
Alco (automobile) 142; and 1909 park race 65, 71, 78–79; and 1909 Vanderbilt Cup 100; and 1910 park race 100; and 1910 Vanderbilt Cup 104
American (automobile) 79–83, 85, 90
American Automobile Association (AAA) 91, 114, 135–136, 139, 148, 173; chosen as sanctioning body 22–24; conflict with ACA 22–24, 27, 63; and Barney Oldfield 66, 174; and Lee Oldfield 146–147; participation of women 111–112; and Philadelphia Motor Speedway 184; and results of 1911 park race 166–167; starter controversy 75, 149–150, 155
American Locomotive (automobile) 24 30, 34, 44, 45, 47, *48*
American Locomotive Company 24, 65, 100, 105
American Motor Car Company 65
American Philosophical Society 4
Anderson, Gil 141, 155–157, 161, 163

Apperson (automobile): and 1908 park race 26, 29, 34, 36, 41–47; and 1909 park race 64, 68, 70, 74, 79, 82, 87, 89, 90, 106, 109; and 1910 park race 108, 109, 117, 120
Apperson Brothers Company 26, 103
Archer, Andrew 123
Argue, Robert 82
Army-Navy Game 61–62, 78, 132, 171
Association of Licensed Automobile Manufacturers (ALAM) 65–66
attendance: at 1908 practice 30, 34; at 1908 race 39, 55; at 1909 practice 74; at 1909 race 77–78; at 1910 practice 105, 110, 112; at 1910 race 115–116; at 1911 practice 147–148; at 1911 race 151
Autolight Motor Supply Company 59, 95
Automobile Club of America (ACA) 22–23, 27, 63, 150
Automobile Row 13, 17, 24
The Automobile 13, 17, 46, 54, 59

B. C. K. Motor Company 64
Bailey, Banks & Biddle 28–29, 59, 63, 132
Bailey Cup (trophy) 29, 50
Ball, William H. 180, 182
Baltzell, E. Digby 171
Bartlett, G. Douglass 6, 23, 176
Basle, Charles 142, 151, 154, 155, 158
Bates, Charles 121
Bean, W. Ward 82
Beardsley, Ralph 107–108, 118, 120–121
Beitler, Lewis E. 6–7, 21
Bellevue-Stratford Hotel 129, 131, 166

Belmont Avenue 13, 21, 32–33; accidents on 80–81, 156, 161, 163; breakdowns on 43, 84; pits located on 40, 44, 59; roadwork on 60–61, 71, 109
Belmont Waterworks 27, 32, 123, *156*
Bennett, Gordon 3, 4
Benson, William R. 61
Benz (automobile) 2, 24; and 1909 park race 64, 66, 74, 79, 81, 83, 91, 141; and 1910 Grand Prize 133; and 1910 park race 101, 105, 108, 112, 117, 118, 125; and 1910 Vanderbilt Cup 104; and 1911 park race 142–143, *146*, 153, 157, *163*, 164
Benz, Karl 62
Benz Import Company 66, 100, 133–134
Bergdoll (automobile) 143–144
Bergdoll, Charles A. 24; and 1910 park race 105, 118–119; and 1911 park race 143–144
Bergdoll, Elizabeth 64, 67, 68
Bergdoll, Erwin: and 1908 park race 26, 35, 40–41; and 1909 park race 64, 66, 68, 80, 83; and 1910 park race 105, 108, 112, 117, 119–125, 128; and 1911 park race 141–145, *146*, 147–148, 150, 153, *154*, 155–158, 161–165, *163*, *164*, *166*, 167–168
Bergdoll, Grover 24; and 1911 park race 143, 144, 147, 149, 154–155
Bergdoll, Louis J. 65, 105, 143; and 1908 park race 24, 26–27, 30, 34, 40–41, 44–47, *48*; and 1909 park race 64, 70, 79–80, 83–84, 86, 89
Bergdoll, Louis J., Motor Company 24, 64, 105, 143–144, 147
Berger, Leander D. 131, 137
Betts, Charles L., Jr. 182, 185
Betz, John F. III 132; and 1909 park race 64–65, 67, 70, 74, 80–81, 83, 86–89; and 1910 park race 104–105, 108, 111, 112, 117, 119; and 1911 park race 142–144, 147, 155–157, *156*, *158*; and Philadelphia Motor Speedway 182
Bitner, Herb 30, 35, 43
Blankenberg, Rudolph 177–183
Block, Lou 105
Blockson, S. 108, 111
Bosch Magneto Company 166
Boulevard Garage 141, 167
Bowen, Thomas 145
Briarcliff (NY) 68
Brighton Beach (NY) 4, 30, 32–33, 108; scene of accident 56; scene of unsanctioned race 27, 32–33
Brill, Herman 27
Brown, Senator 135
Brownlee, George G. 140
Bruce-Brown, David 66
Buick (automobile) 66, 68, 71, *71*, 79, 88, 89
Buick Motor Car Company 66–68
Bureau of Highways 61
Burman, Robert 101, 188; and 1909 park race 66–68, 71, *71*, 79, 81, 83, 89
Burt, Nathaniel 10–11
Butler, S. M. 135, 139, 150

Case (automobile) 141, 154–155, *160*, 161
Casey, Jack 111
Catholic Fountain 32, 46, 163
Centennial Exhibition 1, 8, 13, 77, 187
Chadwick (automobile): and 1908 park race 27, 34–35, 41, 45; and 1909 park race 64, 70, 80–81, *82*, 83, *87*, 90–91; and 1910 park race 108, 111, 117–118, 122, 126–128, *127*, 131
Chadwick Engineering Works 27, 64, 101, 111, 129
Chalmers-Detroit (automobile) 65, 71–73, *72*, 79–81, *80*, 84, 87, *88* 91, 93, 94
Chalmers-Detroit Company 65, 95, 107
Chalmers-Fanning Motor Car Company 65
Chamounix Bridge 84
Chandler, William 160–161
Chestnut Street Opera House 131
Chevrolet, Louis 66–68, 71, 79, 82–83, 88
Chicago Times Herald 4
Chicago-Milwaukee Contest 4
Children's Aid Society 58
Children's Playgrounds 137
City Avenue 13, 32, 33, 121, *162*; accidents on 80, 83, 156, 161, 163; roadwork on 109, 144
City Hall 7, 11–13, 19, 67, 131–132
Clay, Henry 91–92, 102, 109, 116, 131
Clothier, Morris 152
Cobe, Harry 108, 111–112, 117, 121, 125, 127
Cobe, Mrs. Harry 111–112
Coffey, John C. 65, 68, *73*, 79, 83
Coffin, H. E. 93
Coghlan, W. J. 111
Cole (automobile): and 1910 park race 103, 109, 111, 117–118, 121, 125; and 1911 park race 142, 154, 158
Cole Motor Company 103
Columbia (automobile): and 1909 park race 65, 68, 79, 83; and 1910 Vanderbilt Cup 104
Columbia Bridge 32
Columbia Motor Car Company 65
Common Council, Philadelphia 179; endorse race 19, 180–183; funds for trophies 102, 113
Connelly, John P. 182
Continental Tires 40, 51
Coombs, Jack 116
Corbin (automobile) 112, 118, 121
Corbin Vehicle Company 107
Covington, Ed 123
Cumner, Arthur B. 27, 35
Cuyler, Thomas DeWitt 99, 176–179, 182–183

Davis, Carleton E. 180
Davis, George: and 1908 park race 26, 29, 34–37, 40–41, 44–47; and 1910 park race 109, 117, 120, 127–128
Davis, W. Wayne 13, 16, 41
Dawson, Joe 106, 111, 114, 118, 121, 123
Dayton Motor Company 24
Deguise, H. A. 125
De Hymel, Tobin 188; and 1910 park race 106–107, 118–121, 123–125, 127

DePalma, Ralph 2, 70, 101, 141; and 1911 park race 146–147, 151, *153*, 154–157, 159–161, 165
Diamond Rubber Company 51–52, 176
Dingley, Bert 101; and 1909 park race 65, 68, 71–74, *72*, 79, *80*, 81–83, 87–91, *88*, *93*, 95
Dingley, Mrs. Bert 72–74, 91, 96–97
Disbrow, Louis 147, 155, 157–159, 161,*163*, 165
Disston, Henry Albert 116, 152
Dorrance, Arthur 116, 152
Drach, Robert 65, 74, 79, 80–84, 86–87, 90
Duncan, Captain Hayes H. 67, 105, 108, 114, 143
Dunlap, Fred C.: as Fairmount Park Commissioner 139, 171, 177, 179–180; as 1911 race referee 151, 166–167
DuPont, P. F. 24
Durham, Israel 15
Dwyer, F. E. 69

E. M. F. (automobile) 144–145
Eisenhower, A. S. 99, 179
Electric Vehicle Company 65
Elgin (IL) 100, 133, 140, 188
Elm Avenue 32, 40, *70*
Elverson, James, Jr. 99, 177, 180–183
Endicott, Bill 103, 111, 112, 118, 120
Endicott, Harry 103, 111, 117, 121, 123–125
Etheridge, Glenn: in 1908 park race 47, 50, 52; in 1909 park race *73*, 90–91, *92*; in 1910 park race 120–121, 129
Evening Times Fob Medal 50
Everitt-Metzger-Flanders 144–145

Faber, Frank 154
Fairmount Park *9*; creation of 8; safety, reputation for 133–134, 167, 188; *see also* Fairmount Park Commission
Fairmount Park Commission 180; allows automobiles in park 9; creation of 8; and Grand Prize Race 135; make up of 11–12, 15, 63, 177–179, 189; and 1908 race 6–7, 12–13, 17, 19–21, 29, 41, 54–55; and 1909 race 57, 62; and 1910 race 97, 98, 99; and 1911 race 139, 137; and proposal for 1912 race 177; and proposal for 1913 race 180–181; and proposal for 1914 race 182–183; resolution to ban race 169–176; and tickets for race 62–63, 97, 129–130
Fairmount Park Guard 67, *69*, 78, 96, 143, 180
Fairmount Park Guard Pension Fund 138–139, 180
Fairmount Park Race Course, description of 12–13, *14, 20*, 21, *22*
Fairmount Park Trolley 9, 55
Fairmount Waterworks 8, *9*
Falls Bridge 40, 78
Fanning, Mr. 95
Ferguson, William L. 186
Fiat (automobile) 141, 142, 144, 149, 154–155, 157, *158*
52nd Street 32, *70*, *71*, 145; accidents on 88, 125; breakdowns on 120

Firestone Tires 51–52, *53*, 128
Fisk Tires 51
Fitch, Edward H. 176
Flink, James J. 22
Florida, Jim 107; and 1908 park race 26, 29, 32, 34, 41, 43–47, *49*, 52; and 1909 park race 68, 70
Folwell, P. D. 27, 114, 167
Ford (automobile) 66, 105, 118, 122, 125
Ford, Henry 65, 105
Founders' Week 7, 8, 13, 15–16, 19, 21, 24, 54–55, 57; described 5, 6
Founders' Week Cup (trophy) 28, 50, *51, 52*
Franklin Field 61, 78, 171, 181
Franklin Motor Company 103, 109
Free Library of Philadelphia 4
Freeman, Samuel T. 59
French, L. Eugene 27, 64
French Grand Prix 66, 107, 131
Frey, H. P. 107, 111–112, 117, 124–125, 128
Frick, William 122–123
Froelich, Jesse 66, 133
Furness, Horace Howard 174

Gantert, G. Hilton: and dispute with AAA 75, 149–150, *150*; as 1909 starter 78–80, *80*, 95; as 1910 starter 117–118, *119*, 131; as 1911 starter 153–154, 164, *164*
Gellard, Ernest 111–112, 117, 124–125, 127, 131
George's Hill 13, 32, 42, 60, *70*, 115, *124*, 166
German Hospital 87
Gleason, William F. 102
Globe Printing Company 26, 60
Goetz, Harry 120
Gordon Bennett Races 3, 64, 142
Grand Prize Race 2, 96; compared to Fairmount Park 100, 187; 1908 Grand Prize Race 23, 66–68; 1910 Grand Prize Race 105, 133–136; 1912 Grand Prize Race 181, 189
Grant, Harry: and 1909 park race 65, 68, 71, 78–79; and 1909 Vanderbilt Cup 100; and 1910 park race 100, 105; and 1910 Vanderbilt Cup 104, 105–106; and 1911 park race 142–143, 151, 153, 155, 157, *159*, 159–160
Grennan, Jack 71

Hahn, Sgt. Harry 67
Hall, Al: and 1909 race 64, 67–68, 75, 80; and 1910 race 105, 108, 112
Hall, Fred 42
Hamilton Auto Company 24
Hammel, Alfred 147
Hanshue, Harris M. 103, 108, 117, 120
Harbach, H. C. 66, 95, 99, 112, 131, 136
Hardart, Frank 58, 59, 182
Hardesty, Harold 111–112, 117, 120
Harding, Hugh L.: and 1909 park race 68, 70, 74, 79, 82, *84*, 87, 89, 90, 95; and 1910 park race 106, 114, 117, 120
Harkins, Jack 27, 34–35, 41

Harper's Magazine 10
Harrigan, Joe 81
Harris, Frank 44
Harroun, Ray 2, 140; and 1910 park race 106, 111, 117–120, 123–124, 128, 130
Harroun, Mrs. Ray 117
Haupt, Willie: and 1909 park race 64, 70, 79, *80*, 81, 83; and 1910 park race 108, 112, 117, 119, 125
Hayes, E. O. 65, 79, 84–85, *85*
Hazlett, James 100
Heacock, Joseph Linden 183–185
Heacock & Hokanson 183
Hearne, Eddie 101, 118
Herbert, W. B. 27
Herr, Donald 141, 143–144, 154, *154*, 156–157, 159, 161, 165–166
Hewitt, William 116
Hicks, George W. B. 5, 7, 41
Historical Society of Pennsylvania 4
Hitemayer, Robert E. 107
Hodson, Frank 141, 147, 149
Holme, Thomas 4
Horseless Age 128
Horticultural Hall 13, 21
Hotel Walton 24, *25*, 59, 67, 93, 112, 114–115, 145, 149, 151–152, 166
Howard, Charles: and 1909 park race 64, 74, 79, 81, 83, 91; and 1911 park race 141
Hower, Mr. 66
Hughes, Hughie 141–143, 145, 148–149, 151, 155–157, 159–161, 165–166
Huyette, Paul 131, 176
Hyers, James 158

Ideal Motor Company 141
Illinois Trophy Race 140
Indianapolis 500 *see* Indianapolis Motor Speedway
Indianapolis Motor Speedway 106; Indianapolis 500 140, 141, 181; Philadelphia Motor Speedway, model for 183–185, 189; Prest-O-Light Trophy Dash 67; safety of 96; seeks Grand Prize Race 134
Ireland, Edgar C. 29, 41, 44
Isotta Import Company 68
Isotta-Fraschini 68, 71, 80, 83, 89, 91

J. E. Caldwell Company 29
J. I. Case Threshing Machine Company 141
J. M. Quinby Company 68, 91
Jackson (automobile) 103, 108, 117
Jackson Automobile Company 103, 108
Jagersberger, Joseph: and 1910 park race 107, 108, 116–117, 123–125, 127; and 1911 park race 141, 144, 154, 156–157, 159, *160*, 161–162
James, Archibald T. 172
Jefferson Medical College 6
Johnson, Arthur *85*
Johnson, F. M. 27

Johnson, Frank 80, 125, *146*, *154*, 165
Johnson, John G. 179
Johnson, Philip 59
Jones, Harry 115
Jordan, Harry 95
Justice, Theodore 182–183

Keir, Joseph 117
Keith, Sydney W. 58, 99, 177–178, 180, 182
Keith's Theatre 94
Kittrell, C. H. 112
Kline Kar (automobile) 64, 75
Knight, Harry 109, 112, 118, 125, 127
Koopman, Harry 141, 147
Kowalker, John 79
Kulick, Frank 105, 118, 122, 125

La Roche, Max 35, 41, 43
Langhorne (PA) 189–190
Lansdowne Drive 42, *72*
Larzelere, B. B. 64
Leinau, Malin 64, 79, 81–82, *82*, 86–87
Library Company of Philadelphia 4
Lit, James D. 116, 152
Lit Brothers Department Store 116, 132
Locomobile (automobile) 2, 65; and 1908 park race 26, 29, 32, 34–35, 41, 43–47, *49*, 52; and 1908 Vanderbilt Cup 54
Locomobile Company 26, 70
Long Island (NY) 68, 107; compared to Philadelphia 2, 55, 169; end of racing on 133–134, 143, 150; as scene of Grand Prize Race 133–134; as scene of Vanderbilt Cup 4, 23, 53, 61, 100, 103, 104, 141
Long Island Motor Club 141
Long Island Motor Parkway Sweepstakes 26–27
Longstreth, W. C., Motor Car Company 65, 111
Longstreth, William C. 65, 105
Lorimer, Lee 65, 68, 73, 80, 84
Lowell (MA) 65, 68
Lozier (automobile): 2; and 1908 park race 27, *34*, 35, *36*, 41–45, 47, 51, 61; and 1909 race 67, 74, 80–81; and 1910 park race 117, 119, 121, 123–127; and 1911 park race 140, 142, 154–155, 159, *159*, 161, 166
Lozier, H. A. 27
Lozier Motor Company 27, 33, 64, 67, 108, 140
Lukacs, John 10–11, 16, 171
Lynch, Harry 42
Lytle, Herbert 64, 68, 90

MacDonald & Campbell Company 29, 59
MacDonald & Campbell Trophy: 1908 trophy 29, 50; 1909 trophy 59, *60*, 91, *92*, 95
Maher, James T. 178
Mallot, Scott 121–122
Manker, Billie 126
Market Street Merchants Association 182–183
Marmon (automobile) 141; and 1910 park race 106, 111, 117–118, 120–121, 123

Martin, Thomas S. 130, 135
Massapequa Race 107
Matheson (automobile) 13, 16, 27, 36
Matheson Company 27
Matson, Joe 107, 112, 118, 121
Matthews, Harry S. 143, 155, *162*, 165
Maucher, Bert 24, 26, 29, 31–32, 34, 41, 47
Maxwell (automobile) 30, 35, 41–43
Maxwell & Berlet 131
Maxwell-Briscoe Motor Company 24
Maynes, Robert 27
McCurdy, George 179–183
McLaughlin, Chief 102
McNichol, James P. 15–17, 41, 116, 152, 178
Megraw, John 105, 108, 117
Memorial Hall 13, *69*, 187
Mercedes (automobile): and 1910 park race 108, 116, 124; and 1911 park race 141–143, *148*, 155, 157, 159, *159*, 162–163, 167
Mercer (automobile) 2; and 1910 park race 107, 110, 112, 117, 124; and 1911 park race 141–142, 145–146, 149, *153*, *154*, 154–157, 159–160, 165
Mercer Automobile Company 107, 112, 141, 146
Merciful Savior for Crippled Children, Home of the 102
Methodist Episcopal Home 32
Michelin Tires 51, 165
Michener, Harry 27, 35–36, *36*, 41–42, 51
Milwaukee (WI) 181, 189
Mitchell, Al 101, 105, 108, 118–122, 129
Monson, Adolph 141
Montgomery Avenue 27, *156*
Morgan, W. J. 90
Morse, Irving J. 26, 32
Motor Age 92, 173, 176
Motor Cups Holding Company 134–135
The Motor World 95, 97
Mt. Sinai Hospital 102
Mulford, Ralph 67–68, 188; and 1909 park race 27, 33–36, *34*, 41–42, 44–45, 47, 50; and 1910 park race 108–109, 114, 117–119, 120–129, *128*, 131, ; and 1911 park race 140, 142–143, 145, 147–148, 151–159, 160–167
Mullen, W. C. 105, 108, 117, 120–121
Municipal Hospital 88
Munsey's Magazine 11
Munyon, James M. 26

Narrangansett Track (RI) 66
Nash, C. W. Hardwood 112
Nasium, Jim *see* Wolfe, Edgar F.
National (automobile): and 1910 park race 111, 117, 119–122, *124*, 125; and 1911 park race 140–141, 143, 153–157, 159–161, *163*, 165
National Motor Vehicle Company 107, 140
Nauber, Charles 44
Neff, Dr. Joseph S. 58, 63, 95, 97–98, 102, 137
Neill Drive 28, 78, 188; accidents on 40, 47, 83, 111, 121, 129, 145, 147, 161; breakdowns on 43, 45, 81, 124, 126; described 13, *31*, 32, *33*, 69, 82, *163*; roadwork on 109
New York Herald 3
New York–Paris Race 27, 107
Newton, Mahlon W. 182
Nordyke & Marmon Company 106
Norristown Automobile Club 132
North American Trophy 50
North Concourse 13, 21

Ohio (automobile) 143, 155, 159, *162*
Ohio Motor Company 143
Oldfield, Barney 65–66, 146, 167, 169, 174, 188
Oldfield, Lee 141–142, 145–147, 149, 154, 172
O'Leary, Timothy 109, 116
Oliver, William, Jr. 112
Otto (automobile) 112, 118, 122
oval racing *see* track racing
Overpeck, J. R. 27, 40–41
Owen, Dr. Hubley R. 28, 60

Padula, Vincent P. 107–108, 117–118, 122, 125, 127, 128, 131
Palmer & Singer Manufacturing Company 26
Palmer-Singer (automobile): and 1908 park race 26, 29, 41–45, *46*, 47; and 1909 park race 64, 68, 69, 79, 82, 91
Paris-Bordeaux Contest 3
Paris-Madrid Contest 3
Paris-Rouen Contest 3
Parker, George P.: and 1908 park race 36; and 1911 park race 143, 148, 155, 159, 162, *162*, 165
Parkin, Joe, Jr. 80, *82*, 83–84, 86, 88–90, 95
Parkin, Joe, Sr. 80
Parkside Avenue 13, 32, 40, *71*, 151; accidents on 88, 125, 156; breakdowns on 120; roadwork on 60–61
Patchke, Cyrus R. 26, 33, 35, 41, 47, 50–51
patricians 172, 176, 178–179, 181, 189; definition of 10–12, 58, 171, 174–175
Peerless (automobile) 24, 26, 29, 41–42, 66
Penn, William: depictions of 28, *52*, 131, 132; founding of Philadelphia 4, 11, 12
Pennsylvania (automobile) 30, 41, *43*, 45
Pennsylvania Hospital 6
Pennsylvania Motor Car Company 27, 64
Pennsylvania National Guard 7, 60, 78
Pennsylvania Railroad 5, 10, 115, 184
Pennsylvania Society for the Prevention of Tuberculosis 58
Pennsylvania State Legislature 6
Penrose, Bois 16, 178
Pepper, George Wharton 174–175
Percival, "Doc" 134
Le Petit Journal 3
Pfeister, Fred 161
Philadelphia: conservative reputation 10–12, 17, 21; founding of 4–5; industry 5, 12; politics 15, 21; as scene of auto races 4, 187, 189; 225th anniversary of 4, 5

Philadelphia & Reading Railroad 5, 13, 31–32, 45, 111, 120–121
Philadelphia Auto Company 26, 64
Philadelphia Automobile Trade Association 136, 139
Philadelphia Chamber of Commerce 184
Philadelphia Country Club 32, *31*
Philadelphia Evening Bulletin 35, 47, 63, 68, 78, 100, 116, 145
Philadelphia Evening Times 29, 31, 54, 77, 85, 103, 112, 129, 134, 145, 172–173
Philadelphia Hotel Association 182
Philadelphia Inquirer 1, 78, 92, 103, 126, 178
Philadelphia Motor Company 142
Philadelphia Motor Speedway 181–186, *185*, *186*
Philadelphia Motor Speedway Association 181–186
Philadelphia North American 116
Philadelphia Public Ledger 12, 40, 59, 61–62, 64, 137
Philadelphia Record 21, 27, 29, 39, 124
Philadelphia Record Trophy 50
Philadelphia Trophy 131
Philadelphia Zoological Gardens 9
Playgrounds Committee 102
Point Breeze 4, 12, 33, 67, 107, 112, 126, 141, 147, 189
Police 173, 188; availability for race 177, 180–181; 1908 activity 41, 56; 1909 activity 68, 77–78, 85–86, 88, *88*, 91–92, 96; 1910 activity 104, 108–109, 111, 117; 1911 activity 145, 147–148, 152, 161, 165; *see also* Fairmount Park Guard
Police Pension Fund 102, 138–139, 180
Pollack, James: and attempts to revive race 177–180; 1908 proposal 6, 19–20; 1909 proposal 57, 97; 1910 proposal 99, 100; and resolution to ban race 171–172
Popular Mechanics 174
Presbyterian Hospital 44
Prest-O-Light Trophy Dash *see* Indianapolis Motor Speedway
Price, Eli Kirk, Jr. 57, 58, 99, 177–182
Price, William 116
program 135–137, *138*, 139–140
Proud, Mr. (Announcer) *119*, 127
Public Health & Charities, Department of 58, 98, 99
Pullman (automobile): and 1908 park race 27, 29, 35, 41, 43–44; and 1909 park race 64–65; and 1910 park race 111–112, 117, 120, 124
Pullman Motor Car Company 27, 112

Quaker City Motor Club: and banning of race 169–173, 176; choose circuit 13; fear resistance to race 10–12, 169; income from program 135–137; preparations for 1908 park race 17, 22–23, 27–29, 35, 54–56; preparations for 1909 park race 58–64, 66–68, 70, 75, 93; preparations for 1910 park race 97, 100–103, 129–132; preparations for 1911 park race *130*, 139–141, *140*, 144–147, 149–152; and 1911 protest of results 166–167; proposal of 1908 park race 6–13, 21; proposal of 1909 park race 54, 57–58; proposal of 1910 park race 99–100; proposal of 1911 park race 137, 139; proposal of 1912 park race 177, 180; proposal of 1913 park race 180; proposal of 1914 park race 182–183; seek Grand Prize Race 134–135; trial runs 4

Ransley, Harry 179
Rayfield Carburetor 140
Reed & Barton 131
reliability runs *see* trial runs
Remy Company 140
Repplier, Agnes 11, 174, 190
Resta, Dario 185
Reyburn, John E. *16*, 178–179; background 15–16; and 1908 park race 27, 41, 48, 50, *51*, 54; and 1909 park race 58, 62–63, 82, 93, 109; and 1910 park race 97, 99, 100, 102, 109–110, 113, 115–116, 131–132; and 1911 park race 139–140, 153–154; planning of Founders' Week 4, 5; and program controversy 136–137; seeks Grand Prize Race 134–135; supports race 7, 12–13, 17, 97, 172, 180
Reyburn, Mrs. John E. 15, 41, 48, 116
Reynolds, Stephen 103
Rich, George P. 174–175
Ringler, Harvey 141–143, 145–146, 153, 182
Rittenhouse Square 10, 16, 171, 178–179
road course: definition of 3
Roberts, Montague 107, 117, 120
Roberts, Mortimer 107, 117, 121, 123–125
Robertson, George 2, 105, 107, 127, 153, 188; and Brighton Beach 56; and 1908 park race 32–36, 41, 43–48, *49*, 50–53, *51*, 56; and 1908 Vanderbilt Cup 54, 63; and 1909 park race 64–65, 70, 73–74, *73*, 78–79, *80*, 81–84, 87–94, *90*, *92*, *93*, 96; and 1910 park race 101, 104, 112, 116, 134; and 1910 Vanderbilt Cup 103–104; and 1911 park race 157; retires from racing 108, 116
Robertson, Mrs. George 90
Rollston, William 162
Ross, Robert E.: and Grand Prize Race 134–135; and 1909 park race 61, 63, 66–68, 95; and 1910 park race 102, 109, *110*, 114–115, 131; resigns from motor club 135–136, 139
Rush Hospital 58

St. Joseph Hospital 123
St. Mary Hospital 102
St. Timothy Hospital 121, 145
Salzman, George 27, 35–36, 40–42, 44, *45*, 64
Santa Monica (CA) 103, 152, 181, 189
Savannah (GA) 2, 23, 66, 68, 96, 100, 133–136, 189
Savannah Automobile Club 134

Schleiffer, E. F. 103, 108
Schroeder, Charles A. 23, 64
Schroeder, Edward 143; as Wosser, T. J. 107, 116
Schuylkill River 6, 8, 9
Selden (automobile) 69–70, *71*, 80–81, 91
Selden, George B. 65, 69
Selden Motor Car Company 69
Selden Patent 65
Select Council, Philadelphia 19, 102, 113, 179–180, 182–183
Seyler, Fred 120
Seymour, Joe 67, 74, 80, 81
Simmerman, Dr. George F. 111
Simplex (automobile) 132, 142, 144; and 1909 race 64, 70, *73*, 79, *80*, 87, *90*, 91–92; and 1910 race 104–105, 107–108, 117–118, 120–121
Simplex Automobile Company 32, 65, 105
Smith Memorial 13, 21, 31, 35, *72*, 112, 152
Snowden, A. Louden 6, 19, 57, 99, 179, 180–182
South Concourse 13, 21, 28, 30, 32, 35, 59–60, *79*, 82, *94*, 105, 111, 117–119, *122*, 143, *146*, 152, 155, 163, 167; accidents 72, 86, 112, 149; breakdowns on 43–44; roadwork on 61; safety issues *69*, 109
The Speedway (horse racing track) 6
Staines, Roy 29, 35
Stetson, George Henry 59, 95, 182
stock chassis: definition of 8
Stoddard-Dayton (automobile) 24, 29, 41, 44, 117–119, 120, 123
Stoddard-Dayton Company 106
Stotesbury, Edward T. 169, 177–178, 180, 182
Strang, Louis 68, 70, 80, 83, 86, *86*, 89, 91, 188
Strawberry Mansion Bridge 32, 55, 89, 160
Stuart, Edwin Sydney 78, 102
Studebaker (automobile) 26, 30, 41, 46–47, 61
Studebaker Brothers Company 26, 144–145
Stutz (automobile) 141, 155
Suhrmann, Louis *153*, *154*
Superintendence & Police, Fairmount Park Commission, Committee on: and 1908 race proposal 12, 19, 21; and 1909 race proposal 57; and 1910 race proposal 99; and 1914 race proposal 182; and resolution to ban race 171, 176–178
Swain, Charles J. 23, 28
Sweet Briar 13, 21, 29, *30*, 31, *48*, *86*, 111, 188; accidents at 30, 35, 71–72, 82, 84–85, *85*, 120–122; breakdowns at 44, 74, 81, 83, 89, 126, 159–162, 164; crowds at 40, 78, 109, 115–116; roadwork at 60
Syracuse (NY) 146, 149, 172

Taft, William Howard 61, 102
Taylor, John B. 56, 116
Thomas (automobile) 27, 35, 40–44, *45*, 51, 64, 70, 79–81, *80*, 83, 86, 107
Thomas Company 27

Thompson, Samuel Gustine 57–58, 63, 171, 173
Tierney, Luke 86
Tioga Automobile Company 140
Tompkins, George 74, 119
Tower, Jack 144–145
track racing (oval racing) 4, 181
Tracy, Joe 26, 32
trial runs: description of 3

University of Pennsylvania 4, 10, 59, 61, 170–172

Vanderbilt, William K., Jr. 4, 24, 133–136
Vanderbilt Cup 12, 64, 67–68, 141–143, 149, 153, 181, 185; compared to Fairmount Park 2, 7–8, 17, 21–22, 55–56, 61, 96, 103, 105, 108–110, 129, 167, 169, 174, 187, 189; history of 4, 23; 1908 Vanderbilt Cup 26, 53, 56, 63, 75; 1909 Vanderbilt Cup 96; 1910 Vanderbilt Cup 100, 103–107, 109–110, 133
Vodges, Jesse T. 61

Wagner, Fred J. 75, 149–150
Wallace, William: and 1908 park race 26, 29, 41–42, 44–45, *46*, 47; and 1909 park race 64, 68–69, *70*, 71–72, 79, 91; and 1911 park race 143, 147, 149, 157, 159–160
Walton, Hotel *see* Hotel Walton
Washington Square 10, 16
Webster, George S. 100, 177–178, 180, 182
Welch (automobile) 26, 35, 40, 64, 66–67, 75, 80
Welch Motor Car Company 26
Weldon & Bauer 141
Werntz, Stella 145
Wescott (automobile) 109, 112, 118
West Philadelphia Homeopathic Hospital 121, 125
West River Drive 9, 13, 31–32, 69, 78, *84*, *106*, 109, 111, 123, *156*; accidents on 35, 42, 71–72, 82, 89, 145, 147, 161; breakdowns on 87, *87*, 126, 164, ; roadwork on 27, 54, 60
White, J. William *170*, 182; appointed to Fairmount Park Commission 63; background 170–171; opinion of drivers and spectators 181, 189; resolution to ban race 169–181, 189, 190
White Haven Sanatorium 58
Widener, Peter A. B. 179
Wilcox, H. S. 107, 111, 117, 121–122, 125
Willoughby, Robert 163, 167
Windrim, John T. 116
Wishart, Spencer 141, 148, *148*, 155–159, *159*, 161–167, 188,
Wolfe, Edgar F.: as Jim Nasium *144*
Woodside Park 9
Wosser, T. J. *see* Schroeder, Edward
Wynnefield Avenue 120, 144
Wynnewood Avenue 47, 71, 115

Yerger, Frank: and 1908 park race 26, 30, 34,

41, 46–47; and 1909 park race 61, 68; and 1910 park race 112, 115, 118, 122, 128
Young, Charles 69–70, *71*, 80–81, 91
Young, John 125

Zengle, Len 188; and 1908 park race 27, 30, 41, *43*, 45; and 1909 park race 64, 68, 70, 80–84, *87*, 89, 91, 95; and 1910 park race 105, 108, 111–112, 117, 120–121, 123–132, *124*, *127*; and 1911 park race 140–141, 145, 147–148, 151–158, 160, 162–165